ADVANCE PRAISE FOR THE TRIB

"Many have commented on the growing tr⋯
But perhaps no one has done it as creatively ⋯
Rush Limbaugh's persistent race-baiting and "othering" of the Obama Presidency, this book provides invaluable insights into how right-wing backlash
against the first black president set the stage for the rise of Donald Trump. A
must read for anyone interested in understanding racial politics and polarization in the Obama and Trump eras."—**MICHAEL TESLER**, co-author of
*Identity Crisis: The 2016 Presidential Campaign and the Battle for the Meaning
of Americ*a

"In this prescient and well-researched book, Ian Reifowitz traces the roots of
America's current problems with racism to the vile invective Rush Limbaugh
used to describe Barack Obama, the nation's first Black President. Skillfully
explaining how conservative talk-show race-baiting led to the naked racism
of Trump's America, Reifowitz shows that the recent rise of white supremacy
and white nationalism is inextricably linked to the power of language – and
that the right-wing needs this type of incendiary racism to survive. The *Tribalization of Politics* is a fantastic reminder that racism has always been alive
and well in America, it's just been obscured by rhetorical tricks and coded
speech. This is a must-read for anyone seeking to understand how the US
has reached its lowest point in race relations since the Civil Rights Movement."—**KERI LEIGH MERRITT**, author of *Masterless Men: Poor Whites
and Slavery in the Antebellum South*

"What does it mean to be a white person in the United States today? Since
the civil rights era, progressives have answered that it means nothing more or
less than to be a co-equal member of society. But on the right, the answer is
far scarier--and no one has more powerfully frightened whites with tales of
racial peril than Rush Limbaugh, to his immense profit. Ian Reifowitz in this
stunning book shows what democracy is up against."
—**IAN HANEY LÓPEZ**, author of *Dog Whistle Politics: How Coded Racial
Appeals Have Reinvented Racism and Wrecked the Middle Class*

"Donald Trump's racially charged campaign and presidency didn't emerge from a vacuum. Reifowitz documents how Trump follows on years of racialized rhetoric on conservative talk radio. This is important reading for anyone who wants to understand how American politics became so riven by 'identity politics.'"—**JOHN SIDES**, co-author of *Identity Crisis: The 2016 Presidential Campaign and the Battle for the Meaning of America*

"Ian Reifowitz provides a compelling analysis of the power of racialized rhetoric by examining Rush Limbaugh's comments about former President Barack Obama. Reifowitz's comprehensive study provides a wealth of information in a scholarly book that is also entertaining. He supports his arguments well and shows the manner in which the language of an influential radio commentator characterized the nation's first African American president as the 'other,' an 'agitator,' and 'angry' and thus paved the way for the election of President Trump."—**SHARON D. WRIGHT AUSTIN**, author of *The Caribbeanization of Black Politics: Race, Group Consciousness, and Political Participation in America*

"Ian Reifowitz's insightful new book shows how the anti-immigrant, race-baiting rhetoric of America's premier conservative talk show host, Rush Limbaugh, paved the way for Donald Trump's winning campaign for president. It persuasively demonstrates that Trump was not an anomaly, but exploited racial fears and resentments that Limbaugh had stoked since the beginning of the Obama administration."—**ALLAN LICHTMAN**, author of *The Case for Impeachment*

THE TRIBALIZATION OF POLITICS

How Rush Limbaugh's Race-Baiting

Rhetoric on the Obama Presidency Paved

the Way for Trump

Ian Reifowitz

Foreword by
Markos Moulitsas

PUBLISHING
New York, NY

Ig Publishing
Box 2547
New York, NY 10163
www.igpub.com

ISBN: 978-1-63246091-2

CONTENTS

Donald Trump owns conservative media 100 percent, lock-stock-and barrel. Full of bluster and bombast, Trump uses modern media tools like Twitter to directly blast the nation with his unfiltered, uninformed, and uncivil message at full-volume.

To those outside the conservative media bubble, it may seem as though Trump is the entire ball game. Sure, *Fox News* is a presence, but the news channel has reconstituted itself these days as State Media, singular in purpose—to prop up Trump's candidacy. Whatever the "conservative" message might be these days, it doesn't exist without Trump. It is Trump who sets the agenda. It is Trump who determines the message. And it is Trump who decides who can best sell it. Ten out of 10 times, it's Trump.

Thus, in this world of Trump, Trump, Trump, and more Trump, it is easy for the uninitiated to forget that in addition to the president's Twitter account, conservatives have built a massive media machine to promote a message that is often at odds with reality and the American mainstream. Forged in the aftermath of Barry Goldwater's 1964 landslide loss, this massive network of conservative TV, radio, print, and online outlets have allowed them to build an alternate reality so powerful and convincing, that entire swaths of the country are held in thrall.

A Pew study in 2017 found that *40 percent* of Trump voters relied on *Fox News* as their main source of news. Meanwhile, only 3 percent of Hillary Clinton voters relied on *any* cable news channel as their primary source of information. Conservative websites like the *Daily Caller* and *Breitbart* reach millions more. Social media (like Facebook and Twitter) is awash in conservative voices, further amplified by Russian bots. And the Dark Web has given voice to the darkest fringes of the conservative world, from white supremacists to conspiracy theorists like the QAnon crew, convinced of a deep-state conspiracy against Trump fueled by child-sex traffickers like . . . Hillary Clinton.

But nothing reaches more conservative voices than AM radio. Once the province of music stations, the emergence of FM radio led to a mass-migration to the higher-quality band that left AM radio in severe decline. Talk radio didn't require that same level of quality, and station operators embraced the format. The elimination of the Fairness Doctrine in 1987 made it possible for conservatives to take over the dial without concern that political balance was required. And in 1988, a certain Rush Limbaugh launched his nationally syndicated show.

It is hard to overstate just how dramatically important Limbaugh has been in defining conservative thought and ideology, with an audience that has, at times, reached into the *tens of millions*. No single conservative personality, outside of modern-day Trump, has had this kind of reach or influence. And unlike *Fox News*, which actively makes conservatives stupid, Limbaugh's method of misinformation has always been rooted in a more solid foundation of truthiness.

A 2007 survey by Pew Research found that Limbaugh listeners demonstrated among the highest knowledge levels in response to a battery of political current affairs questions, with 79 percent having either a high or moderate level. Among *Fox News* viewers, that number was only 65 percent, second-to-last, with nightly network news watchers faring worse. (Here's a funny aside: the most informed were watchers of Comedy Central's *The Daily Show* and *Colbert Report*, also at 79 percent combined, but with a larger number of "high" levels of knowledge.)

But knowing the names of the vice president, governor, and Speaker of the House is only base-level knowledge. Limbaugh may accurately impart such information, but as this book shows, his pernicious twisting of facts, out-of-context quotes, and toxic editorializing have done far worse damage to the country than whether someone knows or doesn't know the name of the Chief Justice of the Supreme Court.

If you are anything like me, the sheer amount of misinformation stated by Rush Limbaugh in the pages ahead will shock and anger you, deeply. Not just about how Limbaugh twisted the truth. As Ian notes early on, Limbaugh launched his coverage of the Obama presidency with four simple words: "I hope he fails." With that goal in mind, nothing would stop Limbaugh from spending the next years reinforcing the narrative of failure. The truth never stood a chance.

What makes this so infuriating is that Limbaugh decided that lies and policy differences weren't enough to make Obama a failure. Instead, he had to *other* him, turning white America against him, and he did that with pure, unfiltered, unadultured racism.

I was shocked when Ian first told me about this project. "He's literally going to go through *eight years* of Rush Limbaugh transcripts?" I was shocked again when he told me he was finished. *"He actually read eight years of Rush Limbaugh transcripts?"* But that was nothing like the jolt from seeing the results of that thankless labor—his comprehensive transcribing of Limbaugh's hate, always in full context. What these pages show are the words of a white supremacist, and you'll find yourself, like me, wondering how the hell he has gotten away with talking like a KKK Grand Dragon in modern-day America.

There's nothing subtle about what you're about to read. For example, when Barack Obama talked about the disparities in policing between white and black Americans—as objective and uncontroversial an observation as possible—Limbaugh happily ranted about the President carrying out "a purposeful effort here to divide of [sic] people of this country along racial lines." Pointing out racism, to conservatives, is always worse than the actual racism itself. When the president invited Muslim American leaders to the State of the Union Address, Limbaugh claimed that Obama did so " to remind you that you lost . . . to remind you that it isn't your country anymore . . . to remind you and put an exclamation point behind your country's changing no matter what the hell you think about it." It wasn't a unifying gesture very much in character with Obama's theme of one America ("There are no red states or blue states, just the United States"), it was really Obama mocking white America for their impending demographic doom.

"You", of course, refers to his white and mostly male audience. But if you need a more explicit example, how about Limbaugh screeching about how Obama and liberals think that white America is "inherently corrupt ... has always been racist and bigoted, and so it must be chipped away at, it must be destroyed and it must be properly categorized." Or how liberals and Obama "simply say that anybody nonwhite makes something better, whether it does or not ... We're gonna make things better by reducing the numbers of white people ... and we're gonna start sprinkling diversity in there."

I don't mean to steal Ian's thunder, since you'll come across those quotes later in the book, but it's helpful to prepare yourself for what's inside these pages. This isn't a question of ideological disagreements over the effects of a higher marginal tax rate on the wealthy, or even whether climate change is real (it is) or a hoax. This is someone with the ear and respect of a huge segment of the American public telling them that liberals literally want to eliminate white people. And with the rest of the conservative media machine reinforcing that message, it suddenly becomes obvious why so much of white America turned to Donald Trump in 2016—it was a matter of survival. It was either Trump, warts and all, or the demise of their way of life thanks to liberal Democrats doing the bidding of murderous brown and black people. The ugly, racist, spiteful, and bigoted words you will read in this book worked.

Now to be clear, Limbaugh didn't pioneer racism. Republicans have long used race as a tool for attaining power. When President Lyndon B. Johnson signed the Civil Rights Act of 1964, he supposedly said, "We have lost the South for a generation." Johnson wasn't pessimistic enough, as Republicans to this day have continued to profit from their "Southern Strategy"—that is, using racism to turn southern white voters against the Democratic Party. Amazingly, while Democrats *still* outnumber Republicans in most southern states in voter registration, those legacy "Dixiecrats" are firmly in the Republican camp today.

It was no mistake or coincidence that Ronald Reagan unveiled his "states' rights" speech during his 1980 presidential bid at a county fair just outside Philadelphia, Mississippi, the same town in which three civil rights workers were assassinated by white supremacists in 1964. As Bob Herbert wrote in the *New York Times* in 2007, "Everybody watching the 1980 campaign knew what Reagan was signaling at the fair. [It] was understood that when politicians started chirping about 'states' rights' to white people in places like Neshoba County they were saying that when it comes down to you and the blacks, we're with you." Those appeals worked. Mississippi was a swing state at the time, and Reagan won it narrowly, by just under 12,000 votes.

It was a strategy so nakedly obvious that Republicans didn't even bother to hide it, leading then-Republican National Committee Chairman Ken Mehlman in 2005 to issue an apology to the NAACP, "Some Republicans gave up on winning the African American vote, looking the other way or trying to benefit politically from racial polarization. I am here today as the Republican chairman to tell you we were wrong."

But those were empty words, and Republicans have had little incentive to stop benefiting from racial polarization. Indeed, those benefits have only *grown*. In 2008, Sen. John McCain won Mississippi (a battleground state in 1980!) 56-43, with just 11 percent of whites voting for Barack Obama. In 2012, Romney won the state 56-44, with an even lower *ten* percent of whites voting for Obama. And in 2016? Trump won 58-40. And while no exit polls were conducted, the increased margin wasn't African Americans switching their votes to Trump.

While few (if any) states are as racially polarized as Mississippi, the rest of the South still suffers from massive racial disparities. In 2016, only 24 percent of whites voted for Hillary Clinton in South Carolina, 27 percent in Kentucky, and 21 percent in Georgia. The Southern Strategy, Mehlman's apology notwithstanding, continues to bear fruit for Republicans—not just at the presidential level, but also in the Senate, where the large number of rural white states will continue to provide Republicans an unfair and unwarranted structural advantage well into the future. (Fun fact: California, with a population of 40 million, has two US senators. The 21 smallest states combined have about 40 million residents, and 42 senators. Among those, Republicans have a 25-17 advantage.) It pays to keep the nation polarized along racial lines, and will continue to pay off into the foreseeable future.

In that context, Limbaugh isn't an anomaly, but he has been instrumental in bringing explicit racism out of the shadows. Ronald Reagan's speech in Mississippi, on its surface, seemed benign enough. Republicans spoke in code—"dog whistles" in political parlance—in order to keep up proper public pretences. Anyone in the South knew "states' rights" meant keeping the federal government from invalidating racist Jim Crow laws, desegregating schools, and protecting the franchise for voters of color via the Voting Rights Act of 1965. To Americans outside the South, "states' rights", well, they had no clue *what* that was. But whatever it was, it seemed innocuous enough.

There are many other ways conservatives surreptitiously inject race into the public sphere: adopting state flags with the Confederate battle flag's Stars and Bars, demanding Obama's birth certificate (white people don't have their American bona fides questioned), calling black victims of police violence "thugs," and speaking about the "working class" when referring to white rural Americans, as if they're the only ones who work—the list is endless. When it comes to hidden racism, conservatives can be a creative bunch, and their handiwork was a regular staple in the political sphere.

For example, in the 1988 presidential election, George H. W. Bush's campaign manager Lee Atwater, an infamous campaign strategist and future Republican Party Chair, deployed quite possibly the most successful dog whistle in recent history. Willie Horton, who is black, raped a white woman and murdered her husband during a brutal home invasion while furloughed from a Massachusetts prison, under a program supported by Democratic nominee Michael Dukakis (though originally enacted by a Republican governor). As political science professor Claire Jean Kim said in 2012, "the insinuation is, if you elect Gov. Dukakis as president, we're going to have black rapists running amok in the country."

Still, as successful as this efforts was, there were serious long-term problems brewing. "You start out in 1954 by saying, 'Nigger, nigger, nigger.'" Atwater said in a 1981 recording dug up in 2012 by *The Nation*. "By 1968 you can't say 'nigger'—that hurts you, backfires. So you say stuff like, uh, forced busing, states' rights, and all that stuff, and you're getting so abstract. Now, you're talking about cutting taxes, and all these things you're talking about are totally economic things and a byproduct of them is, blacks get hurt worse than whites . . . 'We want to cut this,' is much more abstract than even the busing thing, uh, and a hell of a lot more abstract than 'Nigger, nigger.'"

Abstract worked well enough in 1981 and into the 90s too. But then Obama won in 2008, and then again in 2012. While some praised this new "post-racial" America, the conservative base was restless, unhappy with secret coded language. They were tired of being treated like lepers. They wanted the real deal, to be out and proud. And that's what Limbaugh fed and nurtured over eight years of Obama. With the base primed and ready for the reddest of red meat, all they needed was a candidate too racist, too crass, and too stupid to mask his feelings and intentions. In walked Donald Trump, launching his campaign with an explicitly racist message, "When Mexico sends its people, they're not sending their best. They're not sending you. They're not sending you. They're sending people that have lots of problems, and they're bringing those problems with us. They're bringing drugs. They're bringing crime. They're rapists. And some, I assume, are good people."

The Republican establishment blanched at Trump's grand entrance; it ran counter to the GOP's nascent efforts to broaden its appeal beyond its core white Southern male base. Just two years prior, in the wake of Obama's reelection victory, the Republican Party had issued an "autopsy" report arguing that "If Hispanic Americans hear that the GOP doesn't want them in the United States, they won't pay attention to our next sentence. It doesn't matter what we say about education, jobs or the economy; if Hispanics think that we do not want them here, they will close their ears to our policies." A 2013 *Time* cover of Cuban-American Florida Sen. Marco Rubio was captioned, "The Republican Savior," and the party establishment was giddy over both his candidacy, and that of Jeb Bush, a fluent Spanish-speaker married to a Mexican-American. Trump's bombastic racism was screwing up those plans!

We know how this story ended—the party base was so smitten by that overt racism, replacing dog whistles with dog whips, that it ignored Trump's weak conservative bona fides and outright flaws. The party of family values, including its Christian-Right wing, enthusiastically endorsed perhaps the most morally degenerate person in the entire country, a man who had unprotected sex with porn stars while his wife was home with their baby. The party of national security enthusiastically embraced a man so compromised by Russia, that the nation's security agencies literally investigated whether he was a Russian agent.

None of that mattered. In the end, racism trumped everything.

On his deathbed in 1991, Lee Atwater apologized to Michael Dukakis for the campaign he waged on Bush's behalf. "In 1988, fighting Dukakis, I said that I 'would strip the bark off the little bastard' and 'make Willie Horton his running mate.' I am sorry for both statements: the first for its naked cruelty, the second because it makes me sound racist, which I am not." Of course he was a racist. Engaging in race-baiting, racially divisive behavior is inherently racist, and there is a special place in hell for people who foment racial hatred and division.

Perhaps someday Limbaugh will look back on his body of work and have pangs of regret. Perhaps he will say to himself that he wasn't really a racist or a bigot. How could he be? He had the openly gay Elton John perform at his *fourth* wedding! But like Atwater, his legacy is his work, and this book doesn't sugarcoat.

After Trump's inauguration, Limbaugh was elated. The victory, he said, represented "a reclamation project, reclaiming this country from the people the Democrat Party has been attempting to turn it over to." White conservatives had turned back the black and brown hordes that had been using the Democratic Party to capture America. Or something.

Ian is an optimistic fellow, refusing to give up on Limbaugh's listeners. He says that it is "foolish for Democrats to write off . . . large swaths of Trump voters as incorrigible racists." As a Latino on the receiving end of Limbaugh's and Trump's vitriol, it's harder for me to be optimistic. But hope is eternal, and there is no political goal more beautiful than that of truly achieving a more perfect union.

This book shows what racial tribal politics looks like, and we don't have a choice but to do better.

MARKOS MOULITSAS
Founder and Publisher, Daily Kos

PREFACE

This book stands as the culmination of a decade of work researching and writing about Barack Obama, his ideas, and responses from his detractors. My most recent title, *Obama's America: A Transformative Vision of Our National Identity*, examined the forty-fourth president's writings and speeches on how Americans defined their collective sense of national community. I argued that Obama sought to recharacterize our national identity by emphasizing both inclusion and unity across existing group boundaries in ways and to a degree that even recent presidents had not. The book also included a section that explored how critics—from the left and right—attacked Obama in ways that addressed American national identity. In writing those sections, I developed an interest in examining conservative rhetoric aimed at President Obama, in particular, on how some on the right, especially Rush Limbaugh, portrayed him in a way designed to exacerbate white racial anxiety about a black president, or depicted Obama as a foreign "other," outside the bounds of traditional Americanness.

That interest, combined with the desire to continue exploring the Obama presidency, evolved into this book. My primary source base was transcripts of the *Rush Limbaugh Show*, which airs three hours a day, more than 200 days a year. The main argument I make here—about

conservatives exploiting white anxiety regarding changing demograph-
ics for political gain—is one I began formulating in a 2013 article for *In
These Times*. That article drew on what I had learned writing *Obama's
America* as well as my first book, *Imagining an Austrian Nation: Joseph
Samuel Bloch and the Search for a Multiethnic Austrian Identity, 1846–
1919*, which examined the attempt to cultivate a common national
identity to bring together the many peoples of another multiethnic
state, Austria-Hungary.

The *In These Times* article explored the parallels between the ethnic Germans of early twentieth century Austria and white Americans in
the age of Obama. Both groups experienced a relative loss of power and
status. Some members of each group came to feel a sense of racial alienation as other groups who had been previously excluded from political power began to achieve at least a measure of it. I closed the article
by speculating that, despite the parallels between Austro-German racial
nationalists and American white nationalists, a Nazi-style takeover here
was improbable. Regarding the latter, however, I did argue that "these
extremists need not turn us into a racialist, genocidal totalitarian state
in order to cause serious damage to the fabric of our society . . . We
ignore their alienation at our peril."

At that point, four years into the Obama presidency, Rush
Limbaugh had already been steadily bombarding his audience with
countless rants contrasting his own imagined definition of a once-great
America and the very different America that the supposedly radical
black redistributionist Barack Obama was turning us into. Limbaugh's
aim was to heighten the anxiety felt by his conservative, mainly white
audience.

I had no inkling that the president who followed Obama would be
a man who literally took the rationale and rhetoric for his run directly

from the Limbaugh playbook. In a speech that should have immediately ended his campaign, but instead launched him to the top of the Republican primary polls, Donald Trump declared, in announcing his candidacy for presidency on June 16, 2015, that, "When Mexico sends its people, they're not sending their best . . . They're bringing drugs. They're bringing crime. They're rapists. And some, I assume, are good people."

On that day, and in so much of his campaign rhetoric that followed, Donald Trump spoke the language of racially resentful and alienated whites, language Rush Limbaugh had been broadcasting to millions of Americans five days a week since Barack Obama had become president in 2009. Trump presented himself as the champion of those whites in the struggle against their enemies, people like Barack Obama and other liberals, as well as those whom liberals championed—particularly, Americans of color and immigrants. Trump's road to the White House was significantly smoother than it would otherwise have been because Limbaugh had already paved the way for him. Going forward, the clash between the Obama and Limbaugh/Trump definitions of America will remain central to our public discourse for the foreseeable future.

INTRODUCTION

"How did we get here?" is one of the essential questions right now in American politics. How did we go from a society that elected Barack Obama twice to one that, popular vote loss aside, elected Donald Trump? Although there are no simple answers, we do know that white anxiety, fear, and anger aimed at non-whites and about demographic change became far more strongly correlated with support for the Republican Party between 2008 and 2016. We also know that the right-wing media played an outsized role in encouraging this development, specifically through the way they talked about President Obama. During those years, the individual media figure who played the largest role was Rush Limbaugh.

While Obama was in office, Limbaugh constantly talked about the president using a technique that scholars call "racial priming." In other words, Limbaugh race-baited.[1] The host's aim was to convince his audience that Obama was some kind of anti-white, anti-American, radical, Marxist black nationalist, and possibly a secret Muslim to boot. This was neither a bug nor a supporting element of Limbaugh's presentation, but instead stood as a central feature deployed strategically in order to accomplish a very specific task, a task reflected in the title of this book. The tribalization of politics is exactly what Limbaugh set out to achieve.

Tribalization refers to a transformation much more profound than merely convincing Americans to be partisans who vote based on a shared set of policy preferences. It means cleaving America in two, and, in the case of Limbaugh, creating a conservative tribe animated by political ideology, but more so by racial and cultural resentment that feeds a hatred of the opposing tribe. When speaking about Obama, Limbaugh's primary goal was to advance the tribalization of our politics. His efforts helped ;ay the groundwork for the election in 2016 of a man who essentially adopted the host's view of the Obama presidency.

"I hope he fails"

In 2009, Limbaugh's response to the new president reflected his decision—made well in advance—to oppose and undermine Obama and his administration in every way possible. On January 16, four days before the inauguration, the host of the *Rush Limbaugh Show* regaled his audience with the story of being asked by a "major print publication" to produce a four-hundred-word piece on his "hope for the Obama presidency." He then declared: "I don't need 400 words, I need four: I hope he fails."[2] Over the next few years, Limbaugh repeated his "I hope he fails" line often, citing it as evidence of his bravery and power. As the host said on September 21, 2011, "I was the lone wolf . . . There was nobody, nobody . . . before The Pharaoh was immaculated [*sic*], that would dare utter the slightest negative word."

On Inauguration Day, Limbaugh also brought up the matter of race in discussing why he wanted the new president to fail. "Why do I want blanket success?" he asked. "It's just because this guy's father was black? Is that why we're supposed to all hope for his success?" Right from the start, Limbaugh's plan was transparent—to depict Obama as an ideological extremist who used his race to suppress dissent, i.e., to make it politically incorrect for anyone to criticize him. Limbaugh's anti-Obama rhetoric made him the widely acknowledged "de facto leader" of the Republican Party, a moniker pundits began assigning to him a week into the Obama presidency.[3] Limbaugh's influence quickly seeped into the Obama administration. On January 23, 2009, during a White House meeting where he was trying to win Republican support for his economic policies, Obama offered that, "You can't just listen to Rush Limbaugh and get things done."[4] When the remark became public, it only enhanced the host's stature on the right. On January 26, Limbaugh decried Obama for trying to "marginalize me . . . and have me as the nationwide conservative extremist."

Although President Obama ran for reelection against Mitt Romney in 2012, and grappled with Republican congressional leaders such as Mitch McConnell, John Boehner, and later Paul Ryan on a host of issues, it was Rush Limbaugh who stood as the most consistent and formidable ideological foe he faced over the course of his eight years in office. At the end of his presidency, Obama lamented that people who opposed him were all too often "responding to a fictional character named Barack Obama who they see on Fox News or who they hear about through Rush Limbaugh."[5] Comments such as these led Limbaugh to declare repeatedly, as he did, for example, on October 17, 2016, that he lives "rent-free in Obama's head."

Race-Baiting Works

Rush Limbaugh's push to tribalize American politics, not only by high-lighting policy or ideological disagreements but also by exacerbating cultural and racial division, goes back much further than the emergence of Barack Obama as a national figure. Nevertheless, to say that Obama's years in the White House saw that push break new ground would be an understatement. Limbaugh's most direct objective in service of that goal was to define the president in a way that would scare his audience, which consists mostly of white men—80 percent of them identified as conservative and 72 percent as male in a 2009 Pew survey.[6]

Racial fear stands at the core of Limbaugh's telling of the story of the Obama Administration. And white conservatives have been listening. According to Brown University political scientist Michael Tesler, "even after controlling for economic conservatism, moral traditionalism, religious beliefs and activity, and military support, racial attitudes became significantly stronger predictors of white partisanship in the Age of Obama . . . the effect of racial attitudes on party identification increased relative to nonracial predispositions." He added that this development was seen most strongly among "low-information Americans who had not consistently connected their racial predispositions to their partisan attachments in the pre-Obama period."[7] In sum, Tesler found that the data "suggest that Democrats and Republicans had increasingly *separate realities* about race in the Age of Obama—a logical upshot of the spillover of racialization into mass politics."[8] For just one example, Tesler's analysis of survey data, including one study in which the same individuals were interviewed on two separate occasions, indicated that respondents' beliefs in July 2012 about how the economy was doing strongly correlated with racial resentment—even after controlling for ideology and party affiliation. This had not been the case in the first interviews, done in December 2007.[9]

Tesler found that this "spillover of racialization" extended so far that it affected the way people viewed—I wish I were joking—the president's dog. Tesler ran an experiment in which 1,000 people looked at a picture of the First Dog, Bo Obama, and were asked how they felt about it.[10] Half were told to whom the dog belonged, while the other half were told that it was Senator Ted Kennedy's dog, Splash. Both were Portuguese water dogs, and both owners were well-known liberal Democrats. Tesler cross-referenced the answers respondents gave with their responses to prompts that gauged racial resentment, including one that sounded exactly like something Limbaugh himself would say: "it's really a matter of some people not trying hard enough; if blacks would only try harder, they could be just as well off as whites." Tesler found that Bo's favorability score was 50 percentage points lower among those who expressed the most racial resentment compared to the score he got from the least racially resentful. For Splash, the gap was only 20 points. In other words, more racially resentful whites disliked the picture of a dog when they thought it belonged to Obama rather than another, arguably more liberal politician, who was white.

A detailed, nuanced exploration of Limbaugh's racialized rhetoric about Obama offers valuable insight into how the conservative media machine operates. The reach of Limbaugh's message, both during the Obama presidency and for the three decades prior, has made him the single most potent media voice worsening the tribalization of our politics. He has done this by strengthening the connection between white racial resentment and support for Republican candidates and causes. He was alt-right before the term even existed. Additionally, Limbaugh has spawned multiple other media voices who spread a similar message built around the politicization of racial anxiety and hatred, with some on the fringe forging an even more radical path. Limbaugh planted the seed in what has now grown into a full-blown extremist ecosystem. He has thus played a major part in one of the most impactful transformations in American politics, one that places hate at its center.

An examination of American National Election Survey (ANES) data collected in 1988 (the year Limbaugh's show began broadcasting nationally), 1992, 2000, 2004, 2008, 2012, and 2016 demonstrates the accuracy of this assessment.[11] Political scientists Adam Enders and Jamil Scott found that, while the overall level of white racial resentment held at an essentially constant level over these years, those whites who expressed resentment have grown far more likely to identify as Republican, and those who do not have become much more Democratic. The data shows this to be the case both in terms of whom one votes for as well as how one views various policy issues.

Along the same lines, Vanderbilt University political scientists Marc Hetherington and Drew Engelhardt analyzed the data on racial resentment and partisan affiliation in white respondents over time.[12] In 1986 there was not a tremendous difference in racial resentment between white Democrats and white Republicans; members of both parties were spread out along the spectrum of racial resentment, and in fact Democrats outnumbered Republicans at both the high and low ends. By 2016 there were far more Americans at either extreme, with white Republican racial resentment having shot up, and more Democrats expressing very low levels of resentment.

Political scientist Lee Drutman found a similar pattern when he compared the change in the Republican and Democratic favorability rating of Hispanics. Republican opinion went from about three to four points lower than that of Democrats in the early 2000s to eleven points lower than Democrats' views by 2016—a period during which Democrats' views of Hispanics stayed roughly constant.[13] While this data does not explicitly measure white attitudes, the comparison is nonetheless useful.

Although we cannot lay the responsibility for these shifts on Limbaugh alone, he does bear a significant part of it. Most likely, he is both driving and reacting to this trend. But either way, these shifts are a major development, and helps us understand why Limbaugh talked the way he did about race and President Obama.

There are strong indications that this trend toward tribalization might have been responsible for helping to elect Donald Trump. According to Hetherington and Engelhardt

it is not surprising that a candidate who is well known for questioning President Obama's citizenship and suggested that a Black Lives Matter protestor at one of his rallies be 'roughed up' and said that black youths have 'never done more poorly' because 'there's no spirit' would be attractive to a party that these days is dripping with racial resentment.[14]

John Sides, a professor of political science at George Washington University, examined surveys of 8,000 Americans interviewed in 2011 and 2012 who were also re-interviewed after the 2016 election. Tracking changes over time, Sides found that only three things had a greater effect on how white respondents voted for president in 2016 than in 2012: 1) racial resentment toward African Americans; 2) how favorably they felt about Muslims; and 3) their level of support for a path to citizenship for undocumented immigrants, as well as attitudes about the undocumented and immigration in general.[15]

Other data from the 2016 race further demonstrates the impact of white racial resentment. Tesler found that, among Republican primary voters—who are overwhelmingly white—voting for Trump correlated with: 1) racial resentment toward blacks; 2) unfavorable sentiments toward Muslims; and 3) support for forcibly sending undocumented immigrants out of the United States (These should sound familiar). Such sentiments had been, relatively speaking, nowhere near as significant a factor in determining GOP primary voters' support for the previous two Republican nominees.[16]

Finally, University of California political scientist Lynn Vavreck, along with Sides and Tesler, analyzed ANES data collected in late January 2016. They found that GOP primary voters who placed little importance on their white identity were highly unlikely to express support for Trump, while the percentage who supported Trump grew in almost exact proportion to the importance those voters placed on being white.[17] More broadly, in their comprehensive analysis of voter opinion and the 2016 election, the authors argued that Trump's victory resulted to a good degree from the advantage he gained from the activation of white identity, in particular among the whites without a college degree who made up a disproportionate share of the voting population in key states like Wisconsin, Michigan, and Pennsylvania. Moving a total of 39,000 votes in those states from Trump to Clinton would have made her president. Sides, Tesler, and Vavreck contended that the two major party candidates staking out such strongly opposing views on "identity-inflected issues" resulted in voters seeing a greater gap between them on those issues than between the Democrat and Republican in any presidential election since ANES began surveying voters on the matter in 1972. This is true despite voters seeing a smaller gap in terms of overall ideology between the major party candidates in 2016 compared to 2012.[18] In other words, racial identity and attitudes mattered most.

Regarding the general election, after examining ANES data, Philip Klinkner, a political science professor at Hamilton College, reached a similar conclusion regarding white racial resentment, namely that voters who expressed "high levels" thereof were more likely to vote for Trump than for Romney four years earlier, and the reverse was true for those who expressed "low and moderate levels."[19] Likewise, Tesler found that a belief that whites were "unfairly" treated compared to non-whites "appeared to be an unusually strong predictor of support for Donald Trump in the general election."[20] The authors of another paper found "no statistically significant relationship" between respondents' expressing racist or sexist beliefs and how favorably they felt about 2008 Republican nominee John McCain or Mitt Romney, but did find a "quite strong" relationship when it came to Trump.[21] Trump campaigned differently than Romney and McCain. Specifically, he was willing and able follow the path prepared for him by race-baiting tribalizers like Limbaugh. In that sense, Limbaugh begat President Trump.

The story Limbaugh has told—sold, really—to tens of millions includes far more than simply the idea that Obama was a bad president. At its heart, the host's rhetoric was designed to divide Americans from one another by placing them into separate tribes based in large part on race and religion, to "other" Obama personally, and to characterize his beliefs and policies, as well as those who supported them, as standing in direct opposition to traditional America. Or at least America as defined by Limbaugh. In short, the way Rush Limbaugh spoke about the Obama presidency was so important because, for a great many Americans, he spoke the truth. And in November 2016, they acted upon that truth.

THE TRIBALIZATION OF POLITICS

Chapter One

BLACKENING THE RADICAL, SECRET MUSLIM PRESIDENT

Rush Limbaugh doesn't do rallies. He had long ago "sworn off" such things, the host told his listeners the day before the 2018 midterm elections. That night, however, was different. President Donald Trump had come to Limbaugh's hometown of Cape Girardeau, Missouri, for his final pre-election rally. The host was there to introduce his president.

Clapping his hands, waving his arms, and pumping his fist, Limbaugh moved from one side of the stage to the other. The crowd cheered with gusto for its native son. "It is the night of a lifetime," he told them. He briefly relived the glorious 2016 victory, and then hurled a couple of obligatory shots at Hillary Clinton—he accused her of colluding with Russia to rig that election—(the crowd, as you might expect, broke into a chant of "Lock! Her! Up!")—before taking aim at Barack Obama, Joe Biden, and the mainstream media. Limbaugh then brought up the issue that Trump and his party had put at the center of their closing argument leading into the midterms. It was the only policy issue the host mentioned during his ten minutes of remarks: The Caravan.

There was no need to describe it in any further detail. Those attending a Trump rally would almost certainly have heard all about the couple of thousand refugees who had fled Honduras and were heading north, across Mexico, toward our southern border. Trump, Republican candidates, and the right-wing media—including Limbaugh—had for weeks been using the specter of brown hordes trampling our borders to scare the daylights out of their base. The caravan was the conservatives' core campaign tactic.

"We are a nation at risk in the dangerous world, and much of the risk we face is internal," Limbaugh intoned, citing the caravan as the prime example of that danger. The host went on to summarize his and Trump's worldview, from which flowed their response to the caravan and just about every other issue: "We are defending an America that has strayed from our founding . . . It has to do with culture. It has to do with protecting and defending the Constitution." The traditional America created by its founders is at risk. The enemy is internal. They want to destroy America's culture, its laws, and its institutions. They will stop at nothing in order to achieve that objective.

Finally, the music began playing over the loudspeakers as Limbaugh built to a crescendo and declared, "Raise the roof, 'cause here he comes: the president of the United States, Donald J. Trump!" Limbaugh had prepared the crowd for Trump on a stage in Missouri that night, in the same way that he had spent eight years preparing tens of millions of Americans for Trump with his race-baiting rhetoric about Trump's predecessor, Barack Obama.

"I am the least racist host you'll ever find."

Three hours a day, for well over two hundred days a year, Rush Limbaugh deploys words as political weapons in his campaign to tribalize American politics. And a favorite tactic of his has long been race-baiting. Limbaugh has a well-documented record of using racially coded or outright racist language that long predated the election of our first black president. In the 1970s, working as a DJ under the name Jeff Christie, he once snapped at a female black listener he was having difficulty understanding, "take that bone out of your nose and call me back."[1] More recently, he offered that it was "time to get rid of" the National Basketball Association, saying that the league should instead be called "the TBA, the Thug Basketball Association," and that we should "stop calling them teams. Call 'em gangs." As for the NFL, the host stated in 2007 that "all too often looks like a game between the Bloods and the Crips without any weapons. There, I said it."[2]

As for political figures, Limbaugh has taken numerous shots over the years at civil rights leader Reverend Jesse Jackson. The host asked his audience more than a quarter-century ago: "Have you ever noticed how all newspaper composite pictures of wanted criminals resemble Jesse Jackson?" In a 1990 interview, Limbaugh was asked about this remark. He pleaded not guilty to the charge he had been race-baiting: "You may interpret it as that, but I, no, honest-to-God, that's not how I intended it at all . . . I am the least racist host you'll ever find."[3] Likewise, President Donald Trump told reporters in January 2018 that "I am the least racist person you have ever interviewed."[4] Trump has expressed such sentiments multiple times over the years; that particular occasion had been prompted by reports that he had characterized Haiti and parts of Africa as "shithole countries" and wondered why the U.S. could not take in more immigrants from Norway rather than those places. Like Trump, Limbaugh invests a great deal of energy in convincing anyone listening that he is "the least racist," for obvious reasons. His race-baiting speaks for itself, but proclaiming himself a white supremacist would limit his commercial appeal; therefore, he has consistently characterized himself as "colorblind."

Is Limbaugh a racist or not? In reality, it does not matter whether he is a David Duke-style true believer or someone who agonizes every night about what he said that afternoon. Either way, Limbaugh uses racism—playing and preying on primal prejudices and racial anxieties, especially about African Americans—to rile his audience up. Michael Gerson, a former George W. Bush speechwriter, made the same assertion in regards to Trump: "There is no difference in public influence between a politician who is a racist and one who appeals to racist sentiments with racist arguments. The harm to the country—measured in division and fear—is the same."[5]

Race-baiting and "othering" stand at the heart of the tribalizing story Limbaugh told about the Obama presidency. He relied on these tactics when discussing almost every major policy issue—even ones that were not race-specific—not to mention plenty of issues that had nothing to do with policy at all. Why does this matter? Because these tactics worked. Journalist Ezra Klein noted that scholars who have studied "racial priming" broadly agree that getting white voters to reflect on their whiteness makes them more conservative politically.[6] Limbaugh's underlying purpose in discussing race and Obama was to do just that, to heighten his older, overwhelmingly white audience's identification with their white identity by scaring them about the black president who—the host reminded them repeatedly— wanted to take what they had earned and give it to black people as part of a radical plan to transform the traditional America they knew and loved.

Rush to Judgment

Since Talkers, a radio industry magazine, began keeping such records in 1991, Rush Limbaugh has consistently had the largest audience of any radio talk show host, something that remains true today.[7] The consensus estimate is that he had about twenty million listeners a week in the 1990s—before the internet increased the number of media options—and still reached thirteen to fourteen million during Obama's years in the White House.[8]

Numbers, however, do not begin to fully measure Limbaugh's influence on our politics and society. In short, no individual media figure has had such reach over the past quarter-century. An authoritative 2010 analysis by Kathleen Hall Jamieson and Joseph N. Capella of the University of Pennsylvania identified Limbaugh, along with *Fox News* and the opinion pages of the *Wall Street Journal*—the latter two media behemoths with staffs that dwarf Limbaugh's—as "constitut[ing] a conservative media establishment."[9] And Limbaugh never loomed larger than when—from his studio—he took command of the Republican opposition to the forty-fourth president of the United States.

On January 19, 2009, the day before Obama's inauguration, Limbaugh spoke with *Fox News* host Sean Hannity. In a few sentences, Limbaugh defined Obama's view of America, using themes he would repeat ad nauseam over the next eight years:

> We're a country comprised of human beings that the Democrat Party and the left have attempted to arrange into groups of victims, and that's who [Obama] appeals to, and the victims are the people waiting around for some grievance to be resolved . . . and he is parlaying that. So I think the fact that he's African-American—his father was black—to me, it's irrelevant. This is the greatest country on earth. We want to keep it that way . . . It is that way for specific reasons . . . and I'm very much concerned that our greatness is going to be redefined in such a way that it won't be great, that we're just going to become average.

America is great, Limbaugh continued, and "we want to keep it that way." President Obama, on the other hand, wants to destroy our country by addressing the grievances of disadvantaged groups and redistributing power from those who have held it to those who have not. Obama is black, and African Americans are the primary group whose grievances he is going to resolve. Of course, his blackness was "irrelevant" to Limbaugh, the "least racist host you'll ever find." He added that Obama's blackness mattered to him only because it supposedly protected the president from criticism, from real, honest scrutiny:

> We are being told that we have to hope he succeeds . . . ; that we have to bend over, grab the ankles, bend over forward, backward, whichever; because his father was black, because this is the first black president . . . The racism that everybody thinks exists on our side of the aisle has been on full display throughout their primary campaign . . . they've done a great job, the media has, of covering up his deficiencies. He's too big to fail, and so whatever goes wrong, blame it on Bush, blame it on . . . I mean, MSNBC's new life will be criticizing you and me, because they can't criticize him.

It is all here, in these two paragraphs, deployed in service of the host's push to tribalize American politics. We see the race-baiting and fear-mongering, the notion that being black gives one power that is denied to whites, as well as the language of emasculation and subjugation—thanks to Obama, "we" will have to "bend over, grab the ankles."

Limbaugh returned on dozens of occasions to similar images, along with repeated references to castration. For example, he described the "New Castrati" as "men with no guts who have just been bullied by women and the power structure and liberalism in general . . . 'De-balled' if you will,'" as well as slamming "cuckolded" Republicans, or, in another formation, "cuckservatives."[10] This last term also has racist connotations. In a certain type of pornography, a "cuckold" or "cuck" is a white man who watches someone else—usually a black man—have intercourse with his wife. Conservatives who use the term are well aware of this meaning.[11] "Cuckservative" broke into the mainstream media after Limbaugh's mention.[12]

On countless occasions Limbaugh hammered the point that the president and his allies—both in the Democratic Party and among civil rights leaders, whom the host termed "race hustlers"—tried to paint any criticism of Obama as, by definition, racist. Doing so was part of how, Limbaugh claimed, Obama, blacks, and liberals made race relations worse: "This is the beginning of the ginning up of the race machine. The translation here is: 'Limbaugh wanted Obama to fail because he's black' . . . they're gonna play the card . . . as often as they can. Any opposition to Obama is race-based or racist . . . That's all they've got. And that's how they hope to gin up the white guilt."[13]

Despite facing these slings and arrows, Limbaugh pledged that he would stand up to any attempt to censor the president's critics. Democrats, he claimed, on July 17, 2013, sought to "silence" potential critics of Obama by branding any attack as motivated solely by racism. Eight days later, the host accused "the left" of wanting "race problems" to remain unsolved, and in fact wanting to make them worse. Why? Because "too many people make money off of racial strife, and therefore they're always going to promote it."[14]

In Limbaugh's mind, one of the most important truths he would tell about Obama was that the president was responsible for aggravating racial tensions, for encouraging and fomenting racism rather than bringing about the "post-racial" America that Limbaugh said his election was supposed to usher in. On May 28, 2009, the host laid out this perspective quite clearly, noting that many Americans hoped that electing the first black president would significantly weaken racial conflict. However, Limbaugh knew better: "I said no. It's going to exacerbate it . . . We are going to have more race related problems in this country than we have ever had." And the reason for that, Limbaugh said, was Obama's own beliefs and policies regarding race.

To Limbaugh, a post-racial America would mean that no one talked about racism. That was his definition. Whether racism actually existed was irrelevant; the real problem was that people talked about it. On May 26, 2010, the host reminded his audience that he had predicted that electing President Obama would not "end all this racist talk." He continued that now "everything's about race. Everything is about skin color to these people, or however they classify people, however they seek to group them, whatever, they're victims."

Limbaugh contrasted Obama with conservatives like himself, saying that only one of the two even noticed race. On July 30, 2009, the host said that the president was "as race-oriented as you can be. We conservatives are colorblind. We don't even see people that way. He started it."[15] Later in the same segment, Limbaugh quoted from Obama's book, *Dreams from My Father*, to supposedly demonstrate the racial "tactic" the president used on white people:

President Obama is so race-obsessed he writes a book about the father he never really knew subtitled "A Story of Race and Inheritance." . . . Page 94–95 of the book *Dreams from My Father: A Story of Race and Inheritance*: 'It was usually an effective tactic, another one of those tricks I had learned: People were satisfied so long as you were courteous and smiled and made no sudden moves. They were more than satisfied; they were relieved—such a pleasant surprise to find a well-mannered young black man who didn't seem angry all the time.' That's him describing an 'effective tactic' to deal with white people.

But Limbaugh's telling, though he read the quotation itself accurately, was false. Obama was actually reflecting on a "tactic" he used to calm his mother when she was concerned after one of his friends had been arrested. Limbaugh, not Obama, said the tactic was an approach used on white people specifically. Obama just said "people." The goal of the segment was to ensure that the audience did not believe that Obama wanted to improve race relations.

Throughout both of Obama's terms, Limbaugh hammered into his listeners the idea that the president set out to increase racial division in America. He criticized Barack and Michelle Obama by saying that "everything has to be about race with these people! You know, we were supposed to be post-racial with the election of Obama. We're supposed to have put all that behind us . . . instead, as I knew would be the case, it's gotten worse by design." The host also agreed with the assessment of another commentator who wrote that Obama, "adopted a rhetoric and an agenda that is predicated on dividing up the country according to tribal grievances . . . [and] has nearly torn the country apart . . . no other recent president has offered such a level of polarizing and divisive racial bombast."[16]

Did America hear divisive racial rhetoric during the Obama presidency? Absolutely. But the rhetoric came not from the president, but rather from conservative opponents such as Limbaugh, whose audience regularly heard the host criticize Obama for not bringing about the post-racial America the president had supposedly promised. (It is important to note that Obama actually made no such promise; he told journalist Richard Wolffe in an interview published in 2009 that America's racial problems "aren't just solved by electing a black president."[17]) In addition to the aforementioned quotations, Limbaugh blamed Obama for not improving race relations, even for exacerbating racial divisions, nine times in 2010, once in 2011, twice in 2013, five times in 2014, twice in 2015, and again in September 2016.[18]

The New Black Panther Party

Limbaugh did not just offer a broad condemnation of President Obama on the matter of race but also furthered the tribalization of our politics by directly tying the president to groups and individuals whom the host depicted as representing black radicalism, professing anti-white ideas, and pursuing anti-white aims. This is what I mean when I refer to the "blackening" of Obama. The way Limbaugh assembled and used this cast of characters, repeatedly linking the president to one or more of them, was part of a carefully crafted strategy designed to maximize the number of listeners. For the audience, the dramatization of this alleged linkage became like a soap opera that not only indoctrinated them politically but kept them coming back to hear the next episode.

Given its size and relative lack of influence, the New Black Panther Party (NBPP)—which has no institutional connection to the Black Panther Party founded in the 1960s—played an outsized role in Limbaugh's history of Obama and race. The party's role centered around the host's accusation that the president and Eric Holder, U.S. Attorney General from 2009 to April 2015, ignored voter intimidation allegedly perpetrated outside a Philadelphia polling station by two members of the NBPP in 2008. In July 2010, Limbaugh heaped praise upon J. Christian Adams, a former Department of Justice (DOJ) official, Republican activist, and, more recently, a member of President Trump's controversial, short-lived commission investigating voter fraud.Adams had criticized the DOJ's decision to not file charges in the case. Adams claimed the DOJ declined to prosecute wholly on the grounds of race. The host called him a "whistleblower . . . a pretty gutsy guy" and played audio in which Adams also accused the DOJ of practicing widespread bias: "Some of my [former] co-workers argued that the law should not be used against black wrongdoers because of the long history of slavery and segregation. Less charitable individuals called it 'payback time.'" Limbaugh made clear he agreed with these sentiments, concluding that Obama saw race relations in America in similar terms: "It's payback time . . . he's been raised, educated, and believes on his own that this country has been (as you know) immoral and unjust . . . There's no question that payback is what this administration is all about." Adding fuel to the fire of white racial resentment he was stoking, Limbaugh also threw in that "O.J. Simpson was payback," though neither Obama nor Holder had any connection to the Simpson murder trial.[19]

After the U.S. Commission on Civil Rights investigated the DOJ's handling of the NBPP case, conservative appointee Abigail Thernstrom called the incident in Philadelphia "small potatoes" because there was no evidence that any voter was actually intimidated, let alone prevented from voting. Regarding Adams' charges of DOJ bias, Thernstrom said there was no evidence to back the claims.[20] Nevertheless, the New Black Panthers story is an example—far from the only one—of Limbaugh telling his audience that the Obama administration used its power to favor black people over white people. That the story as he told it was false did not stop the host from using it to make his point.

Limbaugh referred to the New Black Panthers—almost always connecting them to the president—on numerous additional occasions, including four times in 2009, ten times in 2010, six in 2011, three in 2012, twice in 2013, seven times in 2014 and, after taking a break for a year, five more times in 2016.[21] Virtually every time Limbaugh mentioned the NBPP, he tied them to Obama. On April 16, 2010, the host sarcastically thanked Obama for his "never-ending support of the New Black Panthers." On July 7, 2010, the host played audio of King Samir Shabazz, head of the NBPP's Philadelphia chapter, and one of the two men who had been involved in the alleged voter intimidation case in Philadelphia, saying: "I hate white people. All of them! Every last iota of a cracker, I hate him! You want freedom? You're going to have to kill some crackers! You're going to have to kill some of their babies." Limbaugh also mentioned the Philadelphia case and referenced "the voter fraud that happened in 2008." The next day he referenced Shabazz again, voter fraud, and then Obama. The host brought up both Shabazz and Obama—tying one to the other—multiple times in subsequent weeks. On September 29, 2010, Limbaugh again played audio of Shabazz expressing his hatred of whites, along with a denunciation of "Fox Jews—I'm sorry—*Fox News*," along with "most of the media blood suckers, liars, and cruciFox Jews." (Conservative agitators historically strive to exacerbate tensions between blacks and Jews, two reliably Democratic groups. Limbaugh's specific goal here was to cause Jews to question their support for Obama by tying him to a vicious anti-Semite.)

On October 3, 2011, Limbaugh talked about a "*Breitbart* exclusive" report that the president had "appeared with and marched with members" of the NBPP in 2007. Limbaugh skipped over the fact that this was an event commemorating the forty-second anniversary of the march across Edmund Pettis Bridge in Selma, a seminal event in the civil rights movement. Thousands of people were there, and it was no more an Obama event than it was an NBPP event. Limbaugh also brought up Obama and the NBPP when discussing a number of other controversial, race-related incidents.

Talking about the New Black Panthers—which the U.S. Commission on Civil Rights, the Anti-Defamation League, and the Southern Poverty Law Center (SPLC) have all characterized as a hate group—and connecting the group directly to President Obama so often was part of Limbaugh's larger tribalization strategy. Specifially, it a was a way for the host to remind his mostly white audience about the dangers they faced from black radicalism, thus heightening their sense of racial identity and their opposition to the president.

ACORN and "Chicago Thug Politics"

Those who get their information only from the *Rush Limbaugh Show* might be forgiven for thinking that the Association of Community Organizations for Reform Now, popularly known as ACORN, was— before being brought down by intrepid conservative activists in 2009 and 2010—one of the single most powerful institutions in American politics and society.

The group, established in 1970, did make a significant impact advocating for lower-income and working-class Americans on issues such as housing, and had a particular focus on getting lower-income people registered and out to vote. That was until right-wing provocateur James O'Keefe and his associate Hannah Giles produced videos that they falsely edited to make it look like O'Keefe—while dressed as a pimp—had gotten advice from low-level ACORN staffers about how prostitutes might avoid tax laws.[22] (In reality, O'Keefe was conservatively dressed during the encounter, but the image proved indelible.) The organization subsequently lost so much funding that it was forced to disband in 2010. Because of its voter drives in poor, disproportionately Democratic areas, ACORN had long been a target of Republicans. (Following the release of the O'Keefe videos, independent investigations were conducted which found no criminal wrongdoing by ACORN or any of its employees.)

In September 2008, before Obama was even elected, Limbaugh offered that ACORN was "an ultra-radical left-wing fraudulent voter registration operation that is caught routinely, frequently cheating, registering illegals, registering people multiple times . . . That's Chicago thug politics . . . And that's what he [Obama] was doing in the community. He was learning from the bottom up, gutter Democrat Party politics." A few days later, the host added that "Groups like ACORN . . . exist for the express purpose of committing voting fraud."[23] Limbaugh also mentioned on several occasions that Obama had worked for ACORN early in his career. Following the president's inauguration, on January 27, 2009, Limbaugh defined ACORN as "Obama's army . . . Obama's ground machine."

The concept of the "Chicago thug" was one that Limbaugh repeatedly used when referring to Obama, frequently along with mentions of ACORN. The following are just a few examples out of many:

- "thugs from Chicago running our country"
- "the Chicago thugocracy . . . Obama is one of them."
- "[Obama's] tactics are those of a thug."
- "Obama . . . use[s] thuggery, bribes, all kinds of kickbacks, ACORN type . . . Chicago organizer tactics."
- "Obama is a Chicago thug who is forcing his policies on people

with bribes, kickbacks, and all kinds of things at the legislative level."[24]

Political reporter and commentator Jamelle Bouie wrote in 2014 that "thug" had become the "new N-word."[25] Thus, Limbaugh was using "Chicago thug" to code the president as a black man who had learned his thuggery "in the community" i.e. from ACORN, a radical, black organization. In other words, Limbaugh was telling his listeners that the president was just another black criminal.

Limbaugh also blamed ACORN for helping to cause the mortgage crash of 2008 that brought about the Great Recession. This is a wholly false claim.[26] Nevertheless, it is one the host repeated with regularity. As he explained, for example, on September 29, 2008, it went back to the Community Reinvestment Act (CRA), which, in Limbaugh's words, "was meant to encourage banks to make loans to high-risk borrowers, often minorities living in unstable neighborhoods." The CRA, Limbaugh claimed, enabled "radical groups like ACORN . . . to abuse the law" by making banks lend large amounts of money in "subprime" loans to "often uncreditworthy [sic] poor and minority customers." Limbaugh further contended that the law gave ACORN the ability to block a bank from merging or expanding by claiming it was out of compliance with the CRA: "intimidation tactics, public charges of racism and threats to use CRA to block business expansion have enabled ACORN to extract hundreds of millions of dollars in loans and contributions from America's financial institutions." Limbaugh connected then-candidate Obama to the organization, saying, "Of course Obama is as close to ACORN as anybody can be, closer to ACORN than anybody ever seeking the presidency." In the host's view, ACORN shook down banks on behalf of blacks and other minorities, and thus, by extension, so did Obama.

What else was ACORN guilty of, from Limbaugh's perspective? Helping their poor, minority constituency steal from the rest of us. "Look, everybody thinks it's the rich who are the tax cheats," Limbaugh said on September 15, 2009, "but the ACORN babes are helping people cheat on their taxes ... America's poor are gaming and cheating the IRS." (This was a lie that has been widely debunked.[27]) And of course, Obama shared their ideology completely, as Limbaugh made clear during the same broadcast: "What ACORN's doing is the work Obama is doing, but they got caught. You know, Obama is ACORN." Limbaugh repeated the idea that "Obama is ACORN," using those exact words, two and four days later.

When ACORN did finally come under scrutiny from Congress— ultimately leading to the passage of legislation signed by President Obama that made it illegal for the federal government to authorize any money for the organization—Limbaugh again exaggerated its relationship to the president, saying on September 17, 2009: "We all have the tape [note: Limbaugh didn't play it here] of Obama going to meet ACORN and telling them they were going to be fundamentally involved in setting the agenda of his presidency." In reality, at an Iowa forum for presidential candidates in December 2007, then-U.S. Senator Obama told a gathering of 5,000 community organizers—a number of whom were presumably members of ACORN—that, if he were elected, "during the transition, we're going to be calling all of you in to help us shape the agenda."[28] Contrary to what Limbaugh relayed to his audience, Obama did not specifically tell ACORN anything.

On June 30, 2009, Limbaugh went on a tirade in which he shared with his audience what he claimed was the real rationale for the connection between Obama and ACORN. "Anybody who thinks that he

[Obama] intends to just constitutionally go away in 2016 is nuts," he began. "I think that's what all this ACORN stuff is all about. I think giving ACORN money, fraudulent voter registration, whatever it's going to take, these are people who seek power for reasons other than to serve. They seek to rule." In other words, black radicals and, as previous comments in the same segment made clear, uneducated minorities who worshipped Obama ("a cult-like bunch") were going to overthrow the Constitution so that Obama could rule, presumably for life. (Limbaugh explored the idea of Obama trying to stay in office beyond 2016 six other times.[29])

Related to ACORN, Limbaugh brought up community organizing as a way to take a swipe at Obama on thirty-nine different dates during his presidency.[30] (Even as late as January 16, 2014—nearly four years after he had helped drive ACORN out of business—Limbaugh was still nonsensically raving about the president "call[ing] his community organizer buddies at ACORN.") Most Americans likely had a vague understanding that as a young man the president had spent a few years doing a job with that title, and that it involved working with predominantly low-income communities in Chicago. In Limbaugh's world, this work somehow provided evidence that the president was a dangerous extremist:

- "We elected an agitator . . . a community organizer . . . an authoritarian."
- "I mean, President Obama's a lifelong political agitator. What do political agitators do but get people angry? That's what a community organizer is."
- "What's a community organizer? It's intimidation, it's bullying, it is shaking down other people for money. Community

organizers are bullies, making Obama a bully!"
- Community organizing "means agitating, rabble-rousing, and organizing rabble-rousing and agitating."[31]

Like connecting Obama to ACORN, talking about the president as a community organizer was another way for Limbaugh to paint him as an angry black radical who wanted to redistribute power and resources from whites to blacks.

"Vote Fraud Experts Extraordinaire"

One of the most nefarious charges Limbaugh leveled against community organizers broadly and ACORN specifically was that they engaged in widespread voter fraud. He called them "the get-out-the-vote bunch, the fraud voter registration bunch," and "vote fraud experts extraordinaire."[32]

But connecting Obama to election rigging indirectly through ACORN was not enough for the host. The president had, according to Limbaugh, gotten his own hands dirty: "Obama's success begins and ends with corrupting the voting process, and not just the November elections . . . Barack Obama or his proxies will stop at nothing to delegitimize the voting process and that's primarily what ACORN is all about."[33] In fact, ACORN became an absolute bugaboo as a result of exaggerations and outright lies like those leveled by Limbaugh—who connected ACORN to voter fraud eleven times in 2009, including on Election Day, and twice more the following year[34]—and others on the right. A poll done by Public Policy Polling (PPP) in 2009 found that 52 percent of Republicans believed ACORN had stolen the 2008 election for Obama. (He won by 9.5 million votes.) PPP did another poll almost four years later and found that 49 percent of Republicans believed ACORN had done the same thing again for Obama in 2012.[35] Although ACORN had disappeared in 2010, Limbaugh clearly helped make an impression that lasted even beyond the existence of the organization itself.

Exaggerating the prevalence of voter fraud was a common tactic for Limbaugh. For example, when stringent voter ID laws passed in a number of states across the country, he specifically mentioned fraud as a justification on three different occasions.[36] Numerous investigations have shown that the type of fraud voter ID laws address—namely a voter presenting a false ID in order to vote in someone else's name—occurs so infrequently that it essentially does not exist.[37] Loyola Law Professor Justin Levitt found that 31 credible allegations—not even convictions—of voter fraud were made from 2000 to 2014, a period when well over one billion votes were cast in U.S. elections.[38] A peer-reviewed study by University of Massachusetts-Boston professors Keith G. Bentele and Erin E. O'Brien called the process of passing voter ID laws "highly partisan, strategic, and racialized affairs," in which "the targeted demobilization of minority voters and African Americans is a central driver."[39] A federal appeals court decision striking down a North Carolina voter ID law in July 2016 concluded that its "provisions target African Americans with almost surgical precision."[40] Despite the overwhelming evidence to the contrary, in Limbaugh's view, angry black militants—of whom Obama was one—were stealing elections.

The fear-mongering spread by Limbaugh, among others on the right,[41] about widespread voter fraud committed by members of minority groups on behalf of Democrats helped prepare the ground for Republican voters to believe Donald Trump when, in the weeks before the 2016 election, he repeatedly predicted that such groups would commit voter fraud and steal the election from him.[42] Limbaugh echoed

Trump on October 18, 2016, just three weeks before the election, offering a Greatest Hits collection of what he had been saying for years:

> We all know that dead people vote . . . Democrats oppose voter ID . . . oppose purging the voter registration rolls . . . want amnesty for illegal immigrants to put them on voter registration rolls . . . Remember Philadelphia and the New Black Panther Party standing outside a polling place intimidating people into . . . not going in unless they were gonna vote for Obama?

After the election, in which Trump lost the popular vote to Hillary Clinton by about 3 million, he claimed—without evidence—on November 27, 2016 that he actually would have won the popular vote if the millions of supposedly illegal votes cast were thrown out. On January 24, 2017, the White House press secretary stated that Trump continued to believe this. That same day, Limbaugh defended Trump and repeated the false claim that "voter fraud [is] out there and it's been documented." The next day Trump announced his intention to create the aforementioned commission to investigate supposed voter fraud. The commission was disbanded on January 3, 2018, having produced no evidence of fraud.

Jeremiah Wright, Jesse Jackson, Al Sharpton, and Louis Farrakhan

The Reverend Jeremiah Wright, Jr. had been the president's long-time pastor. Obama had attended Chicago's Trinity United Church of Christ for some twenty years, beginning in the late 1980s, and had grown close to Wright. In March 2008, at which point Obama had by no means secured the Democratic nomination for president, ABC News broadcast a story that included video excerpts of Wright saying harshly critical things about this country during his sermons. The clips showed him declaring, for example, "No, no, no, not God bless America, God damn America—that's in the Bible—for killing innocent people. God damn America, for treating us citizens as less than human."[43]

In order to save his campaign, Obama had to make clear that he rejected these sentiments, which were toxic to many voters. As a result, he made his now famous Philadelphia race speech, "A More Perfect Union," in which he distanced himself from Wright, explaining that "the profound mistake of Reverend Wright's sermons is not that he spoke about racism in our society. It's that he spoke as if our society was static; as if no progress has been made."[44] In late April 2008, Wright made additional inflammatory statements, and Obama broke with him completely, formally leaving Trinity Church.

Nevertheless, Limbaugh spent the entirety of Obama's two terms accusing the president of still believing the same things about America as Wright. For the host, there was no better way to paint Obama as an America-hater than to tie the president to his former pastor. By doing so over and over, Limbaugh created a tribalizing piece of shorthand—saying "Reverend Wright" conjured images of Obama, the anti-American president. Thus, Limbaugh constantly identified Wright as Obama's "mentor," and "his preacher"—not "former"—as if their break had never happened. Once, the host simply declared, "Jeremiah Wright is Obama." Limbaugh also claimed that the pastor was "telling [Obama] to say" things and that Obama was a "arrogant, radical guy who is angry" and "reveals that he has a bunch of chips on his shoulder, and we know his wife does, and we know Reverend Wright does."[45]

Limbaugh made a habit of saying that the president had a "chip on his shoulder about race," as he did less than a month after the inauguration, on February 17, 2009. Limbaugh used those or comparable words about Barack or Michelle Obama eleven more times in 2009, seven times in 2010 (including on October 26 when he also contended that Obama was "keeping alive" the "race business"), six times in 2011, once each in 2012 and 2013, six times in 2014, seven in 2015, and twice in 2016. The last occasion made clear how central this idea was to the story of Obama that Limbaugh told: "He [Obama]'s got a chip on his shoulder about this entire country from the founding forward because he thinks it's unjust and illegitimate, was a slave state (and still is) and therefore is heavily balanced and abused against African-Americans."[46] Limbaugh's purpose was to paint Obama as a black radical whose anger about racism was reflected in his administration's policies. The host also approvingly quoted an essay that described the "real racism perpetrated by the likes of Eric Holder, Barack Obama, and Jeremiah Wright."[47]

Limbaugh also used Wright to paint the president as an anti-Semite, stating that "[Obama] listened to Jeremiah Wright's anti-Jew, anti-American sermons for 20 years." He continued: "The anti-Jew rhetoric" in today's America comes from "the left" and those "close to Barack Obama." Likewise, Limbaugh cited "the anti-Semitic stuff" Wright had uttered over the years, for which "Obama's never apologized."[48] In addition to the many mentions cited throughout this book, Limbaugh also made reference to Reverend Wright thirty-two times in 2009, twenty-five times in 2010, twenty-three times in 2011, eight times the following year, six in 2013, seven in both 2014 and 2015, and four in 2016.[49]

Although Reverend Wright was Limbaugh's top choice, two other "radical" black figures he frequently linked the president to were Jesse Jackson and Reverend Al Sharpton. The host connected the president or his administration to Jackson, Sharpton, or both, on at least thirty-five broadcasts during the Obama presidency.[50] Limbaugh started even before Obama had wrapped up the Democratic presidential nomination, asserting in March 2008 that "[t]here's no difference in Obama and Al Sharpton; there's no difference in Obama and Jesse Jackson. It's just Obama had a much better mask than those guys."[51]

Limbaugh once used Sharpton to blacken Obama when talking about foreign policy, in a segment that had zero to do with race. He accused the administration of snubbing the Dalai Lama during a White House visit by escorting him "out a back door . . . Meanwhile, Al Sharpton goes out the front do'. Yes, I spoke with a little Negro dialect there. I can do that when I want to."[52] The implication was that the black man who lived in the White House showed Sharpton more respect than he did the Dalai Lama.

Another black figure with whom Limbaugh tarred Obama was Louis Farrakhan. The Southern Poverty Law Center has characterized Farrakhan as "an anti-Semite" and described the organization he leads, the Nation of Islam, as "based on a . . . fundamentally anti-white theology."[53] Limbaugh nevertheless called him one of the president's "mentors" on January 28, 2009, just a week after the inauguration. Limbaugh also asked on April 19, 2010: "What was the racial makeup of the Million Man March? Louis Farrakhan was the leader, a Jew hater without peer, Obama a proud attendee." The host failed to note that Obama also condemned antisemitism, specifically among African Americans, in the same 1995 *Chicago Reader* interview where the president discussed his attendance at the march.[55]

Limbaugh also connected Farrakhan to Wright—and thus doubly to Obama—multiple times. For example, he claimed: "That's his [Obama's] mind-set. That's the mind-set of his preacher [Wright]. It's the mind-set of Calypso Louie [Farrakhan]." ("Calypso Louie" referred to Farrakhan's prior career as a songwriter and performer of calypso music. Limbaugh loves to give his subjects nicknames.) Another time, Limbaugh noted that the person who performed Obama's baptism as a Christian was "a man who gave Farrakhan a lifetime achievement award named after him, the Jeremiah Wright Award." Even eight years after Obama took office, Limbaugh was still tying him and Wright to Farrakhan. "Obama's pastor cherishes Calypso Louie Farrakhan, and Obama cherishes Reverend Wright," the host said in 2016.[55] Limbaugh's goal here was to heighten his white audience's sense of racial paranoia, and then direct the animosity that flowed from it at the president. Limbaugh had already told his listeners that Obama = Wright, Obama = Jackson, Obama = Sharpton, and that Obama was at least strongly influenced by Farrakhan. Consequently, any time he criticized one of them for advocating on behalf of blacks and against whites, or for what he, with no trace of irony, would call "race-baiting," the host was essentially criticizing Obama as well, even when he did not mention the president specifically.

Limbaugh also occasionally linked Obama to white radical figures to get his racially divisive points across. Bill Ayers admitted to participating in the bombings of government facilities as part of the Weather Underground in the 1960s. Ayers and Obama had some professional interactions in Chicago early in the latter's career. Although Ayers is white, Limbaugh used his connection to Obama—in addition to Wright and other black figures—to paint Obama as a secret radical trying to hide his real beliefs. The host, with similar intent, also referenced the influence on the president of Saul Alinsky, another white radical and the author of *Rules for Radicals* (the seminal text on community organizing).

Tiger Woods? Yes, Tiger Woods

The notion of Obama as a secret radical supported an idea Limbaugh frequently sought to implant in his audience, namely that the president was something other than what he seemed. For example, on February 23, 2009, the host stated that "He [Obama] is the exact opposite of the way he is portrayed... [he] has ambitions that are not being reported on ... [His] associations, voting record, life, all tell us precisely that none of us should be surprised at anything... he's trying to achieve." On March 11, 2010, Limbaugh declared that the American people "now realize that they were fooled and elected somebody who's totally unlike the man they thought they were electing." On October 11, 2010, he called President Obama "a Manchurian Candidate here designed to destroy the country."[56] Here's the host on March 8, 2011: "If [Obama] was being honest since he's been elected, he would have been impeached because none of it is what anybody bargained for when they went to the polls in 2008."

On the matter of depicting the president as being not what he appeared to be—or, as Limbaugh put it on December 8, 2009, "the man behind the curtain . . . the real Barack Obama,"—the host suggested parallels with another public figure with whom Obama seemed, on the surface, to share something when it came to matters of race: Tiger Woods. Both had black fathers (although Woods' has some white ancestry while Obama's was a dark-skinned African) and non-black mothers (Obama's was white, while Woods' was of Thai, Chinese, and Dutch origin). The two men have talked, albeit using different terms, about moving beyond traditional, absolutist ways of understanding racial identity. Seemingly a lifetime ago, Woods referred to his racial identity as "Cablinasian," a combination of the words Caucasian, black, American Indian, and Asian.

On the same December 8, 2009 show, which was just days after Woods's infidelity became a major media story, Limbaugh approvingly brought up an article by conservative writer Lisa Schiffren (who also authored the 1992 speech in which Vice President Dan Quayle criticized TV's *Murphy Brown* for glorifying single motherhood): "If I were watching the public's disgust with the newly revealed Tiger Woods from an office in the West Wing, I'd be concerned." Why? Because, as Limbaugh's audience heard, Obama's campaign

> explicitly attempt[ed] to borrow from the then-universal Tiger Woods appeal to allay any discomfort voters might have had with a mixed-race politician. They constructed a persona that would make the American electorate comfortable with a barely-known, first-term senator with a left-wing voting record, a deliberately obscured personal and professional past, and no traditional qualifications for high office.

The host then added that "just as there were people who knew the real Tiger, there are people who know the real Barack Obama." Two days later, another quick mention hinted at Woods' cheating on his wife by having sex with white women: "So Obama goes over there and, you know, there aren't a whole lot of African-Americans on the Nobel Peace Committee, there aren't a whole lot of African-Americans in Denmark, Norway over there, a lot of blondes, Tiger Woods would know about it." Limbaugh went back to the Woods–Obama connection ten days later, on December 18, 2009. This segment offered a prototypical example of Limbaugh insinuating something truly obscene but giving himself just enough cover to say that he did not actually say it. "The parallels between Barack Obama and Tiger Woods are stunning," Limbaugh began. "We don't know if there's rampant sex romps going on with Obama. We doubt that. But everything else . . . We don't know who he is. We don't know anything about the man other than his years agitating the community in Chicago, the things he's written about in his books." According to Limbaugh, Obama had secrets, and was definitely a shady character of some sort. More specifically, Obama was like Woods, another multiracial, light-skinned black guy, and if Tiger was having affairs with white women, well . . . While Limbaugh did say, "We doubt that" in order to give himself cover, by simply teasing the possibility, he was encouraging his listeners to wonder whether Obama— just like Woods—might well be having "sex romps" with white women.

Limbaugh here was evoking one of the most dangerous, hateful, racist tropes in the history of our country: the sexually aggressive black man who pursues white women. The fear and rage that this trope unleashed resulted in the lynching of thousands of black men accused, in some cases, of doing little more than looking a bit too long at a white woman. The brutal 1955 murder of Emmett Till falls into this category. His funeral—with its open casket that put the violence of white supremacy on full display—shocked the nation. It is hard to believe that Limbaugh did not know exactly what he was doing.

The host continued to use the trope of the sexually aggressive black man frequently when mentioning Obama and Woods. On February 19, 2010, Limbaugh stated that,"Now, *Fox* was running this, but Obama's been broomed for Tiger's porn star mistress. I dig it." "Broomed" means abandoned, so this was ostensibly about *Fox News* moving from covering the president to another topic, but Limbaugh saw an opportunity to mention Joslyn James, the white porn star mistress of Tiger Woods, and Obama in the same sentence.

Similarly, on February 18, 2013, the host talked at length about the president having had a private (i.e., no press allowed) golf outing in Florida with Woods the day before. Limbaugh joked about having been on a Florida highway and seeing "a busload of women" travelling in the general direction of the course the two were playing on, before covering himself by adding, "I'm not leveling any accusations." After a break, Limbaugh said he'd received a number of emails saying, in summary, "'Rush, come on! Obama's a very loyal and devoted husband. He doesn't care about women.' Maybe not, but who else was up there?" Then the host replayed the Obama–Woods "sex romps" segment and concluded with: "At some point the same unmasking that has happened to Tiger Woods will happen to Barack Obama." Limbaugh went on: "I predicted that, at some point, the veil would be lifted on Obama. I still say this. I thought it would happen by now, but it hasn't yet. But it has been on Tiger . . . When the media makes you, the media can break you—and that is going to be true of Obama at some point."

Is He Is, or Is He Ain't a Secret Muslim?

Another "veil" that Limbaugh insinuated would be lifted from the president was that he was not a Christian, but instead, a secret Muslim. On one show in 2010, the host mentioned seven different times that Obama had once described the Arabic language Muslim call to prayer as one of the prettiest sounds on earth. From 2011 to 2016, Limbaugh questioned the president's Christianity on multiple occasions, including after Obama had spoken about it at length at an Easter Prayer Breakfast; again when criticizing Obama for not condemning "militant Islam" after the terrorist attack on the *Charlie Hebdo* office in Paris; again while criticizing how Obama dealt with violent acts committed by police (something that ostensibly had nothing to do with Islam); and finally, in a diatribe that ended with a mention of Reverend Wright.[57]

In discussing the Muslim burial rituals American military personnel performed on the body of Osama Bin Laden, Limbaugh—in a remark he characterized as a "media tweak" (one of his favorite strategies to defuse criticism when he wants to be especially outrageous)—opined that, "whenever it comes down to deciding between American or Muslim sensitivities, Obama always seems to side with the Muslim sensitivities." The host went farther down this road when talking about economics, contending that the president's approach to the banking industry was "exactly how Sharia law sees it . . . making money off of money is sinful."[57] That Obama expressed no such belief is irrelevant; the point was to tie him to Islam. Michael Tesler noted that because opponents such as Limbaugh "persistently painted [Obama] as the 'other' (e.g., Muslim and/or foreign born) . . . attitudes toward Muslims continued to be an especially potent predictor of support for and opposition to" him in 2012, as it had been in 2008.[59]

Limbaugh also harped on very fringe in-jokes or references that his conservative audience would understand to make his "Obama is a secret Muslim" point. He mentioned that the president once accidentally referred to the "57 United States"[60]—the same number as there are member states in the Organization of the Islamic Cooperative. According to a right-wing conspiracy theory so widespread that Texas Republican Representative Louie Gohmert referred to it on the floor of the House, this was a slip-up that unintentionally revealed Obama's "secret Muslim" status. Limbaugh did not go that far, but there was no need because conservatives already knew the rumor. He just had to say "57 states" and—if the spirit moved him—chuckle.

Limbaugh also referred to the president as "Imam Obama," asking why, since it was acceptable to refer to Bill Clinton as the first black president, couldn't he "call Imam Obama America's first Muslim president?

Clinton wasn't black . . . Obama says he's not a Muslim, he's a Christian." The host came up with "Imam Barack Hussein Obamadinejad," incorporating the name of Iran's Muslim president Mahmoud Ahmadinejad, and offered that Obama "might believe he's the 12th imam" (a major religious figure in some branches of Islam). Limbaugh also described this one as a "media tweak."[61] He used the term imam to describe Obama on five other occasions.[62] Limbaugh also claimed several times that the president spoke more respectfully and positively about Islam and Muslims than Christianity and Christians. In one instance, the host alleged that "the president is directly and indirectly promoting religious beliefs that are hostile to Western values."[63] Of course, Reverend Wright came up a few seconds later.

If connecting Obama to Islam and to Reverend Wright were not enough, Limbaugh at times sought to connect all three. On August 19, 2010, he questioned the president's faith by stating that Wright preached "a weird brand of Christianity. Reverend Wright's church? Black theology is what comes out of that pulpit, which is, you know, not exactly mainstream Christianity." The next day, Limbaugh made the point more directly, offering that, "Reverend Wright used to be a Muslim and now he's a black liberation theologist [sic]. Which is some sort of Christianity, but he used to be Muslim." About a minute later, in a long exposition, Limbaugh revisited the same point to further question Obama's Christianity:

> You see, Obama's Christianity is the opposite of obvious . . . He has a Muslim name: "Barack Hussein Obama." He had a Muslim father and an extended Muslim family in Kenya. He was partly raised and educated in Indonesia by a Muslim stepfather. He has Muslim half-sisters and brothers, one of whom continues

to reside in a three-by-five-foot hut in Kenya [Limbaugh returned again and again to this "brother living in a hut" to insult Obama for supposedly not helping his family].

His mother was a self-proclaimed and unaffiliated atheist. Obama professed no religion and belonged to no church until he joined Reverend Wright's Trinity Church in Chicago, [Wright] was a Muslim who converted to black liberation theology, which is a highly exotic . . . form of Christianity in the American, even black American, context. . . .

Obama's great literary intellectual role model was Malcolm X. One of Obama's religious advisors is a Chicago Muslim, Eboo Patel. Imam Faisal Abdul Rauf . . . the controversial Muslim leader behind the plan to build the Islamic Center and mosque a couple blocks from Ground Zero wrote the afterward to Eboo Patel's 2006 book: *Building the Interfaith Youth Movement: Beyond Dialogue to Action.* So the Ground Zero mosque imam wrote the afterward to Obama's religious advisor's book. The religious advisor is a Muslim. . . .

Now, having said all that, none of what I have said means that Obama's a Muslim and none of it means that Obama's not a sincere Christian. If he's going to say that he is, fine. We will accept that he's a Christian.

The last three sentences allowed Limbaugh to protect himself against charges he called Obama a Muslim, or that he directly questioned Obama's Christian faith. This is a textbook example of how Limbaugh operates, walking right up to a line by repeating things "other people" are saying and then giving himself cover, in the most technical and limited sense, by not stating he agrees.

Limbaugh followed exactly that blueprint when criticized by MSNBC host Chris Matthews on this very language on August 25, 2010, replying that the sole instance when he spoke about Obama being Muslim was when he quoted Libyan dictator Muammar Khadafy. The host claimed he never called the president a Muslim, and added that his goal was to "help" the media by educating them about why so many Americans believed that falsehood. Limbaugh then went ahead and repeated the charges about Obama's Christianity and Reverend Wright. Here (and again the next day) he both defended himself and made sure anyone who missed the previous show now got the point. This tactic was also a favorite of Trump's ("some people say") throughout the years he questioned the president's birthplace. He also used this blueprint in his campaign for the White House, and has continued to do so as president.

During the same week in 2010, Limbaugh again made the Obama–Wright–Muslim connection. Referencing a remark made about U.S. foreign policy by an American Muslim activist, the host averred on August 23, 2010: "So US [sic] has more blood on its hands than Al-Qaeda . . . This sounds like Jeremiah Wright: 'America's chickens have come home to roost' quote, unquote." (This was one of the most widely quoted lines from Wright's sermons that were featured in the 2008 ABC broadcast.)

Later that day, Limbaugh further discussed why so many believed the president was Muslim and/or doubted he was a Christian:

It's really not hard to understand . . . Folks have not forgotten Jeremiah Wright. When Obama says he's a Christian there are a lot of people that don't believe him, and just because he got elected president doesn't mean they've forgotten it . . . Jeremiah Wright, people heard the tapes, mainstream ruling class try to ignore them. "Ah, doesn't, that's a long time ago. Obama didn't hear a word Wright said in 20 years."

We don't believe Obama when he says that he didn't hear any of that incendiary language when he was in the church . . . We're not that gullible . . . What is the only proof we have that Obama's a Christian? Well, okay, his word, his word. But Jeremiah Wright is the only proof that we have that he's a Christian. Obama described Wright as his spiritual mentor. Well, sorry, media, we've heard Jeremiah Wright. We know what Jeremiah Wright said. We know what he thinks of America.

September 18, 2015, saw Limbaugh again ponder whether Obama might really be a Muslim: "And the media say, 'He said he's a Christian!' Okay, fine. Let's leave it at that, then. I don't know. It's not my job. But . . . Obama has gone out of his way to try to tell people that ISIS is not Islam and they're not Muslims . . . He's hell-bent on people thinking that." Limbaugh said the same thing again on October 13, 2016, this time as part of a defense of Trump and an attack on Hillary Clinton.

Limbaugh's speculations about Obama's faith made serious inroads with his conservative audience. A PPP survey from August 2015 found that 54 percent of GOP primary voters believed that the president was a Muslim, while a further 32 percent were not sure. Only 14 percent correctly stated that Obama was Christian.[64] The results of a CNN/ORC poll conducted a couple of weeks later were somewhat more uplifting, with a mere 43 percent of Republicans believing Obama was a member of the Muslim faith.[65] As for what such beliefs tell us about partisan preferences, an analysis of the American National Election Studies found that, among white respondents, 89 percent of those who believed Obama was Muslim had a more positive opinion of Donald Trump than Hillary Clinton. By comparison, among those who identified as Republican, the figure was actually two points lower.[66]

There's also evidence that suggests the belief that Obama was Muslim represented racial bigotry in another form. Michael Tesler found that 13 percent of those voters who stated that Islam was Obama's religion offered his blackness as the reason they would vote for someone else in 2012. However, 60 percent of those same voters cited his supposed Muslimness as the reason they would not vote for him.[67]

From Limbaugh to Trump

Rush Limbaugh saw the opening on white anxiety right from the start of Obama's presidency, and pushed harder and more effectively to exploit it than anyone else in the media. In doing so, he helped lay the groundwork for the man who, capitalizing on racial and cultural resentments with a skill that would have made George Wallace proud, rose from birther-in-chief to commander-in-chief.

President Trump has followed Limbaugh's tribalizing path by campaigning and—as his reaction to the August 2017 white nationalist terrorist attack that killed protestor Heather Heyer in Charlottesville, Virginia, among many other examples, makes clear—governing on the basis of white identity politics. Trump earned praise from numerous white supremacists, including David Duke and Richard Spencer, for his comment, made after the violence that followed a march organized by neo-Nazis, that there were "very fine people on both sides."[68] As Pulitzer

Prize winning columnist Eugene Robinson put it: "making whites feel embattled and aggrieved is central to the Trump presidency."[69]

As for Limbaugh, on August 16, 2017, he excused the Charlottesville remark by saying that "Trump was probably trying to be accommodating, and he was trying to identify both sides as being somewhat guilty and somewhat responsible." The host rarely if ever extended that level of understanding to remarks of Obama's that generated controversy. Instead, Limbaugh took every opportunity to twist such comments in ways that further tribalized our politics along racial and cultural lines.

Going beyond Trump, the rising tide of white racial resentment that Limbaugh and others like him have nurtured is feeding a level of extremism reflected in the swelling ranks of violent hate groups. In June 2017, even before Charlottesville, Arie Perliger, Director of Security Studies at the University of Massachusetts-Lowell, offered that his research, conducted at the Combating Terrorism Center at West Point, "show[s] that the significant growth in far-right violence in recent years is happening at the base of the iceberg."[70] More recently, in November 2018, the *Washington Post* examined data on global terrorism and concluded that "violence by white supremacists and other far-right attackers has been on the rise since Barack Obama's presidency—and has surged since President Trump took office."[71] This dovetails with an April 2009 Department of Homeland Security report—which was ultimately suppressed as a result of harsh attacks from conservatives, including Limbaugh—that found that, among other causes, the election of a black president who might implement a shift in government policy could serve as "a driving force for rightwing extremist recruitment and radicalization."[72]

Chapter Two

INVENTING THE ANTI-AMERICAN PRESIDENT

Barack Obama loves America. No one could have spoken as eloquently about our country as he has and not be proud of it. Here's one example, from a June 30, 2008 speech he gave in Independence, Missouri:

> For me, as for most Americans, patriotism starts as a gut instinct, a loyalty and love for country that's rooted in some of my earliest memories. And I'm not just talking about the recitations of the Pledge of Allegiance, or the Thanksgiving pageants at school, or... fireworks on the Fourth of July... Rather, as wonderful as these things may be, I'm referring to the way the American ideal wove its way throughout the lessons of my family, the lessons that my family taught me as a child.

During the speech, Obama noted that some had "challenged" his love of country. The soon to be president accused those people of being motivated by "the desire ... to score political points and raise fears and doubts about who I am and what I stand for."[1] While this line could be applied to many pundits and politicians on the right, no figure did more to raise doubts and fears about the nation's first black president than Rush Limbaugh, who waged an eight-year tribalization campaign to brand Obama as anti-American in the minds of his listeners.

Limbaugh used a multitude of tactics to try and achieve his aims. He claimed that the president hated America because of its history of racism. He questioned the president's birthplace. And he accused Obama of wanting to redistribute resources from whites to minorities, most specifically to African Americans, in order to right historical wrongs.

In order to establish a basis for Obama's "anti-Americanism," Limbaugh declared that the president rejected the original principles of our country, as well as the Constitution itself, and the [white] men who crafted it. "Obama talks about 'remaking' America [which] means destroying these traditions, institutions that have defined America and its greatness since the founding," the host stated in July 2009. He added in December that the president was not proud of our country: "America as talked about by Barack Obama—is an America of guilt . . . guilty of racism, sexism, bigotry, homophobia, discrimination, imperialism, colonialism." Two years later, Limbaugh asserted that Obama believed America was "criminal."[2] The host also said that the president considered America to be "exceptionally evil." For good measure, he included Michelle Obama as well, citing her "bilious disgust with America."[3]

Going further down the anti-Americanism road, the host declared in 2010 alone that:

- "We thought that Obama was our first post-American president. We might have underestimated him. Our first anti-American president."
- "He [Obama] hates America."
- "He [Obama] doesn't like much of what's American."
- ". . . by virtue of its character, America was evil . . . I've always

believed Obama felt this"

- "Barack Obama and his crowd see this country as a great Satan."[4]

Limbaugh also told his audience that Obama's hatred of America would drive the president to tear down our most sacred institutions. On September 10, 2009, Limbaugh spoke as if he were President Obama, explaining what he claimed the president believed and would do if given the chance, i.e., if he were able to get rid of the Constitution:

> The whole notion of individual rights and limited government is nothing more than a racist invention of white slaveholders known as the Founding Fathers. We know that our Founding Fathers were racists. We never agreed to their Constitution. Did you vote for it? No. It was imposed on us from one generation to the next. So, forget about it or else our agenda of redistribution of wealth and big centralized government will be obstructed by something as inconsequential as the highest law in the land which we don't respect; which we didn't vote for; which we think is a sham; which we think is racist, sexist, bigoted, and homophobic. The first thing I could do if I had a chance is rip the Constitution to shreds. Now, I know we're not to the point where I can do that yet in front of you.

Limbaugh followed this up in March 2011 by asking if the military had a "contingency plan for—I don't want to say an anti-American president, 'cause that's gonna cloud my real intent here." After being criticized for appearing to call for a military coup, the host fell back on his usual shtick, that this "was a media tweak ... That's what's called stirring the excrement."[5] Limbaugh's walk back aside, the idea of some kind of "deep state"—an unelected element within the government working against the leaders chosen by the people—was obviously okay with the host if the president was named Barack Obama. On the other hand, Limbaugh has repeatedly attacked the so-called deep state for supposedly working to undermine the Trump presidency.[6] The host has also condemned what he called the "silent coup" against Trump.[7]

Additionally, Limbaugh accused Obama of not being able to let go of the past when it came to racism: "He [Obama] still holds that against this country, and that's one of the reasons he's got this country in his crosshairs." The host also claimed that the president saw America as "a country of immorality . . . a nation that has not gotten beyond its slavery past . . . not gotten beyond its immorality, its racism, its sexism, its bigotry and homophobia. He looks at this country and he's got a chip on his shoulder."[8] Limbaugh also asserted in January 2012 that "Barack Obama thinks this country has been inherently unfair since its founding . . . Barack Obama believes that the Founders and the white majority of this country, since its founding, have been inherently unfair, have screwed everybody else, have taken everything for themselves."[9]

Even after Obama had won reelection, Limbaugh, on December 20, 2012, continued to focus on the president's supposed belief in the "unfairness" of America:

Obama is selling the country was founded unfairly and unjustly. The country was founded as a rigged game, a stacked deck. And the people who founded it—we all know who they were—arranged it so that the country was always gonna be theirs. And then what did they do? They ran around the world, and they took from that country and they took from that country and stole this resource and monopolized that resource, and tortured their opponents in war. That's how we became a superpower and we don't deserve that, and these people who benefited from this unfair founding, it's time they paid their fair share now . . . It's time to make the rich pay their fair share. It's clear that Obama selling the notion that what's wrong in this country is that one to 2 percent of the people have always had all the money. It's time to take it back from 'em. And that'll fix everything. That's transformative . . . in terms of matters of race, we're heading back to the pre-Civil Rights Act days.

Here, Limbaugh condemned Obama both as a hater of America and as a straight-forward racist. Crucially, he connected these ideas to the president's economic message, in which Obama asked the wealthiest to pay their "fair share" of taxes. The host did something similar on June 26, 2014, when he claimed that the president had

a big problem with the traditional culture of this country . . . it is an unjust, immoral culture, dominated by an unjust, immoral majority, which has gotten rich and powerful on the backs of the poor, the misbegotten . . . It's time now to transfer power unfairly acquired by . . . the majority and give it to the people it was stolen from.

Similar language about the president supposedly hating America because of its history of racism frequently abounded from the mouth of Limbaugh. A few examples among the many topics that provoked such slander: a high school class in Wisconsin that, according to Limbaugh, "promoted a critical race theory that alleges white people are oppressors"; the president's remarks at the Standing Rock Indian Reservation in which he acknowledged that, when it came to dealing with Native tribes, the United States "often didn't give the nation-to-nation relationship the respect that it deserved"; and a Pew Research Center poll that found liberals were less likely than conservatives to express often that they were proud of being American. One such attack came at the end of a harangue that was not inspired by any particular event, but was instead Limbaugh simply offering a long analysis of why liberals like Obama "oppose" and "hate" the Constitution—the answer was "slavery."[10]

On December 17, 2014, Limbaugh ripped Obama for having mentioned that he had once been mistaken for a valet. "Why does he have to continue to diminish . . . this country?" the host thundered, "The president playing the victim card, racial victim card? . . . But anything in the service of diminishing the United States, anything that serves to illustrate this country as less than perfect and less than what it should be, they [the Obamas] will not miss those opportunities." Limbaugh failed to mention that the president, in keeping with his long-standing practice, also praised our country's progress on racism in the same interview: "The small irritations or indignities that we experience are nothing compared to what a previous generation experienced."[11]

The host also used Michelle Obama as a pawn to brand her husband as someone who sought to use racism to divide America. Limbaugh criticized remarks the First Lady made about how she had felt unwelcome at museums as a young person because she was black, then connected those statements to President Obama's comments about his "My Brother's Keeper" initiative, which provided support for young black and Latino men and boys. The host condemned the president for talking about "boys and young men of color being treated differently by law enforcement when it comes to stops and arrests," and claimed that both Obamas were carrying out "a purposeful effort here to divide of [sic] people of this country along racial lines." To Limbaugh, highlighting the existence of racial disparities was what divided Americans, not the actual disparities themselves.[12]

Similarly, in response to the president being asked in 2015 why questions of national identity seemed to be coming up more often than they had in the past, Limbaugh alleged that Obama was "redefining 'who we are' because . . . 'who we were' was evil, immoral, unjust, corrupt." Under Obama, the host opined, "all of the victims of all of that corruption . . . will soon be running the country and will have their chance at payback." In January 2016, after playing audio of the president talking about politics in Washington being divided, Limbaugh blamed Obama for the state of things, slamming his "undisguised, now, efforts at transforming and changing this country into something it was not founded to be. And all of this disunity, this division? It's justified, it's warranted, just like the anger associated with it is totally justified and warranted, and understandable. And it is unique to Obama. He has brought it about."[13]

Later in the same segment, after citing the president for having invited leaders from a Muslim American organization to attend the State of the Union address, Limbaugh added that Obama did this to be "purposefully provocative," to "remind you that you lost . . . to remind you that it isn't your country anymore . . . to remind you and put an exclamation point behind your country's changing no matter what the hell you think about it, and take a load of this." That was Limbaugh's tribalization at its most naked. When Obama acted or talked about America in a more inclusive way than had traditionally been done,

Limbaugh framed it as his essentially poking white Americans about their lost power.

On March 30, 2016, Limbaugh pounced again, following the president's comments at a National Prescription Drug Abuse and Heroin Summit about how Americans perceived drug addiction differently when thinking about white compared to nonwhite addicts. Limbaugh accused the president of having "a giant problem with this country that is institutional, that dates all the way back to the founding. It is rooted in what he thinks . . .was institutionally incorporated in the founding . . . racism and discrimination and bigotry and white supremacy and all of this." In the broadest terms, the host claimed that "Obamaism is . . . dead set opposed to traditional Americanism, as defined by the way the country was founded." He also asserted that "Obama has been schooled in radicalism, not Americanism," and criticized a 2011 speech the president delivered in Osawatomie, Kansas, laying out his take on economic inequality and government's role in combating it—one that echoed ideas in a speech Teddy Roosevelt had delivered in the same town 101 years earlier—as "alien to American ideals and principles."[14]

The baselessness of these types of charges is clear to anyone who has actually listened to the words of Barack Obama over the past twenty-five years. For example, in the speech that opened this chapter, Obama declared that what "best describes patriotism" is "not just a love of America in the abstract, but a very particular love for, and faith in, the American people. That is why our heart swells with pride at the sight of our flag; why we shed a tear as the lonely notes of Taps sound." However, it wasn't truth or love or pride that Limbaugh was seeking, but rather to further inflame the white resentment of his audience by casting President Obama as someone who hated America, and by extension, them.

"Why doesn't he show his birth certificate?"

The so-called "birther" movement represented another building block in the broad attempt by Obama's opponents to characterize him as loyal to other countries or institutions—i.e. "anti-American." A variety of theories and evidence was proposed by various groups and individuals on the right which all centered on the idea that the president had been born outside of the country, was not a natural-born citizen of the United States, and was thus, under Article II of the U.S. Constitution, ineligible to be president. Political journalist Adam Serwer defined birtherism as a "synthesis" of anti-black, anti-immigrant, and anti-Muslim bigotry that grew among right-wingers, and which characterized Obama as "not merely black but also a foreigner, not just black and foreign but also a secret Muslim."[15] The birther conspiracy gained traction during Obama's campaign for president in 2008, and Limbaugh jumped on board, seeing it as another way to "other" the president and paint him as "not American."

The host first brought up the issue of Obama's birthplace on April 7, 2009, when he quipped that the president was referring to "his country, [the] United States—I don't think he's talking Kenya here." Limbaugh made a similar remark the next day. On a show in June, he offered up a birther joke: "What do Obama and God have in common? Neither has a birth certificate." Limbaugh then performed his usual "I am not saying it, but . . ." dance when he pondered where Obama was born: "Supposedly Hawaii, but we don't have independent confirmation of it. I don't want to go there. God doesn't have a birth certificate, either, so it's no big deal."[16]

Another birther jab came on June 30, when the host mentioned an audience member at a Republican congressman's town meeting who asked why "nobody's interested" in Obama's supposed failure to present his birth certificate. Limbaugh noted that "the crowd went nuts. There's all kinds of stuff bubbling up out there." On July 20, the host added that, "Barack Obama has yet to have to prove he's a citizen. All he'd have to do is show a birth certificate." This comment ignored the fact that on June 13, 2008, Obama had done exactly that when his campaign released the short form version of his birth certificate.[17] Unsurprisingly, this did not put an end to the issue for Limbaugh. On October 9, 2009, when Obama won the Nobel Peace Prize, the host quipped that he was "the second Kenyan" to have won it.

Limbaugh also cast aspersions on Obama's place of birth by making reference to the president with the use of a made-up name. "Little Barry Soetoro is back," the host said in November 2010, "and they're all happy over there in Indonesia." In this case, Limbaugh was referring to Obama's childhood nickname, Barry, and the surname of his stepfather, Lolo Soetoro, an Indonesian man his mother, Ann Dunham, married when Obama was six years old. The family lived in Indonesia, a predominantly Muslim country, for approximately four years. Limbaugh continued: "In India he was introduced by somebody from Kenya, and the woman says, 'As a fellow Kenyan, Mr. President,' of course everybody looked the other way, 'What do you mean fellow Kenyan, we don't want to hear this,' and now little Barry is back." Limbaugh also discussed the birther controversy at length after the media asked Hawaii Democratic Governor Neil Abercrombie about the issue in January 2011. Limbaugh all but embraced the conspiracy. He claimed that no one had "definitively prove[n]" that the president was born in Hawaii, and charged, without evidence, that "most government officials have apparently done their best to seal it all off." The host brought up birtherism three more times over the next two months, and one last time in 2012.[18]

When President Obama released the long form version of his birth certificate on April 27, 2011, he remarked that the country needed to stop being "distracted by sideshows and carnival barkers"—with Donald Trump having emerged as the loudest barker of them all.[19] In the month prior, on at least five occasions, Trump had publicly questioned Obama's birthplace in language that went far beyond even Limbaugh's:

- "Why doesn't he show his birth certificate? There's something on that birth certificate that he doesn't like."
- "He's spent millions of dollars trying to get away from this issue . . . all of a sudden a lot of facts are emerging and I'm starting to wonder myself whether or not he was born in this country."
- "He doesn't have a birth certificate, or if he does, there's something on that certificate that is very bad for him. Now, somebody told me -- and I have no idea if this is bad for him or not, but perhaps it would be -- that where it says 'religion,' it might have 'Muslim.' And if you're a Muslim, you don't change your religion, by the way."
- "I have people that have been studying [Obama's birth certificate] and they cannot believe what they're finding . . . if he wasn't born in this country, which is a real possibility ... then he has pulled one of the great cons in the history of politics."
- "His grandmother in Kenya said, 'Oh, no, he was born in Kenya and I was there and I witnessed the birth.' She's on tape. I think that tape's going to be produced fairly soon. Somebody is coming out with a book in two weeks, it will be very interesting."[20]

Even after the release of the long form birth certificate, Trump continued to indulge in birtherism, either casting doubts on the document's
authenticity or simply questioning Obama's birth without getting specific on at least eight other occasions.[21]

Finally, on September 16, 2016, Trump stated that Obama was,
in fact, born in the United States. Even that turned out to be not so
straightforward, as Trump lied about the origins of the birther conspiracy, falsely claiming that it had been started by "Hillary Clinton and her
campaign of 2008."[22] And that is not the end of it, as after becoming
president, Trump has continued, in private conversations with advis-
ers and at least one senator, to question Obama's birthplace.[23] Beyond
what Trump has said publicly, documents released after his one-time
friend, *National Enquirer* publisher David Pecker, secured immu-
nity from Special Counsel Robert Mueller make clear that as early as
2010 Trump's personal lawyer and fixer, Michael Cohen, got the tab-
loid to promote the birther conspiracy in its pages.[24] In her 2018 memoir, *Becoming*, Michelle Obama wrote that she would "never forgive"
Trump for promoting birtherism.[25]

"The deck is now reverse stacked in perpetuity."

Limbaugh also used a time-honored conservative talking point as a signal that the president sought to advantage blacks as well as other racial
minorities, and disadvantage whites: affirmative action.

Affirmative action—along with racial "quotas"—came up on June
29, 2009, as part of a long tirade that stands as one of the worst examples of Limbaugh playing on white racial fears. He began by calling
Obama and leading Democrats in every branch of government "racists"
and "far left extreme radicals" who thought America had always been
"unjust," and who favored "minorities" in order to counter past discrimination. The host was just getting warmed up:

This is about get even with them time. This is returning the nation's wealth to its rightful owners. This is radical leftism on parade. So when I say does it really matter when Caucasians become a minority, what I mean by this is we already have a governing majority. He's gonna treat them that way. It's reverse racism. We have people who are angry and fit to be tied and they think it's time some people have a lesson taught them and those people happen to be those who have succeeded, those who have achieved, regardless of their race, and those who have been perceived to have all of the power for all of these years, it's time to get even with them. And the parade is on, and you see it happening right before your eyes every day with every piece of legislation that comes forth . . . .

The purpose of the laws now is to achieve the exact opposite. The affirmative action quotas, whatever you want to call it, the intent was never to find equality or to properly compensate . . . Their purpose has not been to level any playing field. It's to reverse it.

The fear that "reverse racism" would worsen as whites approach becoming a numerical minority in this country was something Limbaugh stoked repeatedly in his disproportionately older, conservative, white audience. For example, on March 14, 2012, the host alleged that Obama hoped to enact laws that would treat Americans differently based on their "tribe" or "race" and that the president rejected the idea of equal treatment mandated by the Constitution because he supposedly viewed it as "a rich white man's law." Limbaugh's message was that Obama had it in for whites. On that point, a 2013 poll of nearly 3,000 Americans found that 61 percent of conservative whites and 56 percent of whites over the age of sixty-four believed that whites would face more discrimination as the U.S. becomes more diverse.[26] Fear about their future position makes anxious whites more likely to support political candidates who signal that they will defend their collective status, and to turn away from candidates who appear sympathetic to the interests of non-whites. This in turn makes those anxious whites more likely to vote conservative, which is exactly what Limbaugh's rhetoric aimed to accomplish. Increased white fears also undermine our country's ability to successfully adjust to demographic change. However, the host does not want America to make any such adjustments. Instead, he wants to prevent the change from occurring by keeping America as white as possible.

Limbaugh's audience heard about affirmative action and Obama again when the host said in July 2010 that "we have had affirmative action, we have addressed every grievance 10 to 20 times, and the people who have made us address these grievances have openly said there'll never be enough redress, this has got to happen in perpetuity." In other words, "reverse discrimination" against whites would go on forever if Obama and his allies had their way. The host also lamented "vacation affirmative action," according to which the media would not criticize the first family for taking extravagant vacations because, Limbaugh said sarcastically, it was "only fair and it's only right that members of an abused minority now get their share of the pie." On another show in 2010, Limbaugh talked about the matter in a more traditional sense, saying of Obama: "He's got nobody to do affirmative action for him, nobody to give him an A when he got a D." He did the same thing a few months later, although this time he bumped Obama's grade up a letter, saying that the president had "somebody at Harvard turn [his] C into an A."[27]

An in-depth discussion of affirmative action in October 2010 saw Limbaugh use the issue to undercut the achievements of both President

Obama and First Lady, claiming that being black had advantaged them both. "The way has been paved for Obama, whereas the way has not been paved for me." Note Limbaugh's assertion that a white male, born in 1951, as he was, faced a disadvantage compared to an African American born only a decade later. The host also further defined the Obamas as "them"—separate from "us," i.e., the white people who had supposedly earned their status without the benefit of affirmative action: "Now, my question, do you and I consider the Obamas part of a meritocracy? Do we consider them elites to have come from one of us? We don't, do we? They have nothing in common with us."[28]

Obama's second term featured more mentions by Limbaugh of affirmative action. There was a harangue about Michelle Obama, affirmative action, and her undergraduate attendance at Princeton in which the host painted the first lady as focused on black grievances against the larger society, and claimed that her thesis, titled "Princeton-Educated Blacks and the Black Community," focused on "how Princeton made it miserable for black people." Without using the words "affirmative action," Limbaugh also criticized the president for citing racial discrimination, then argued that efforts to combat it meant that minorities had an advantage over whites: "Well, it's just the exact opposite. The deck is now reverse stacked in perpetuity."[29]

"Think forced reparations here, if you want to understand what actually is going on."

A race-baiting rant by Limbaugh on June 29, 2009, included another key theme he employed in his quest to simultaneously create an "anti-American" Obama and heighten white racial resentment: reparations. He used the concept to emphasize to his audience that Obama was going to plunder the money they had spent their lives working hard to earn and save, and give it to a bunch of—in his words—"non-producers," i.e., black people. Limbaugh theorized that Obama and his Democratic allies were

> smart enough to know that if they call a piece of legislation reparations, it doesn't have a prayer, but if they couch the legislation in fairness and compassion, the usual liberal terms, then people will go for it because they think that they have created enough white guilt at all of the unjust immorality of the history of this country that people sit by and let it happen so that their own personal guilt can be assuaged, regardless of the impact on the country. They're playing this tune very consistently, and they're playing it very well.

Limbaugh's first mention of reparations had come a month earlier, on May 11, 2009, when he described the president's budget as pursuing "more food stamp benefits . . . more unemployment benefits . . . an expanding welfare state . . . to take the nation's wealth and return it to the nation's, quote, 'rightful owners.' Think reparations. Think forced reparations here, if you want to understand what actually is going on." Conservative politicians and media figures have long sought to link food stamps and welfare to black Americans, and have had significant success in doing so.[30] Adding in the term "forced reparations" sent a very clear message that Obama planned to take from whites and give to blacks. Later that same month, the host highlighted where he believed the president had gotten these ideas from, stating that Obama believed that "Jeremiah Wright is right, that this country is racist and the way to get this country fixed is to return the nation's wealth to its rightful owners via high taxes, redistribution, nationalization of industries."[31]

Limbaugh linked "welfare" and "reparations" on numerous other occasions. The host asserted in 2012 that supporters of reparations would never enact a program using that word but instead would "camouflage it, disguise it as some sort of welfare program." He also claimed in 2015 that the president had built a "quasi-reparations infrastructure . . . that will outlast his administration." Limbaugh also brought up the topic indirectly when he noted that Robert Mugabe, the long-serving, corrupt president of Zimbabwe, had enacted a race-based reparations program in his country. As the host described it, Mugabe—whom he identified as a "role model" of Obama's—"took the white people's farms, the only place that had any money." Though he admitted that Obama was not taking the land of white farmers, he still insisted that the president was taking "wealth" from those who had it and giving it to those who did not. Limbaugh also characterized the president as "nothing more than an old school African Colonial who . . . wants to turn this into a Third World country."[32]

A corollary to the attacks over reparations was Limbaugh's claim that Obama wanted to "redistribute" money and resources from whites to blacks. He often mentioned both in the same diatribe, or made clear in some way that any redistribution would be based on race. On March 30, 2009, just after he characterized Obama's actions as coming "right out of Reverend Wright's sermons," Limbaugh said that the president thinks it is his responsibility to

> return the nation's wealth to its rightful, quote, unquote, rightful owners . . . he believes the people who have wealth have stolen it from those who have no wealth. It's been unfairly achieved and accrued, and it's his job to take it and redistribute it . . . When he talks about sacrifice, he's talking about

raising your taxes, taking away your assets, and giving them to other people he thinks you stole them from who are thus more deserving.

Limbaugh frequently railed against this alleged desire of Obama's to "return" America's wealth to its "rightful owners." For example, he averred that the president's economic policies aimed at "the redistribution of wealth . . . He [Obama] seeks to return the nation's wealth to its 'rightful owners'. . . unions, 'working families' (which are unions), minorities, women, whatever. The evil majority in this country—which, in his view, has always been white—needs to be taken down a peg."[33]

Limbaugh added the city of Detroit to his redistribution thesis on October 7, 2009. He claimed that the city's poor and homeless were receiving money to assist them with finding housing thanks to the Obama stimulus plan, which had passed early in the year. The host declared that "this is nothing but redistribution, this is not stimulus. 'Thousands'—thousands!—of people lined up Tuesday [at the Cobo Center]. Some people in line falsely believed they were registering for $3,000 stimulus checks from the Obama administration." When Limbaugh talked about "redistribution"—not to mention Detroit, a city that is more than 80 percent black—his audience understood that he was talking about money going to black people. Michael Tesler determined that "racial resentment was a powerful independent determinant of opposition" to the 2009 stimulus when it was attributed to Obama or presented neutrally (most people already associated it with Obama), but not when characterized as coming from Congressional Democrats.[34]

Limbaugh followed this by playing an interview with a woman on line at the Cobo Center whose voice sounded black:

ROGULSKI: Did you get an application to fill out yet?

WOMAN: I sure did. And I filled it out, and I am waiting to see what the results are going to be.

ROGULSKI: Will you know today how much money you're getting?

WOMAN: No, I won't, but I'm waiting for a phone call.

ROGULSKI: Where's the money coming from?

WOMAN: I believe it's coming from the City of Detroit or the state.

ROGULSKI: Where did they get it from?

WOMAN: Some funds that was forgiven [sic] by Obama.

ROGULSKI: And where did Obama get the funds?

WOMAN: Obama getting the funds from . . . Ummm, I have no idea, to tell you the truth. He's the president.

The following day, Limbaugh played the interview again, along with a second one from the same event that also featured women whose voices sounded black:

ROGULSKI: Why are you here?

WOMAN #1: To get some money.

ROGULSKI: What kind of money?

WOMAN #1: Obama money.

ROGULSKI: Where's it coming from?

WOMAN #1: Obama.

ROGULSKI: And where did Obama get it?

WOMAN #1: I don't know, his stash. I don't know. (laughter) I don't know where he got it from, but he givin' it to us, to help us.

WOMAN #2: And we love him.

WOMAN #1: We love him. That's why we voted for him!

Limbaugh then lamented: "There's your future, America. Obama's America." Also on October 8, a post titled "Free Money From Obama's Stash" that was centered around these two interviews appeared on the website of American Renaissance, which has been characterized as a white supremacist group by the *Washington Post, Fortune,* and the Anti-Defamation League.[35] Limbaugh clearly knew what buttons he was pushing.

On the October 7 show, Limbaugh also dredged up another event that he had mentioned before, a town hall meeting in Fort Myers, Florida on February 10, 2009 where President Obama had spoken about the stimulus. Limbaugh said that "some woman actually stood up and asked him [Obama] when's her new kitchen going to be installed. And another woman stood up: When do I get my new car?" The person the host was referring to was an African American woman named Henrietta Hughes. However, she did not ask the president for a new kitchen. Here is what she actually said: "I have an urgent need, unemployment and homelessness, a very small vehicle for my family and I to live in . . . The housing authority has two years waiting lists, and we need something more than the vehicle and the parks to go to. We need our own kitchen and our own bathroom. Please help."[36] After basically branding her, as John K. Wilson put it, "a 21st Century welfare queen,"[37] Limbaugh then laid out how Hughes' remarks represented everything the president stood for, namely race-based redistribution:

This is a model citizen, as far as Obama is concerned . . . That person is the rightful owner of this nation's wealth . . . that woman has been shafted by the US injustice [sic]: Racism, sexism, bigotry, unfairness, immorality. That woman is in the circumstances she's in because America is a flawed nation. And as such, that woman is going to have what has been rightfully hers all of her life that has never been hers, given to her. That woman is the ideal American citizen. That woman is . . . the type of citizen Obama wants to build his future America on.

Limbaugh followed this by quoting the conservative *Washington Times* saying that the Department of Homeland Security had given ACORN almost $1 million that, in the past, had normally been awarded to fire departments. Limbaugh's audience was being told that Obama was taking money that was supposed to go to putting out fires—maybe on your block!—and giving it to poor, lazy black people looking for a handout. The host did not tell his audience that the grant from the Federal Emergency Management Agency—which ACORN did not receive, in the end—came under its "Fire Prevention and Safety Grants" program, and that the money would have been used to put smoke detectors and carbon monoxide detectors in the homes of lower-income Americans. Thus, it would have helped fight fires. ACORN had received a smaller grant for the same purpose in 2007, during the Bush Administration.[38]

On December 3, 2010, Limbaugh played the Detroit audio again and added: "Now, imagine if people like this weren't allowed to vote? We're just pondering this. We're not suggesting it. Don't anybody go off crazy here. Seriously. What's the old saw: Once people figured out they could vote themselves money from the Treasury, that's the end of it?" He mentioned the line about people "voting themselves money" again on June 21, 2012, when discussing the upcoming presidential race, adding that, "Obama has clearly rolled the dice and said, 'Yeah.

There's more people that want to sit around and be taken care of by me than there are people who want to assume responsibility for themselves.' That's what he's banking on." Limbaugh replayed either the Detroit or Fort Myers audio on thirteen other occasions, including as late as November 2015.[39]

On September 27, 2012, Limbaugh played the Detroit audio, followed by a clip from Cleveland in which another black woman spoke about getting free stuff from Obama:

REPORTER: You got an Obama phone?
WOMAN: (screaming) Yes! Everybody in Cleveland, low minorities, got Obama phone. Keep Obama in president, you know? He gave us a phone!
REPORTER: He gave you a phone?
WOMAN: He gonna do more!
REPORTER: How did he give you a phone?
WOMAN: You sign up. If you're . . . If you on food stamps, you on Social Security, you got low income, you disability . . .
REPORTER: Okay, what's wrong with Romney, again?
WOMAN: Romney, he sucks! Bad!

Limbaugh replayed this on May 13, 2015, and brought up the "Obamaphone" on three other occasions, allowing his audience to hear repeatedly that the president provided free stuff for black people.[40] Never mind that the so-called "Obamaphone" program was not created by Barack Obama. In reality, low income Americans have received heavily discounted telephone service as part of the Lifeline program since President Ronald Reagan—or, as Limbaugh almost always calls him, "Ronaldus Magnus"—established the program in 1985. Furthermore, it was in 2005, under another Republican, George W. Bush, that Lifeline was expanded to include cell phones.

Limbaugh found another way to make his point about race-based redistribution when he talked in 2012 about a new book by Stanley Kurtz,[41] who argued that Obama was implementing

> a very ambitious plan to transform America by undercutting America's suburbs in order to redistribute suburban money back to the cities. Obama has had a lifelong hostility to the suburbs. His community-organizing mentors hated suburbs ... They believe that suburbanites were just greedy racists who didn't want to share their tax money with the urban poor.

This language makes clear that the suburbs stand for whites, and the cities for blacks.

Limbaugh revisited Kurtz's ideas the next day, again a week later, twice in 2013, once in 2014 (when he agreed with Kurtz's assessment that "Obama has a war on the suburbs to take people from the inner city and put them in the suburbs via affordable housing"), and twice in 2015, including one time when he characterized the president as "a guy trying to eliminate suburbs, or at least eliminate the voting power and economic power of suburbia."[42]

"Santa Claus" Obama and Welfare

The use of welfare as a racial dog whistle by conservatives looking to advance the cause of tribalization goes back at least to Ronald Reagan, who in his 1976 presidential run spoke about "welfare queens" behind the wheel of a Cadillac, and "strapping young bucks" feasting on T-bone steaks they had purchased with food stamps.[43] UC Berkeley law professor Ian Haney López explained that starting around that time, some conservative politicians "start[ed] painting welfare as a transfer of wealth to minorities," noting that today, they talk about "food stamps" in similar terms.[44] A prime example of this was Newt Gingrich's 2012 presidential campaign, during which he stated that "the African American community should demand paychecks and not be satisfied with food stamps." Gingrich also derided Obama as "the most effective food stamp president in American history."[45]

More broadly, Limbaugh and other conservatives have long claimed that welfare promotes "dependence" and thus stands in opposition to the traditional American value of self-sufficiency. Thus, connecting Obama to welfare was another way the host could brand the president's political beliefs as anti-American.

One insidious tactic Limbaugh used was to call the president "Santa Claus" in a racialized way, thereby suggesting that he gave presents to black people just because they were black. For example, in 2012, Limbaugh played audio from a Detroit city council meeting, and then summarized what Councilwoman JoAnn Watson had said as follows:

> She's saying, "Obama, bail us out. We voted for you, dude. Bail us out. There's gotta be a quid pro quo . . . We want some bacon. We want some pork." So the city council in Detroit is asking for an Obama bailout, and people get righteously indignant when you say . . . that people voted for Obama because he's Santa Claus.

Limbaugh also called the president "Santa Claus" when arguing that government serving as the "provider for people" had "destroyed the black family." Additionally, Limbaugh's audience heard this from the host: "Half the country that votes is on welfare, and they vote for Santa Claus."[46]

Limbaugh also discussed welfare and the president on February 13, 2009 when he condemned the economic stimulus bill, saying that it "totally gets rid of welfare reform . . . reward[s] state governments for the more people they enroll on [sic] non-work required welfare plans." (Limbaugh and many other conservatives complained that the 2009 stimulus legislation had "abolished" welfare reform because of changes to how the federal government provided funds to states.[47]) In other words, Obama wanted to allow people to receive welfare without working. Limbaugh did not use the words "lazy" or "black," but he did not have to, given the long history of conservatives using "welfare" as a racial dog-whistle. Thus, when the host said "welfare," his audience understood that to mean "black." Four days later, the host went deeper into the matter: "I think race is a central factor in determining Obama's worldview . . . he clearly believes that welfare reform was designed to punish black, inner-city families and people." That is why, according to Limbaugh, the president wanted to get rid of welfare reform.

Limbaugh connected welfare and Obama on numerous other occasions. On January 18, 2010, he said that Obama wished to "expand the safety net, restore things to the status before Reagan . . . These people are all about . . . getting as many people as possible on the welfare state." From February 4, 2010: "He's [Obama is] extending these hands out there and waiting for somebody to take the handouts. Disguised lingo. You have to be in the welfare state to understand the code lingo here, folks. It means the gravy train's going to keep on coming." This segment did double duty, as it painted Obama as redistributing wealth to African Americans, and as someone who was actually more "black" than he let on when he was not speaking in "code." On March 12, 2010,

Limbaugh claimed that under Obama, "welfare reform has significantly been rolled back, has it not? The requirement to work is not near what it was."

On April 28, 2011, after the president mentioned that he had benefited from food stamps—which his mother received for a time when he was a child—Limbaugh pounced: "He [Obama] is a product of the welfare state . . . His adult career has been about expanding the welfare state, whether as a street agitator, community organizer, or president . . . he thinks that the welfare state should replace capitalism." On July 9, 2012, Limbaugh claimed that "We have 48 percent of the people in this country not paying income tax . . . All of these people are eating. . . . And they all have their cell phones . . . And they all have their plasma TVs, and they're all able to sign up for cable and use them. Despite all of the economic malaise . . . We've got an administration which is happily paying for this result." Apparently, the host found it shameful that poor people could both eat and make phone calls. He came back to this issue with actual statistics on September 13, 2013, expressing particular outrage that 83 percent of people in poverty had air-conditioning. This statistic galled him so much that he repeated it three times in about a minute. The fact that people without air conditioning die in heat waves, including hundreds in the Chicago heat wave of 1995, or tens of thousands in the European heat wave of 2003, did not seem to have penetrated Limbaugh's consciousness.[48] He concluded that it was "obvious" that Obama had no interest in "creat[ing] jobs" and would rather "create welfare recipients."

Limbaugh's repeated stressing of welfare and Obama may have influenced Republican presidential candidates prior to Donald Trump. On July 13, 2012, the host told his audience that the White House had announced the previous day that "the traditional work requirements of the new welfare reform law back in 1996, those new work requirements, can be waived or overridden by a legal device called a waiver authority under the Social Security law. Welfare reform has been gutted, ladies and gentlemen." He added four days later: "Obama just gutted it [welfare reform] in a lawless fashion . . . He just took the work requirements out of it last week and nobody said anything." This "new directive" prompted then-presidential candidate Mitt Romney to attack Obama using language that strongly resembled Limbaugh's. Romney ran a television ad with the following narration: "Since 1996 welfare recipients were required to work . . . President Obama quietly ended the work requirement, gutting welfare reform."[49]

The problem was that Romney and Limbaugh had lied about what the provision did. PolitiFact reviewed Romney's claim and branded it a "pants on fire" lie. FactCheck.org likewise found the claim untrue, as did a *CNN* "Fact Check," while the *Washington Post* branded it "Four Pinocchios" (out of four).[50] Additionally, a number of prominent political journalists—as well as scholars who measured audience responses to Romney's welfare ads—called out the campaign for, in this case, directly appealing to white voters' racial resentment.[51]

Even after Romney's loss in the 2012 election, Limbaugh continued to link welfare and Obama. On January 16, 2014, the host stated, "He [Obama] did away with the work requirement for welfare and food benefits . . . You don't have to even look for work to get benefits. You don't have to look for work to get welfare." On November 6, 2015, Limbaugh revisited the false claim that the president had used the stimulus to destroy welfare reform because he believed it was "discriminatory and unfair." Finally, on May 9, 2016, Limbaugh brought up the most base racial stereotype on welfare, suggesting that black Americans are looking for a handout:

> You African-Americans out there who believe that the elec-
> tion of Barack Hussein O was going to mean . . . substantive
> improvement. And I don't mean welfare. I don't mean more
> goodies and benefits. I mean, election of Obama was gonna
> genuinely improve life circumstances for African-Americans.[52]

President Trump's rhetoric and policy approach to welfare, food
stamps, and other forms of government assistance have strongly paralleled that of Limbaugh and like-minded conservatives. In December
2018, an executive order proposed stricter work requirements for those
seeking food stamps. The White House press release announcing the
proposal spoke about "self-sufficiency" and railed against the existing
"system" which, it claimed, promoted "lifelong dependency."[53] As for
his personal rhetoric, on November 29, 2017, Trump repeated some of
the worst lies about supposedly rampant welfare abuse: "I know people
that work three jobs and they live next to somebody who doesn't work
at all. And the person who is not working at all and has no intention of
working at all is making more money and doing better than the person
that's working his and her ass off."[54]

"He's gonna cut this country down to size."

On one show early in Obama's first term, Limbaugh put it all together,
combining the president's supposed hatred of America with his desire
to take from whites and give to blacks. While we have already seen a
lot of hateful words on this specific theme, I would argue that on June
4, 2009, we heard one of the worst examples of a major media figure
fomenting racial animus this country had seen in a long time:

> [Obama] lives and breathes and believes the things that he

says, because that's what he's been taught about this country. His wife, ditto. And those people are all enraged. They're all angry . . . The days of them not having any power are over, and they are angry, and they want to use their power as a means of retribution. That's what Obama's about, gang. He's angry. He's gonna cut this country down to size. He's gonna make it pay for all the multicultural mistakes that it has made, its mistreatment of minorities.

Jamelle Bouie pointed to this specific passage when he identified Limbaugh's racial rhetoric as having laid the groundwork for the election of a president who arguably began his campaign for the White House by serving as the nation's birther-in-chief: "You can draw a direct line to the rise of Trump from the racial hysteria of talk radio—where Rush Limbaugh, a Trump booster, warned that Obama would turn the world upside down."[55] Striking fear in his white audience not only of race-based reparations, but racial retribution, i.e., violence—and connecting it to Obama—is one of the most despicable things Limbaugh has done in his campaign to tribalize our politics.

This was not an isolated example. In a long, multi-topic monologue from January 8, 2013, Limbaugh began with the assertion that many African Americans today

still think that there's slavery going on. There are African Americans today who know that slavery isn't going on but they are still so ticked off that it did that it may as well still be happening. Now, this is done on purpose. The civil rights leaders keep this emotion ginned up. They profit from it, and they are able to advance their political agenda as a result of it.

Limbaugh pivoted to talking about the movie *Django Unchained*, which features a black hero killing large numbers of whites during the time of slavery. The host commented: "you'd think it was pre-Civil War in this country and this movie somehow got made telling the truth and that we better wise up, there are still slaves." Limbaugh then brought up how Jesse Jackson and various Afrocentrists had been "on the warpath against western civilization on campus, universities. The Reverend Jackson was . . . making this claim that western civilization was responsible for racism and slavery and bigotry." Limbaugh went on criticizing Afrocentrism and multiculturalism: "the education system in this country, this multiculturalism curricula has corrupted more than you will ever be able to calculate." He then asserted that Reverend Wright believed the same thing as the multiculturalists: "It's what he's teaching people. It's what he's teaching his flock." And who, of course, was a member of Wright's flock for twenty years? President Barack Obama. Six days later, the host brought up *Django* again, this time playing audio of Louis Farrakhan talking about a "race war." Here we see Limbaugh tying together the bloodthirsty *Django*, Jesse Jackson, Louis Farrakhan, and Jeremiah Wright. He did not even need to use the president's name, as his audience knew exactly about whom he was talking.

This slander continued right through the 2016 presidential campaign. On June 2, 2016, Limbaugh contrasted Obama to Trump on "the concept of America," and repeated a charge he had made in the past, that "Obama doesn't even think in terms of American exceptionalism." He then pushed further on the matter, using ideas he had emphasized throughout the Obama presidency:

If your starting point is America is flawed. If your starting point is America is guilty of whatever the things you think it's guilty of, if you think it's flawed and guilty because of the way we were founded, because of some of the elements in our past such as slavery, colonialization, as Obama would look at it . . . I think that he looks at this country as a country that is owed a little punishment. I think Obama looks at America and sees a place that is an undeserving superpower, needs to be cut down to size.

As America moved into the party conventions that summer, Limbaugh declared on July 12 that Hillary and Bill Clinton, Senator Bernie Sanders (Clinton's main opponent for the Democratic presidential nomination), and Barack Obama all believed "that there's nothing redeemable about America. It has to be 'transformed,' I think is the word Obama uses." Later in that same broadcast, he stated that, "Obama stands with people he thinks have been given the shaft ever since this country was founded. I think his objective is to even the playing field, as he defines it. And the way he does it is to transfer discrimination from one group to the next, rather than end it. His prescription is payback." On July 28, after Obama's speech at the Democratic National Convention—a speech that soared with positive imagery about our country, including the words "America is already great"—Limbaugh dismissed those words as insincere: "That's not Barack Obama. That's not what he believes. That's not who he is . . . Obama is the guy who thinks America's founding was unjust and immoral. He doesn't relish it. He doesn't cherish it."

In that speech, the president also skewered one of the host's core contentions about what exacerbates racial divisions. Obama explained that "acknowledging problems that have festered for decades isn't making race relations worse—it's creating the possibility for people of goodwill to join and make things better."

On Veterans Day, 2016, three days after the election of Donald Trump, Obama set Limbaugh off by praising the diversity of our military in a speech at Arlington National Cemetery. The host didn't seem to care that the president praised the military for exemplifying how America has been able to "forge unity from our great diversity." Here is one of the countless examples of Obama doing what Limbaugh claims he never does, which is to encourage and reinforce unity among all Americans, specifically across lines of race. However, instead of praise, Limbaugh let loose a long rant criticizing the concept of diversity, and condemned former Obama administration official Van Jones for saying that Trump's election represented a "whitelash." (Jones, according to Limbaugh, believed the same things as the president—"Van Jones is Obama is Van Jones."[56]) According to Limbaugh, Obama and liberals think that white America is "inherently corrupt . . . has always been racist and bigoted, and so it must be chipped away at, it must be destroyed and it must be properly categorized." For that reason, Limbaugh claimed that liberals like Obama "simply say that anybody nonwhite makes something better, whether it does or not . . . We're gonna make things better by reducing the numbers of white people . . . and we're gonna start sprinkling diversity in there."

On January 20, 2017, Limbaugh contrasted how the outgoing and incoming presidents viewed America. He claimed Obama saw America as "a rotten place . . . unfair and discriminatory." Trump's inauguration as our forty-fifth president, which took place that day, represented instead "a reclamation project, reclaiming this country from the people the Democrat Party has been attempting to turn it over to." The host also characterized the anti-Trump inauguration protestors as "the obscure minorities that Barack Obama tried to turn this country over to." In other words, Obama hated traditional, white America, and wanted to weaken it. Limbaugh and Trump, however, were going to make it great again.

Chapter Three

HATING COPS, BUT LOVING
BLACK LIVES MATTER

The issue of race rarely remains out of the news in America for very long. During the Obama administration, this offered Limbaugh regular opportunities to tie his race-based criticisms of the president to specific events involving African Americans. The host's goal was to place Obama outside the American mainstream by contending that he stood with black criminals and prisoners—and against law enforcement officials. Limbaugh race-baited in this manner when discussing the president's policies and proposals on police and criminal justice reform, and, in particular, his reaction to a series of racially charged incidents, as well as the emergence of the Black Lives Matter movement.

Limbaugh did not have to wait long after the inauguration to get started on his quest to worsen the tribalization of our politics, as the first summer of the Obama presidency was rocked by a high-profile racial incident: the arrest of Henry Louis Gates, a well-regarded scholar and Harvard professor of African American Studies. On July 16, 2009, Gates, then a fifty-eight year old man who used a cane, came home from a trip abroad to find his front door jammed, leaving him unable to enter his house. With the help of the man who had driven him home, Gates forced the front door open and went inside. Someone observing this activity made a 911 call, reporting a possible break-in, and Cambridge

Police Sergeant James Crowley arrived at the house. After an interaction—the details of which remain in dispute—Crowley arrested Gates. On July 21, the Cambridge Police Department dropped the charges. But the story—which echoes events from 2018, when America began to more rigorously scrutinize whites who call the police on blacks for doing things like waiting at Starbucks, having a barbeque in a park, or taking a nap in the common room of one's own dormitory[1]—was just getting started.

On July 22, President Obama held a press conference about health care. As the very last question, a reporter asked him to comment on Gates's arrest and what, if anything, it revealed about racism and race relations in our country. Obama began his response by highlighting the "incredible progress" our country has made over the years on racial equality—something he did almost every time he talked about race as president—before stating that "race remains a factor" in matters relating to law enforcement and the criminal justice system. He offered this in order to explain why some black and brown Americans might not fully trust police officers, which potentially affected situations that could be "honest misunderstandings." The president was clearly making room for the possibility that Gates's arrest fell into that category. Obama said he did not know what, if anything, racism had to do with the arrest, and he in no way attributed Sergeant Crowley's actions to racial bias. But ultimately one sentence in his whole answer stood out: "The Cambridge police acted stupidly in arresting somebody when there was already proof that they were in their own home."

Limbaugh jumped in with full force, blackening Obama the very next day by saying that his remarks made clear that he "did listen to Reverend Wright all those 20 years." The host averred that, when talking about Gates during his press conference, the president had been "more animated. He came more alive. He was more passionate on that last question . . . about the arrest—and calling the cop stupid? . . . there's an undercurrent here. I think Obama is largely misunderstood by a lot of people. I think his associations in his young life and early adult life matter." Limbaugh also characterized the question as "a setup" because, the host insinuated, Obama had wanted to speak out about the arrest and race: "President Obama is black, and I think he's got a chip on his shoulder. I think there are elements of this country he doesn't like and he never has liked and he's using the power of the presidency to remake the country . . . when that question about Henry Louis Gates and the arrest in his home came up, why, it was passion, excitement, animation, fire!"

What really offended Limbaugh, though, was that Obama brought up the fact that racial disparities and discrimination in the area of criminal justice still existed. This, not their existence, was what was harmful to race relations in the United States, according to Limbaugh. He condemned Obama's comments, saying that they were

> not a force for positive race relations in this country. He's dealing in stereotypes and I am deeply troubled by that . . . what we got was the reaction of a community organizer. We saw the community organizer that is Barack Obama. We got the ACORN reaction last night. We got the militant black reaction . . . Basically we saw a community organizer in action last night.

As we have seen, "community organizer," "militant black," and of course, ACORN, are the kind of terms that Limbaugh used repeatedly to separate Americans into tribes by painting Obama as someone who would employ his power to favor blacks over whites.

Limbaugh also used Gates's arrest to brand Obama as anti-police. By raising the president's supposed hostility toward the police, Limbaugh maintained that Obama

> cement[s] in certain people's minds that there's a constant adversarial relationship with the cops, the cops are bad. My president even says the cops are stupid. President says the cops are racist, the cops profiling and so forth. This is agitation last night, folks . . . Obama is not a force for positive race relations in this country. He is not a uniter.

The host went on to further divide the black president from white Americans by accusing Obama of not knowing what really happened between Gates and Crowley, and having instead

> pop[ped] off, just exactly as he would back in Chicago in the community organizing days. He goes off about racial profiling, all the rest. Based on what? A limited amount of information about a single incident where he's quick to condemn the cop, the whole police department, and white America.

Limbaugh also rebuked Obama for having achieved success in his life and nonetheless having the gall to talk about racial discrimination, as well as for supposedly still seeing himself as a "victim." It's as if that success somehow took away his right—not to mention his responsibility—to speak out against injustice:

> Mr. President, you are not a victim. You are, in fact, the president of the United States. You went to private school. You went

to Ivy League schools. You are a millionaire. You have a charmed life. Congratulations. You're living the American dream. Stop pretending otherwise. If anybody behaved stupidly yesterday it was the president, in even taking the question.

The next day, July 24, Limbaugh went right back to the Gates-Obama controversy. He started by calling out "President Barack Nifong," a reference to Michael Nifong, the Durham County, North Carolina district attorney who had pursued a criminal case against three white Duke University lacrosse players after a black woman accused them of raping her. Ultimately, no charges were brought. North Carolina State Attorney General Roy Cooper (who was elected Governor in 2016) judged the three players to have been "innocent" and Nifong was ultimately removed from office and disbarred due to misconduct. By calling the president "Nifong," Limbaugh was tarring him with the stain of a corrupt government effort to wrongly and unfairly injure white American men who were falsely charged with wrongdoing by a black woman, a slander containing both racial and gender connotations.

Limbaugh then launched into a condemnation—one he made on a regular basis throughout the Obama presidency—of people who voted for Obama because of racial guilt "just to get that legacy of sin due to slavery out of our system to be done with it just wipe the slate clean, at least make them feel better about it." Instead of bringing about a post-racial America, Obama was "behaving as a community organizer and is fanning the flames of race and is calling the police stupid." While the host did not say he was specifically talking about white Obama voters, it was transparent that he was, as it would presumably be white voters who would be upset that the president was acting like a community organizer (by which Limbaugh meant a black radical). He closed the segment by saying of Obama: "He could end this story. But ACORN doesn't apologize. Community agitators don't apologize."

Instead, the story ended when Obama and Vice President Joseph Biden invited Sergeant Crowley and Professor Gates to meet informally on the White House grounds to discuss what had happened in Cambridge. The meeting on July 30 was dubbed the "Beer Summit" which, Gates reported afterward, went well. Laughing, he said of Crowley, "We hit it off right from the very beginning. When he's not arresting you, Sergeant Crowley is a really likable guy."

Limbaugh, however, did not find anything to like about the Beer Summit. He did a long segment on it, quoting passages from Obama's *Dreams From My Father* in which, taken out of context, Obama appears to have spoken harshly about white people. Then he brought up the Summit itself, denigrating it as a "photo-op" aimed at showcasing Obama's desire to ease racial tensions even though, the host claimed, "he's the one that caused all this." Limbaugh then repeated his reference to Obama's memoir and noted that although the president allegedly "loves white people," his true beliefs suggest otherwise. Limbaugh used Gates's arrest to attack Obama on race on several other occasions, including twice more in 2009, and twice in both 2014 and 2016.[2]

Shirley Sherrod

Another major incident involving race that Limbaugh connected to President Obama centered around Shirley Sherrod, an African American official in the Georgia office of the U.S. Department of Agriculture (USDA). On July 19, 2010, Andrew Breitbart, founder of *Breitbart News*, posted a falsely edited video in which Sherrod was supposedly heard openly recounting her act of discrimination against

Roger Spooner, a white farmer, to an audience at a National Association for the Advancement of Colored People (NAACP) meeting. Shortly thereafter, she was fired by the USDA. The full, unedited video, which surfaced within a day, showed that Sherrod had in fact helped Spooner. In an interview, the farmer said that without Sherrod's assistance, he would have lost his farm, and they remained friends.[3] Within days, Sherrod was offered another position at the USDA, which she ultimately declined.

Limbaugh first used the controversy to again tie President Obama to Reverend Wright. The day after the video appeared on *Breitbart,* Limbaugh said Wright's name fifteen times (along with eleven the next day, and once more the day after that). In addition, when discussing the matter on July 20, the host also claimed that Sherrod's supposed anti-white actions reflected Obama Administration policy, warning listeners about "the bigger picture," namely that if you are not black and seek help from a black, Obama-appointed government official, "you might have the same treatment regarding your health care that this poor white farmer got." The Sherrod case, Limbaugh alleged, showed how "the federal bureaucracy . . . these people look at it as having all kinds of power over the rest of us . . . It's not going to be long before these same kinds of people are going to be the people you have to go through to get the health care treatment or whatever access you need to the system." According to Limbaugh, black bureaucrats in a black-run administration would literally have the power of life and death over "the rest of us." These kinds of remarks explain why, according to Michael Tesler, attitudes toward health care reform became racialized during the Obama presidency, as "racial cues work best when issues are structured to fit relevant racial considerations (e.g., a black president giving health insurance to black Americans)."[4] The host's fear-mongering about black, Obamacare bureaucrats arbitrarily denying health care to whites while approving it for blacks paralleled the false charge that Sherrod had discriminated against a white farmer seeking support from the government.

Even after what Sherrod really said came to light and proved to be the opposite of what it had appeared to be in the Breitbart video, Limbaugh did not withdraw or correct anything he had said. Instead, he continued to attack the president, alleging on July 21 that the administration was practicing racism at the highest levels, and asking why Shirley Sherrod was fired "on the basis of racism," while Eric Holder had not been. Limbaugh reminded the audience about Holder and the New Black Panther Party voting case, which he claimed showed that "racism" was the "underlying" reason why the Department of Justice did not bring charges against the NBPP. The host went on to explain why the Obama Administration fired Sherrod so quickly (for which it ultimately apologized): "They had to keep their own credibility up if they're going to sit there and call the Tea Party a bunch of racists and they're gonna call conservatives a bunch of racists . . . [the NAACP] wants to go after Fox News; wants to go after the Tea Party; wants to go after everybody else on the basis that they are racist and it simply has gotten out [sic] hand." Thus, Limbaugh was telling his audience that the real problem of racism in America was that conservatives were being branded as racists.

Limbaugh also not only blamed Obama for having exacerbated racial divisions, but argued that the president, if he wanted to, could end "all this" by simply saying

"Enough, America, stop this . . . We must be better than this. All of this talk about racism here and there is bringing this country down; it's dividing the country; it's tearing it apart." The problem is he wants all that to happen. So he won't do this. And the very fact that the president of the United States does not take one step, does not make one move toward healing any of these divisions is proof positive that he wants them, that he profits from them.

The following day, July 22, Limbaugh said he "must" keep talking about Sherrod, which he called a "distraction," although he did not actually want to. "It's nothing more than the left playing the race card . . . They are keeping alive the divisions in this country and I hate taking the bait." Somehow, a falsely edited video that a right-wing news outlet ran was, to Limbaugh, an example of liberal race-baiting, something he said was being done with President Obama's "direction and approval."

Going further, the host rebuked the president for, in his words, "tribalizing this country. We aren't Americans anymore. We're all members of different racial tribes, and we are to be pitted against each other: Black Americans, White Americans, Asian-Americans, Hispanic-Americans . . . divid[ing] people in this country into various groups, victims, tribes." Limbaugh opined that Obama did this because he wanted to undermine who and what we were as a people, the things that made us "the greatest nation in the history of humanity." Although it was true that someone did aim to tribalize this country, that person was not President Obama.

Trayvon Martin

Neither the Gates nor Sherrod incidents, however, had near the impact on American society that the killing of Trayvon Martin, a seventeen-year-old African American, did. On February 26, 2012, George

Zimmerman shot and killed Martin after an altercation between the two. Zimmerman was a neighborhood watch coordinator for the gated community in Florida where Martin, who was unarmed, was visiting his relatives. Limbaugh covered the aftermath of the event in excruciating detail, including the arrest, trial, and acquittal of Zimmerman. I will focus here only on what the host said about Obama as it related to the incident.

On March 23, 2012, in his first comments on the killing, President Obama spoke of how, if he had a son, "he'd look like Trayvon." The president has two daughters, but he clearly still felt the loss acutely. It was not a theoretical thing for him, but instead the actuation of every black parent's worst fears. Rather than sympathize with the president, however, Limbaugh responded on his next show three days later by accusing liberals of "look[ing] at everything through a political lens," thinking that was "foreign" to him. Then, returning to one of his favorite targets with which to smear Obama, Limbaugh criticized the president for not condemning the New Black Panther Party who, outraged that the local police had not arrested or charged Zimmerman with a crime, had offered a $10,000 bounty for his "capture." The next day, Limbaugh accused the Obama campaign of "exploiting" Martin's death by selling "Obama 2012" hoodies. Martin had been wearing a hoodie the night he died, and subsequently that item of clothing became linked to those advocating for justice on his behalf. The truth was that the reelection campaign had been selling the hoodies on their website for some time before Martin's death, which Limbaugh neglected to mention.[5]

The criticism was harsher the following day, March 28, when Limbaugh endorsed this statement from J. Christian Adams, the former DOJ official who had been involved in the disproven NBPP voter suppression case in Philadelphia: "'No president in our history would have injected himself into a criminal matter using racial code like Obama did.'" Limbaugh asserted that Obama had injected race and politics where it did not belong, just as he and Attorney General Eric Holder supposedly had done in not bringing charges against the NBPP. Because the president talked about racism—using "racial code," as the host put it—he was the one being divisive, he was the real racist. Limbaugh also accused the president of lying about the circumstances surrounding Martin's death in order to exploit racial divisions: "the story that Obama and the Sharptons and Jacksons and so forth wanted to portray." Furthermore, he claimed that the president—or, in Limbaugh's words, "the regime"—"intended" for this to be "a political story that harms Republicans." Obama's statement about having a son who would look like Trayvon was "simply a way to advance the liberal agenda."

Limbaugh returned to the Trayvon Martin-looking-like-the-president's-son meme on several subsequent occasions. On April 11, 2012, after a caller suggested that Obama could have "calm[ed] this whole situation down" by just "calm[ing] down his minions, Al Sharpton and Jesse Jackson," Limbaugh criticized Obama for "stoking" the situation by talking about his "son." The host stated, without evidence, that the president unquestionably "wants this kind of chaos and unrest in the culture." He then speculated that Obama could "calm this down" simply by addressing the matter "in genuine American terms, not racial terms," as other presidents supposedly had done. Note the juxtaposition of what was "racial"—namely, talking about the reality of racial discrimination—and what was "American"—i.e., not doing so.

Limbaugh then slammed Holder—and thus, Obama—for praising Sharpton's actions in response to Martin's killing: "Here's the author of the Tawana Brawley hoax being held up on a pedestal by the attorney general of the United States, who thanks him for his prayers, his partnership, his friendship, and his tireless efforts to speak out for the voiceless." Limbaugh was referring to a 1987 case in which Sharpton had advised a black teenager who, according to all indications, invented rape charges against white male assailants. Here, Limbaugh was pushing both the racial and gender paranoia buttons.

The host also went on at length about Michelle Williams, chief of staff of the Tampa NBPP. He told his audience that Williams had said: "Let me tell you something, the things that is about to happen to these honkeys, these crackers, these pigs, these pink people, these (beep) people, it has been long overdue." Limbaugh repeated Williams's remarks several times, and then added: "That's right. Obama said, 'Yeah, yeah, if I had a son he'd look like Trayvon,' essentially saying, 'My son would have been killed.'" By talking about the threat of anti-white violence, then going straight to the president in the very next sentence, Limbaugh was clearly insinuating a connection between the two.

On February 14, 2013, Limbaugh again used the "my son would look like Travyon" remark to criticize the president, this time for not condemning Christopher Dorner, a black ex-cop who shot several law enforcement officials and their family members during a killing spree that had begun eleven days earlier. Dorner's grievance stemmed from the belief that he had been wrongly drummed out of the Los Angeles Police Department for reporting officers who had allegedly used excessive force. Limbaugh ranted: "Obama can't come out and condemn what this guy's doing. Obama's base loves this guy! Obama's base has made this guy [sic] national hero . . . So Obama . . . can't come out and say if he had a son, he'd look and act like Christopher Dorner." The host also suggested that Dorner represented "the entire social construct that

Obama and the Democrats are behind that this is still . . . a slave nation." In this diatribe Limbaugh tied Obama—and his statement of support for Martin—to anti-police violence committed by a black man.

George Zimmerman's acquittal on charges of second degree murder and manslaughter was announced on Saturday, July 13, 2013. Limbaugh took to the air that Monday and asserted that the Department of Justice was considering federal civil rights charges against Zimmerman only because of racial politics: "With a normal administration, with a normal set of circumstances, the DOJ doesn't have a case. But we're not talking about normal here. It [the Obama Administration] politicizes virtually everything." In fact, the president had made a statement just after the verdict was announced, saying, "we are a nation of laws, and a jury has spoken. I now ask every American to respect the call for calm reflection from two parents who lost their young son."[6] But Limbaugh did not acknowledge Obama's words, and instead took another shot at the president: "I had a dream that the president, Barack Obama, decided to promote racial healing by reaching out and appointing Zimmerman to replace [Secretary of Homeland Security] Janet Napolitano."

On July 17, Limbaugh said he wished that our "first African American" president "would try to rise above" the pressure from black leaders to bring federal charges against Zimmerman and would, instead, "unite everybody." According to Limbaugh, however, "he's not doing that. He's got this constituency to serve. He's got the Congressional Black [Caucus]. He's got the NAACP. Holder, the same thing. They're out there, and they're dangling a carrot in front of these people. 'Don't worry, Zimmerman's not off the hook yet.'" In reality, the host explained, these groups could not really pressure Obama and Holder, because "Obama and Holder lead that movement," and were the chief "race hustlers."

On July 19, 2013, six days after the Zimmerman trial came to an end, Obama revisited his famous statement about having a son who would look like Trayvon. This time he said, "Another way of saying that is Trayvon Martin could have been me thirty-five years ago." On July 22, Limbaugh played this remark within part of a longer statement by the president and then expressed his outrage: "What is all of this could've, would've, might've, it didn't happen to him. What happened to Trayvon Martin did not happen to him . . . This is a blatant attempt . . . to perpetuate the myth within the black community that all blacks remain helpless victims of white supremacy, white racism." The host also talked about how Obama was "no different than Jesse Jackson or Al Sharpton" before characterizing Obama's remark as "utterly irresponsible. It is certainly not healing. It's not even emotionally honest. But it is exactly who I've always thought Obama is."

Later in the broadcast, Limbaugh broadened his remarks from Martin to the larger question of race and Obama, in familiar tribalizing terms:

Remember[,] Obama was portrayed as this post-racial president, post-partisan president. Everything was gonna vanish! There wasn't gonna be any more racism . . . There was gonna be total unity! . . . they really believed that Obama didn't care about race once he became president. When anybody paying attention would know that's the primary thing that animated him. It's the primary thing that informed him, the primary source of his grievance. Obama is grievance politics, and the primary reason for that grievance is race. It's in everything that he's done. It's in every policy.

A month later, another shooting gave Limbaugh an additional chance to bring up Obama and Martin. A white Australian man, Christopher Lane, who was visiting his girlfriend in Oklahoma, was shot and killed by three teenagers, two of whom were minorities. On August 21, 2013, Limbaugh asked why the president had not addressed Lane's death, claiming, "This is a purposeful, willful ignoring of the exact racial components (but in reverse) that happened in the Trayvon Martin shooting." The host accused Obama and his allies of not caring about Martin's killing, and instead only seeing it as "an opportunity to advance their political agenda. [Lane's death] doesn't."

Two days later, Limbaugh criticized the president for not calling Lane's parents, and said he did not know whether Obama had called the family of another white man, an eighty-eight-year-old World War II veteran named Delbert Belton, who that week had been beaten to death by two black teenagers in Spokane, Washington. Again, the implication was that Obama did not care about a crime when the victims were white; he cared only when they "look like Trayvon."

Michael Brown and Ferguson

The hashtag #BlackLivesMatter started appearing on Twitter and other social media outlets shortly after the acquittal of George Zimmerman. The Black Lives Matter (BLM) movement that grew from it gained national and international prominence a year later, as a result of protests organized in response to the killing of Michael Brown. Brown was shot on August 9, 2014, in Ferguson, Missouri, a suburb of St. Louis, by Officer Darren Wilson of the Ferguson Police Department. Protests erupted within hours of the killing. Two days later Limbaugh weighed in, describing the unrest in Ferguson as "a full-fledged, full-scale riot. . . .

Of course. The riots. So history repeats, chaos continues, keep everybody all worked up into a frenzy, it continues. This race-whatever you want to call it in Ferguson, Missouri."

It didn't take long for Limbaugh to blame this "race-whatever" on the president: "Wasn't the election of Obama supposed to mean there wasn't gonna be any more of this? And after, if he had a son, Trayvon Martin, after that, didn't we deal with that in such a way it wasn't going to happen anymore?" Taken at face value, Limbaugh was simply tweaking those who claimed the election of Obama would mean the end of racial strife. In his usual code, however, Limbaugh was telling his audience that Obama never wanted to end racial strife, by which the host meant ending any talk about racism. That was why he said Ferguson was about "keep[ing] everybody all worked up."

During the next day's show, on August 12, Limbaugh went into detail about the promise of the "post-racial America" that Obama's election was supposed to bring about. He cited the many people who supposedly voted for Obama primarily "to end the racial strife that exists in this country . . . we were assured that if we elected the right guy, this kind of stuff wasn't gonna be happening anymore, or it would happen much, much less." Limbaugh also laid the blame for Ferguson at Obama's feet even more directly than he had the day before: "You have people fanning the flames of this to keep it alive because the race business is profitable, and it makes people very powerful, and it keeps them in the public eye." Since Limbaugh had, on multiple occasions, made it clear that Obama believed the same thing as the leaders of the "race business"—Sharpton, Jackson, et al.—this was an obvious shot at the president. The host followed by going after Obama for supposedly talking about race in America no differently than civil rights leaders had fifty years earlier: "There hasn't been any change. There hasn't been any improvement."

Limbaugh continued to hammer Obama about Ferguson over the next several days. On August 18, he attacked the president over the video that appeared to show Brown and another man robbing a convenience store, the incident Officer Wilson had initially been called to investigate.[7] The host stated the video had been "suppressed . . . withheld at the request of the DOJ, meaning Eric Holder, which means Barack Hussein Obama." In Limbaugh's view, the president had put his finger on the scale in favor of a black criminal against a white cop. The president and attorney general did what they did "because they were afraid the facts of the case might damage, or dampen the rage against the cop."

The following day, Limbaugh denounced Obama for seeing Ferguson as "an opportunity . . . Remember, Obama has wistfully spoken of the sixties. He wasn't around then, but he says he wishes he had been. Well, here's a chance to relive some history . . . Obama can finally . . . be down for the struggle." The host also claimed Ferguson provided a political opening for Obama and his party to drum up black support by "play[ing] the race card" and spreading lies. "The myth is that this happens all the time," Limbaugh ranted. "The myth is that young, innocent blacks are gunned down by white police departments every day in this country. Of course, that isn't true. It's far from true. It's nowhere near true!"

Finally, Limbaugh brought up Sharpton and Jackson and mentioned a rumor that Sharpton had demanded money from the Brown family in return for his help with the case. The host danced around whether this was true or not. "Let's say that that's not true, because I can't confirm it, I can't back it up. But I'm telling you, I wouldn't be surprised if it's true." The next words out of Limbaugh's mouth were: "But this is the Democrat Party, folks. The president of the United States is in charge of what's happened here." In other words, it was all on Obama.

Limbaugh then mentioned a number of other faux-scandals and outrages before bringing it all together:

> What do you mean, how did it get past Obama? . . . This is about wiping out anybody who opposes Obama. This isn't Al Sharpton. This isn't Jesse Jackson. They're just tag-alongs now. This is Obama and Holder. But all of this is Barack Obama. Every event, every detail, every occurrence is Obama. And the end result is the end and absence of any opposition. So that's what Ferguson's all about, like all the rest of this has been about . . . He's in charge of all this. I think that it is a structured strategy, well conceived, brilliantly executed strategy for all of this crap to be happening in this country for six years.

In these comments, we see Limbaugh alleging a wide-ranging conspiracy to provoke racial unrest—by citing Sharpton and Jackson, he is making clear that that is what this conspiracy is about—directed and perhaps even micro-managed down to the smallest "detail" by President Obama. The host was raising the specter of Obama being intimately connected with Black Lives Matter—a movement many white Americans saw as a direct threat to their own safety because they believed that BLM's efforts, if successful, would restrict the ability of police officers to do their jobs effectively. This was Limbaugh doing his very best to tribalize American politics by heightening white racial anxiety, and playing on some of the deepest, long-standing fears many white Americans held about African Americans and crime.

The August 20, 2014 show featured a long discussion criticizing the president for deliberating over whether he should go to Ferguson.

Limbaugh also used this to undercut the allegations about police violence made by Black Lives Matter: "If the myth were true, if white cops every week were shooting innocent black kids, do you think Obama would go to one of those things? . . . Do you think Obama would speak up? . . . One of the reasons . . . he doesn't go is 'cause this is not common." The host then returned to the point about people having voted for Obama to bring America into a post-racial era:

> "Stop hating us. Stop judging us. Stop calling us racist. Stop calling us bigots . . . we helped elect [Obama]." And those people today . . . are still being told they're racist, still being told they're bigots, still being told that they support white cops killing black kids. Nothing's changed. In fact, as I say, it may have even gotten worse.

According to Limbaugh, the most important thing that had "gotten worse" was white people unfairly being called racist.

Leading up to the 2014 midterm elections, Limbaugh accused Democrats of looking to events in Ferguson—specifically the grand jury empaneled to decide whether to indict Officer Wilson in Brown's death—to help turn out voters. The host predicted on October 21, 2014, that, if the grand jury did not indict, the Obama-Holder DOJ would make a "major, major" push to find that Wilson committed federal "civil rights violations" against Brown. The next day, Limbaugh said that the entire case had demonstrated the "civil rights coalition's" belief that "smearing and destroying a police officer was necessary and appropriate to Democrats in order to create mobs and property destruction and voter registration, and to turn out the vote."

Robert McCulloch, the St. Louis County Prosecutor, announced on November 24, 2014, that a grand jury had declined to indict Officer Wilson. The following day, Limbaugh began his show by opining that most of the property destroyed or damaged in the riot following McCulloch's announcement was minority-owned. He related what he thought a black person might be thinking that morning:

> After fifty years of loyally supporting the Democrat Party and that resulting in the election of the first brother, Barack Hussein O, all my problems solved, all my loyalty paid off, finally payback time, whatever, it's gonna end, and whatever I've been mad about for all these years is gonna be over, we're gonna fix it. And then six years into it, it's worse, and I'm confused.

As usual, it was Obama's fault—in this case because he had raised the expectations of African Americans and led them to believe it was going to be "payback time." Hence, riots.

Limbaugh then criticized the president's response to McCulloch's announcement. "Everybody thinks Obama called for calm last night . . . Well, he called for calm. But then he went on and spoke for twenty minutes about . . . all the things he thinks are bad in America in terms of race relations and police departments . . . So he started out appealing for calm, and then kind of fed the rage." Limbaugh also said that he was surprised by the decision of the grand jury to not indict Wilson, despite what he described as "enormous pressures exerted by the president's representative, Eric Holder, the attorney general." Finally, he concluded by saying that if Obama

> really cared about unity, he could have done a lot for it last night. If he really cares about bringing people together—if

he really cares about a functioning, orderly society, even if he wants to transform it—he had a golden opportunity last night, and he punted. He had twenty minutes of inane ramblings that were designed subtly to feed the rage.

Limbaugh then went on to play selections from the president's remarks in detail, explaining, in his view, the various ways Obama "fed the rage." Among the things the host criticized Obama for saying was (in Limbaugh's words) that "we got too many white cops in Ferguson . . . if we're gonna have more policing we gotta have more black cops in there because they understand and might behave differently than white cops . . . The cops are not representative of the people who are committing the crime." Additionally, regarding comments Obama made about the police needing to work with local communities rather than against them while the majority were protesting peacefully, Limbaugh characterized the president as blaming the cops: "he's basically asking the cops, just stand aside. You're gonna make matters worse if you show up here."

However, one section of the president's remarks that Limbaugh did not play clearly showed Obama firmly rejecting violence and vandalism, and presenting America as having improved on matters of race, despite still needing to do more:

We have made enormous progress in race relations over the course of the past several decades . . . And to deny that progress . . . is to deny America's capacity for change. But . . . there are still problems and communities of color aren't just making these problems up . . . The law too often feels as if it is being applied in discriminatory fashion. I don't think that's the norm

... But these are real issues ... we need to ... understand them
and figure out how do we make more progress ... That won't
be done by using this as an excuse to vandalize property. And
it certainly won't be done by hurting anybody. So, to those in
Ferguson, there are ways of channeling your concerns con-
structively and there are ways of channeling your concerns
destructively.

The following day, November 26, Limbaugh characterized what was
happening in Ferguson as "barbarism" and accused the president of
believing that it was "legitimate, because a lot of people were upset"
by yet another court decision that went against black Americans. After
repeating the truly scurrilous charge that Obama had "scripted" the
unrest in Ferguson, and connecting him again to Sharpton and Jackson,
the host then went on a long rant about what the president could have
done and why he did not. In the end, Limbaugh said of the rioting and
the president's reaction, "He [Obama] practically excused it."

Nearly a week later, on December 1, Limbaugh discussed a series of
meetings Obama Administration officials had held at the White House
with law enforcement professionals and civil rights leaders, including
Sharpton and Holder. The host claimed that the participants were discussing "how to set up, in American classrooms, memorials to Michael
Brown . . . what they are doing is coming up with five ways to teach
about Michael Brown and Ferguson." Although a number of substantive proposals on policing emerged from the gathering, Limbaugh used
it as another opportunity to blacken the president and advance his tribalization push. Public opinion research data suggests that exactly this
kind of rhetoric helped move some whites who had previously voted
for Obama into Trump's column in 2016.

It might be hard to imagine Obama voters being bigoted, but John Sides, Michael Tesler, and Lynn Vavreck found that significant numbers of whites who voted for Obama in 2012 expressed varying degrees of white racial resentment while also overwhelmingly embracing liberal positions on issues such as taxation and the existence of climate change.[8] The country's racial climate during Obama's second term contributed to this phenomenon of racially resentful white Obama voters shifting to Trump, as Black Lives Matter and Ferguson "kicked off a massive and racially polarizing national debate over police violence against African Americans."[9] Limbaugh took full advantage of that climate, which ultimately benefitted Trump.

"They were . . . throwing gasoline on the flames . . . Hoping for a bigger fire."

Two days later, on December 3, 2014, a grand jury in Staten Island, New York, announced that it would not bring charges against a police officer who had killed Eric Garner, an unarmed black man who had been selling "loosies" (single cigarettes) in front of a convenience store. Garner died while being arrested, the result of being put into a chokehold by NYPD Officer Daniel Pantaleo. His last words were "I can't breathe." On December 8, Limbaugh criticized the president's reaction, falsely charging Obama with portraying America as having not progressed in the past two centuries on racism: "You would think we haven't even started working on these problems, and that's not true . . . And the president taking sides in this in a way that further divides the country I find reprehensible and very unfortunate. But purposeful." Of course, the president's full remarks in Ferguson, and similar words throughout his career, spoke to the opposite of what the host was saying, but anyone who got their news only from Limbaugh did not hear that. The fact that many among his audience fall into that category makes the host's tribalizing efforts—which are aided by the existence of an almost hermetically sealed right-wing media ecosystem—all the more successful.

Limbaugh then criticized the Justice Department, which had sent representatives to Ferguson the day after Michael Brown's death, "ostensibly to have a meeting with community leaders ... That was just a cover for what really went on." The DOJ officials, according to the host, actually talked about "recogniz[ing] the signs of 'white privilege' . . . then gave them guidelines on how to behave and how to react to white privilege." To Limbaugh, discussing white privilege and how blacks might be treated in a discriminatory fashion was a serious problem: "Everybody thought the DOJ going [sic] in there try to mollify things and get answers, dig deep and get to the truth? They were ... throwing gasoline on the flames ... Hoping for a bigger fire ... This is not unifying. It's not problem solving. It's exacerbating problems and it's using people, and it is encouraging anger." Why would Obama do this? To ensure that black people would keep voting Democratic, according to Limbaugh. In reality, the opposite was true, as it was Limbaugh who was "throwing gasoline on the flames" about race to ensure that his largely white audience kept voting Republican. This strategy paid off in the 2016 election, and Trump has continued to follow it as president. As journalist Dylan Matthews noted in an article entitled "Donald Trump Has Every Reason to Keep White People Thinking About Race," a vast corpus of social science research indicates that "even very mild messages or cues that touch on race can alter political opinions . . . priming white people to so much as think about race, even subconsciously, pushes them toward racially regressive views."[10]

On December 20, 2014, two NYPD police officers, Wenjian Liu

and Rafael Ramos, were gunned down in their patrol car by Ismaaiyl Abdullah Brinsley, ostensibly as revenge for the deaths of Garner and Michael Brown. Brinsley fled, and soon committed suicide. Within hours, President Obama issued a statement condemning the attack. On his next show, two days later, Limbaugh acknowledged that the president had condemned the killings "unconditionally," and "called for patient dialogue." Was the host turning over a new leaf? Not so much. Here is how he closed the segment: "He [Obama] went on to ask for a rejection of violence and words that harm. Well, there's a place he might want to start then, and that would be in his own house." Limbaugh continued by twisting what Obama meant by "dialogue"—by which he clearly was referring to discussion of criminal justice and police reform—and accused the president of calling instead for talking with "cop killers." He added: "They've all got blood on their hands . . . Sharpton . . . Everybody who has encouraged this kind of behavior on the part of average citizens against the cops . . . has blood on their hands . . . According to President Obama, white cops are racists." We already know that Sharpton and Obama share the same beliefs on matters of race, in Limbaugh's view, so this was the host's way of taking a double swipe at the president. Incredibly, the next day Limbaugh pretended that he had not talked about the president's condemnation of the murders of Officers Liu and Ramos: "Obama has yet to speak up on the two dead cops. He's still playing golf. He could do a lot to quell this if he wanted to, but he's not doing anything."

Returning to Ferguson, on January 21, 2015, the media reported that the DOJ was planning to recommend that federal civil rights charges not be brought against Officer Wilson in connection with the death of Michael Brown. The next day, Limbaugh declared that the investigation was all just "for show . . . in order to build a bridge to militant activists." He also called it a "smoke screen" designed to lay the groundwork for the feds to investigate the Ferguson Police Department for "alleged systematic discrimination." What the DOJ did, according to Limbaugh, was "extort these police departments into signing consent decrees forcing the police departments to conform their practices to Obama and Eric Holder-approved policing methods in their communities." (Consent decrees are agreements between individual, local police departments and the DOJ, according to which a department deemed to be problematic from a civil rights perspective must undertake reforms and submit to outside monitoring. President Trump's DOJ has sharply limited the use of consent decrees, which Limbaugh praised as "unravel[ling] . . . the extraconstitutional, extrajudicial behavior of the Obama administration."[11]) The host further explained what this would mean: "if Obama-Holder oppose stop-and-frisk, if they do that in Ferguson, they have to stop. They have to stop any intelligence gathering that the DOJ claims is rated [sic] in racism."

Limbaugh continued, averring that the consent decree "essentially ties the police department's hands and punishes or shapes these police departments under the premise that they have been violating the racial and civil rights of the residents for years." He called this "the unreported story," and argued that it would "end up making the police departments back off just a little here, just a little there, in pursuing bad guys . . . it's based in the belief that the United States, as founded, is unjust, immoral, racially segregated, biased country, has created these bad guys." Limbaugh was offering a prediction that ultimately mirrored the highly contested, unproven hypothesis that came to be known as the Ferguson Effect; namely that police officers might be so afraid of being unfairly punished over their interactions with black suspects that they would not engage as heavily as they had previously, which would lead to increased levels of crime.

Going further with this theme that the Obama-Holder DOJ favored black interests over the pursuit of justice, Limbaugh criticized Holder's suggestion (made in an interview published by *Politico* on February 27, 2015) that the standard of proof necessary to bring a federal civil rights charge should be lowered because the federal government ought to become "a better backstop" standing against discrimination.[12] On his show the same day, Limbaugh declared that the attorney general's proposal reveals what he—and thus Obama—really believed, namely that "civil rights prosecutions shouldn't need evidence, because we know them when we see them . . . We know when people are doing things because of race . . . I mean, I say this jokingly, but I wouldn't be surprised if someday Obama issues an executive order eliminating the need for evidence in federal civil rights cases."

When the DOJ finally announced on March 4 that Officer Wilson would not face federal charges, Limbaugh exulted, noting that the report was "unambiguous" and "unequivocal" about Wilson's actions. Still, the host complained on March 5 that the DOJ's final report was "one of the greatest travesties" because it says "the protestors in Ferguson were nevertheless justified . . . because the overall atmosphere in that town is one of racism and bias . . . Except everything they were protesting did not happen. And our report says so. This is gutless . . . Holder is afraid to have a straight conversation about race."

Rallies and protests had followed the DOJ announcement about Wilson and, at one of them, on March 12, 2015, two police officers were ambushed by a gunman. They were seriously wounded, but both survived. On that day's show, Limbaugh had no doubt about whom to blame: "Congratulations are in order. President Obama, Al Sharpton, Attorney General Eric Holder, St. Louis is on fire again . .

. The attorney general sends out this report: Ferguson police department racist. Ferguson police department filled with prejudice . . . What
in the world did they think was gonna happen?" The host charged that
the DOJ had spent months "perpetuating what everybody knew was a
lie," namely that Brown posed no threat to Officer Wilson before the
shots that killed him were fired. He added that the DOJ "had to give
the crowd something in the final report, and they did by pointing out
the Ferguson police department's racist." And that was why, Limbaugh
believed, the officers got shot.

The way these interconnected events often unfolded in stages—a
black man killed by an officer, followed by protests in response and,
on occasion, violence that appeared to be retaliatory; then a decision
from the justice system to not bring charges in the initial killing, followed again by protests in response and, on occasion, more apparent
retaliatory violence—provided Limbaugh with plenty of fodder and
ample freedom to riff back and forth across the issue of Obama's supposed support of black "militancy" against white police officers. In the
host's telling, anything other than Obama unconditionally and force-
fully condemning Black Lives Matter and downplaying the issues the
protestors raised meant that he was encouraging violence against the
police. In reality, nothing Obama could have said would likely have
satisfied Limbaugh, who was on a tribalizing mission.

The following month saw the case of Freddie Gray, who died in
custody following spinal injuries allegedly incurred during a trip in a
Baltimore police van. His death was followed by unrest that included
looting, vandalism, and scattered violence. On April 28, Limbaugh
went back to his old stand-by, saying that Obama "assured us and
promised us [that] this kind of thing was not going to happen anymore," and yet, even with a black president, "we have all this rage and

anger and promises of a new normal."

Two days later, after the president spoke about what was happening in Baltimore, the host offered his take, which included a familiar racial dog whistle, welfare: "It's as Obama has said: If Americans don't see . . . any rioting, if Americans don't see any looting, if the American people don't see anything burning on their TV, they might not realize that billions of more tax dollars are needed on welfare benefits." He added, "I'm paraphrasing, but that's essentially what Obama said."

On his May 1 broadcast, Limbaugh played remarks from Al Sharpton calling for the Justice Department to "step in and take over policing in this country." The host said that this push was part of what liberals meant by "social justice as opposed to real justice." And Limbaugh added, in response to a caller, "Obama basically called for it." Why was the president behind a national takeover of the police? In order to "rein them [police] in . . . really restrain them, because the presumption under which all this is happening is it's the police departments who are guilty."

Limbaugh's May 6, 2015 show included further condemnation of the president, who had recently been in New York, for not meeting with the family of Brian Moore, an NYPD officer gunned down by a man whom Moore and his partner had approached after thinking he might have a weapon in his waistband. The host contrasted not meeting Officer Moore's family with new U.S. Attorney General Loretta Lynch (she had replaced Holder ten days earlier) traveling to Baltimore to meet with the Gray family. Limbaugh's audience now heard that the black president and the new black attorney general cared more about the death of a black man who was under arrest than they did about a white cop who gave his life in the line of duty. This was a classic example of tribalization by Limbaugh.

There was another go-round two days later about the alleged federal takeover of policing under Obama, with Limbaugh noting "he's just gotten started, folks. Obama wants to restrain the police department presence . . . The real reason is for chaos." Limbaugh did not explain what kind of chaos he was referring to, leaving it to his audience's imagination, but did explain that the president "believe[s] that a vivid police department presence is intimidating and provocative and leads to unrest . . . they [police] are . . . a leading factor in a high crime rate and the unfair incarceration rate of young African-American men." The host repeated this argument again fifteen days later, and, without using the term, assigned blame for the so-called Ferguson Effect: "Barack Obama, every Democrat in this country thinks that it's the cops that are responsible for violence just by wearing the uniform and showing up. So the cops, in response, okay, okay, we hear you, they're backing off."

Limabaugh's audience heard similar remarks four more times over the next four weeks.[13] Along these lines, on July 13, 2015, Limbaugh discussed Obama's upcoming visit to a federal penitentiary—the first by a sitting president—and stated that the president believed that the disproportionate incarceration rate for black men resulted from racism. The visit, according to the host, was part of a larger push by Democrats to gain voting rights for felons—along with "illegal aliens" and "any number of so-called disenfranchised groups." Limbaugh said he "wouldn't be surprised if" Obama pardoned "certain prisoners" and sought "to extend the right to vote to our felon community, as the lingo goes." He also speculated that Obama might be prepared to apologize to the inmates. "Remember, according to people like Jesse Jackson and Al Sharpton . . . most of the African-American men have not broken the law. It's a miscarriage of justice . . . You know Obama agrees with that—or if he doesn't, he will say that he does." Limbaugh ended by noting that "with Obama pandering to prisoners . . . attacking police officers and police departments," he had handed another issue to the Republicans "on a silver platter. The issue: Law and order." Donald Trump would emphasize those three words often during his campaign for the White House, and as president.

More broadly, Trump has echoed many of the same themes as Limbaugh on the issues of the police and Black Lives Matter. When asked on August 2, 2015, about the problems of police violence raised by BLM, Trump responded: "Some horrible mistakes are made. At the same time, we have to give power back to the police, because crime is rampant . . . because we have to have law and order . . . You're always going to have bad apples . . . [but] the police have to regain some control of this crime wave and killing wave that we have in this country."[14] (Regarding that so-called crime wave, the U.S. violent crime rate in 2015 was near the historic, four-decade plus nadir it had reached the previous year, and it has remained at a similar level since then.[15]) In a presidential debate on January 14, 2016, Trump offered that the "police are the most mistreated people in this country."[16] On July 18, 2016, he assigned some of the responsibility for the murders of police officers to Black Lives Matter. In an interview, Fox News host Bill O'Reilly asked: "Do you believe the group . . . is a fuse-lighter in the assassinations of these police officers?" and Trump answered: "certainly in certain instances they are. And they certainly have ignited people." Additionally, the then-Republican nominee characterized BLM as a "threat" and charged them with "calling death to police and to kill the police, essentially."[17]

"Barack Obama, Black Lives Matter. All of these things factor into what is happening."

The issue of police officers and black men killing one another took center stage again in the final summer of the Obama presidency. On July 5, 2016, in Baton Rouge, Louisiana, Alton Sterling was shot and killed by police officers while they were holding him down on the ground. A gun was found in Sterling's pocket after the shooting. The following day, Philando Castile was shot and killed by a police officer in a suburb of St. Paul, Minnesota. In that incident, a broken brake light led Officer Jeronimo Yanez to pull over the car Castile was driving. According to police audio, Yanez and his partner thought the driver and passenger resembled suspects in a recent robbery. Castile's girlfriend, Diamond Reynolds, and her four-year old daughter were in the car as well. Castile informed Yanez, who had approached the driver's side window, that he had a gun on him, and the officer told him, "Okay, don't reach for it, then . . . don't pull it out." Castile replied, "I'm not pulling it out," and Reynolds also said, "He's not pulling it out." Yanez then screamed, "Don't pull it out," and shot Castile seven times.[18] Reynolds recorded the incident with her phone and live streamed it on Facebook, where approximately 2.5 million people had seen it by the next afternoon.

The day after Castile's death, July 7, protests occurred around the country, including one in Dallas, Texas. This was initially a peaceful protest, with numerous protestors taking and posting selfies with police officers who posed with them, smiling. As the Dallas march drew to a close, Micah X. Johnson attacked the police officers, killing five and wounding nine others in total, along with two civilians. He had expressed resentment over the killings of black men by police, and had stated a desire to kill white people, and white cops in particular.

The next day, Limbaugh speculated that Attorney General Loretta Lynch, who said she would investigate the Dallas killings as a hate crime, "may well conclude it wasn't a hate crime because Black Lives Matter doesn't hate." The host then, again, talked about how Obama's election was supposed to end "this kind of thing," but had instead made things worse "for predictable reasons." Limbaugh also claimed that the president had used violent language while in office in describing how to organize his supporters, "but he says if they bring a knife you bring a gun [note: In 2008 Obama had paraphrased an oft-quoted line from the movie *The Untouchables*, and that is what the host was referencing here] . . . He was clearly indicating that he's ready to roll. He's ready to rumble out there in his efforts at community organizing." Limbaugh did not directly say that Obama's language had inspired the murders of the police officers in Dallas, but, as we have seen time and time again, he rarely makes his most inflammatory charges directly. Additionally, he criticized the president for not standing up for police officers the way he stood up for Muslims after a Muslim commits a terrorist act. "Where is the equality, fairness . . . I don't think I've ever heard anybody in this Regime counsel restraint and advise, 'No backlash against cops.'"

Limbaugh's next show was Monday, July 11, and the host went after the president again over Dallas and BLM (on this day, Trump also declared: "We must maintain law and order at the highest level or we will cease to have a country, 100 percent . . . I am the law and order candidate."[19]) Limbaugh also brought up some of the president's prior statements that supposedly demonstrated antipathy toward the police, and then shifted to talking about the so-called War on Cops. The host first chided Obama for saying Micah Johnson's motives were "hard to untangle," then questioned whether Obama had "asked us to pause on the basis that it'd be very difficult to untangle the motives, let's say of shooter Dylann Roof?" Roof was a white Christian (his name was on the membership roll of St. Paul's Lutheran Church in Columbia, South Carolina[20]) who wrote a white supremacist manifesto before murdering nine African Americans in a Charleston, South Carolina church a month earlier. Limbaugh's implication was that Obama was more understanding of Johnson than Roof because he was more sympathetic to blacks murdering whites than vice versa. On July 12, Limbaugh again attacked the president and his "minions" for employing supposedly anti-cop rhetoric, of "doing everything they can to whip up hatred against the cops . . . Obama, he's clearly been saying things and acting out as though he, too, is a person with a grievance against the cops." Then he circled back to another favorite theme: "His [Obama's] prescription is payback."

The next day, Limbaugh critiqued the president's address to the nation about Dallas. He thought that Obama had said the right things in the first half of the speech, before delivering a "political sucker punch." According to the host, the president had to "give the impression he was a healer and a unifier before he could pivot to what he really wanted to say." Limbaugh was livid that the president mentioned the death of Sterling and, in his words, "drew a moral equivalence" between that event and the killings of the Dallas police officers. He also criticized Obama, as he had done before, for not telling the "truth" about what had happened in Ferguson; in other words, for not telling the protestors they were wrong because Brown was not the "gentle giant" he was made out to be. Limbaugh claimed, again, that Obama could have prevented the unrest there, but chose not to, and could have also prevented the unrest that erupted after the deaths of Freddie Gray and Eric Garner. Therefore, Obama was to blame for it all: "We don't expect presidents to further and promulgate lies and misinformation for the express purpose of creating and fomenting deadly anger."

On July 18, Limbaugh talked about how, even when the president asked people to "tone down the rhetoric" on the issue of police treatment of African Americans, he was not referring to Black Lives Matter or people like Al Sharpton. Instead, "he honors those people. He brings 'em to the White House. He conducts seminars with them . . . And then, on the same day the president said that police can make the job of being a cop a lot safer by admitting their failures." In other words, Obama was pro-BLM and anti-cop.

After the killing by police of Keith Lamont Scott on September 20, 2016, in Charlotte, North Carolina, largely peaceful protests took place, accompanied by some incidents of violence and unrest. Officers approached Scott, who had exited his car and who, according to police, was holding a gun. They ordered him to drop his weapon, and when he failed to respond, Officer Brentley Vinson shot him. Video could not confirm what, if anything, was in Scott's hands at the time he was shot. Police found a gun with his fingerprints and DNA at the site of the shooting, and Scott was found to be wearing an ankle holster. Limbaugh unsurprisingly criticized the president on the following day's broadcast, covering many of the same points he had used after other incidents of police violence, this time adding the charge that, perhaps, it was a visit to the Obama White House by BLM leaders that had "radicalized" the movement. Limbaugh presented this notion as a question, not a statement, as is his wont. Although the host did not get specific, he was presumably referring to a July 13, 2016 White House forum on policing attended by BLM activists Brittany Packnett and DeRay Mckesson, along with law enforcement officials, elected officials, and other civil rights activists.

The next day the host asked: "Did Obama even ask for calm yesterday? If he did, I missed it . . . It's just like we've asked about Ferguson and elsewhere, we have to ask, 'Where is Obama? Why hasn't Obama spoken out and actually told the facts about what actually happened in Charlotte?'" Limbaugh again blamed the president for all the previous incidents of unrest because he supposedly had not told the truth about how the black men killed by the police were the ones at fault. A day later, after Obama did address the unrest in Charlotte, the host played the president's remarks, including a line where he said that looting and vandalism were "the wrong way" to respond to frustrations about the police and violence. Even Obama saying exactly what the host had called for was not good enough: "It didn't sound very impassioned to me," Limbaugh said. "It doesn't sound like he's that interested to me when you get right down to it."

The same kind of tribalizing rhetoric continued after the election of President Trump. On November 21, 2016, after a weekend when four officers were shot and one, Benjamin Marconi of San Antonio, was killed, Limbaugh brought together many of the incidents covered in this chapter into a kind of closing argument delivered at the end of an eight-year long trial in which—citing Obama's remarks about Henry Louis Gates, Trayvon Martin, and Michael Brown—the host prosecuted the president for the way he spoke about race and the police:

> President Obama has not supported the police departments of this country . . . Obama's Department of Justice has used these incidents as pretexts for taking over local police departments . . . And the pretext for all of this is that . . . police departments are racist. You can go look at statements by Loretta Lynch and before her, Eric Holder, and even Obama. The presumption is that police are racist, that police are shooting African-Americans for the fun of it.

Neither Lynch, Holder, nor Obama had ever said, implied, suggested, or even hinted at the vile notion that cops shot black people "for the fun of it." But that didn't stop Limbaugh from making the accusation, an example of race-baiting as hateful as any he put forth during the Obama presidency. Limbaugh then made clear exactly where the responsibility lay for the cops ambushed, shot, and killed in the line of duty: "Barack Obama, Black Lives Matter. All of these things factor into what is happening."

Chapter Four

OBAMA, THE APOLOGIZER AND APPEASER

Although Rush Limbaugh more often employed racially inflammatory rhetoric when discussing domestic issues, he also used international affairs to "other" Obama. In terms of tribalizing rhetoric, Limbaugh's attacks on the forty-fourth president's foreign policy often focused on the theme that Obama was pro-Muslim—or at least refused to respond vigorously to violent acts of terrorism or other transgressions committed by Muslims.

An example of this supposed pro-Muslim bias came after ISIS unleashed a series of terrorist attacks in and around Paris on November 13, 2015, that killed 130 people. Limbaugh rebuked Obama, stating that the president only got "animated and passionate" when criticizing the notion that we should apply a religious test to refugees in order to keep Muslims out of the country. By contrast, when talking about actually fighting ISIS, the host opined that Obama was "impersonal . . . detached . . . as though he was talking theory and philosophy in the faculty lounge." This wholly subjective assessment fits the larger slander Limbaugh pushed about Obama caring more about Muslim sensibilities than protecting America. Regarding the ISIS attacks in Brussels that killed thirty-two people on March 22, 2016, Limbaugh excoriated the "overall passivity shown toward ISIS by President Obama . . . He has never been proactive in taking on ISIS."[1]

Another line of attack that Limbaugh used against Obama in the foreign policy arena was that the president, because he rejected the traditional conception of America as a force for moral good, had purposefully sought to weaken the U.S. position in the world. This false charge would come up again and again during both of Obama's two terms. For example, on March 27, 2009, Limbaugh accused the Obama Administration of carrying out a foreign policy that ignored American interests, and instead sought to "please the world, including our enemies," and of having offered an "apology for America" on multiple occasions. "Apologizing for America" was a popular theme of Limbaugh's, as the host accused the president of apologizing for our country's sins on thirty-two shows in 2009 alone, often several times during a single broadcast.[2]

After the story broke in 2013 about former Central Intelligence Agency employee and U.S. government consultant Edward Snowden having leaked a massive amount of classified material regarding surveillance being conducted by the National Security Agency as well as foreign governments, Limbaugh took the incident as an opportunity to criticize Obama for not supporting the principles upon which America was constructed: "Do I want somebody in charge of this kind of surveillance who doesn't like this country as it's founded? . . . somebody . . . who is in the middle of trying to transform this country into something the founders never intended it to be?" For the host, the problem was not that the government was conducting widespread surveillance, but that the person giving the order to conduct it was not pro-American. Similarly, when criticizing the Administration's proposals for military spending in 2014, Limbaugh asserted that the president's primary objective was "to tear down the greatness of this country so that we are not better than any other nation."[3]

"Barack Obama's Got Something Against Israel"

One key foreign policy issue that Limbaugh began emphasizing almost immediately after Obama's inauguration was the U.S. relationship with Israel. Basically, the host argued that the president did not support Israel in its struggle to live in peace and security with its neighbors. Of course, painting Obama with an anti-Israel brush was a perfect way for Limbaugh to show that the president was also pro-Muslim. On January 23, 2009, Limbaugh accused the president of having "told Israel to open the borders so the gazookas [sic] from Gaza could get closer to aim their rockets, I guess." He reiterated this point four days later. What Obama had actually said was that "Gaza's border crossings should be open to allow the flow of aid and commerce," but only "with an appropriate monitoring regime" that included international as well as Palestinian monitors, and only as "part of a lasting ceasefire."[4] Limbaugh's audience only heard the part of Obama's statement that supported the host's pro-Muslim tribalizing efforts.

Limbaugh told an even bigger lie a month later when he alleged that Obama had sent $900 million to Hamas—which the U.S. and the European Union have designated a terrorist organization—under the guise of helping the Palestinian population. When Limbaugh repeated this accusation on March 5, he noted that, "Israel is now in our crosshairs." After the Republican National Committee echoed the charge, PolitiFact investigated and rated it as "false."[5]

One of the important events early in the Obama presidency that Limbaugh used to create a tribalizing wedge on the matter of Israel was the so-called "New Beginning" speech. During his run for the presidency, Obama had promised, if elected, to make a significant speech about Islam in a major Muslim capital. The purpose of this gesture was to reach out on behalf of the United States to Muslims throughout the world. The president fulfilled that promise in Cairo, Egypt, on June 4, 2009. Limbaugh offered his thoughts on the speech the same day. Sticking with his general characterization of the president as pro-Muslim and thus anti-American, the host wondered if, given that Obama had "found a way . . . to praise" Islam's contributions to the world, that maybe he could, someday, give a speech about "our accomplishments, too." Limbaugh must have missed the section of the Cairo speech where Obama said that "The United States has been one of the greatest sources of progress that the world has ever known . . . We were founded upon the ideal that all are created equal, and we have shed blood and struggled for centuries to give meaning to those words— within our borders, and around the world."[6]

During the speech, Obama also rejected the Holocaust denial embraced by, most prominently among Muslim political leaders, Mahmoud Ahmadinejad, then Iran's president and a well-known anti-Semite. President Obama talked about how Palestinians had suffered in the decades since the Holocaust, as they lacked self-determination and a state of their own. However, to Limbaugh, this meant that the president was saying, "there are two sides to the Holocaust!" and that Obama was drawing "a moral equivalence between the slaughter of six million Jews and a political circumstance in Palestine that's largely brought on by Palestinian leaders." The "New Beginning" speech also provoked what would become some of Limbaugh's most familiar foreign policy criticisms of Obama: that the president wanted to "cut [America] down to size," redistribute our wealth to poor countries, and weaken Israel.

Limbaugh even brought up Jeremiah Wright to further scare his audience about Obama's supposed bias against Israel. On June 5, 2009, Limbaugh returned to condemning the Cairo speech by citing Wright, this time specifically to brand Obama as anti-Israel: "Barack Obama's got something against Israel. Now, if you look at who mentored him, Jeremiah Wright, you'll find there's a guy who's got something against Israel." Limbaugh highlighted this theme on several other occasions, such as when he said that those who hated Jews are "not part of my circle," but that Obama, by contrast, had "surrounded himself with such people."[7]

Limbaugh continued with his Obama has "something" against Israel theme on June 8, when he stated that the president had "thrown them [Israel] under the bus." In this instance, the host said that the president had "bowed" to the king of Saudi Arabia, and that "Obama has far more roots, heritage, ability to relate to somebody like the king of Saudi Arabia than he does with [Israeli Prime Minister] Benjamin Netanyahu. May we say that without fear being [sic] raked over the coals for it? He said it himself in his Cairo speech. He was surrounded by Muslims growing up in three different countries." Limbaugh spoke again of Obama's "deep Muslim roots" four days later.

The host continued depicting the president as anti-Israel for the entirety of his presidency. Just a few examples out of many: on July 30, 2014, after the announcement of a cease fire during the fighting between Israel and Hamas-controlled Gaza, Limbaugh condemned the administration for, in his words, having "chosen sides, and the side they've chosen is Hamas . . . the administration knows that Hamas is killing its own children with this behavior, and yet they blame Israel." On March 19, 2015, Limbaugh hyped a report that the president had spent money to "turn out the Arab vote" in the Israeli election that had just taken place. The report was later debunked.[8]

Limbaugh also used the U.S. relationship with Iran to try and convince his audience that Obama was anti-Israel. Limbaugh castigated Obama over Iran, saying that the president would allow Tehran to acquire nuclear weapons and that he did not care if Iran threatened Israel. The host brought Iran up frequently, even over issues that had nothing to with the country. For example, in discussing the FBI's successful infiltration of a domestic, homegrown terrorist group that had sought to blow up a synagogue in the Bronx, New York, Limbaugh asked on May 21, 2009: "Jewish-hating Muslim extremists actually try to carry out their threats but somehow we don't think Iran will?"

A March 18, 2011 caller to the Rush Limbaugh Show let fly a series of extreme accusations that the host summarized as "Obama wants an Iranian caliphate," "Obama has sympathies here to the Iranian mullahs" and "with militant Islamists." Limbaugh added the usual disclaimer to distance himself just enough from the comments—"it sounds crazy"— but then went on to say that the caller did "sound a little bit more informed on the Muslim Brotherhood than does our intelligence director . . . He did lay it out pretty effectively . . . I could tell he was a little afraid of saying so. It's a strange thing for an American citizen to think." Calls like these provided the ideal opportunity for Limbaugh to insulate himself, as he could let the ridiculous, baseless calumny hang out there for his audience to digest, then talk in a supportive way about the caller—praising his bravery—without going on record as saying that he necessarily believed him.

It was the nuclear issue, however, on which Limbaugh mostly focused when condemning the president on Iran. On March 5, 2015, the host asked, "Why is giving Iran the nuclear bomb so important to Obama?" and claimed that the president had changed the existing U.S. policy, according to which we had long sought to prevent such a development. He repeated the question a few more times during the segment, before finally giving his audience the answer: "To counter the nuclear dominance of Israel in the region . . . I don't think Obama wants Iran to start nuking people. I think he doesn't trust Israel as the only nuclear power in the region. I think he wants Israel, as a nuclear power, balanced—neutered . . . the whole point of Iran getting a nuclear weapon is Israel."

While discussing the negotiations over the nuclear deal with Iran on March 24, Limbaugh characterized Obama and those who thought like him as believing that "America is on the wrong side of everything and that they can perfect it . . . They hate America the way it was before them. But I don't think they hate America in the sense they want to destroy America as though it would be nuked like the Iranians do." Six days later, the host returned to the Iran-Israel connection to pass along a vicious rumor: "there's a credible train of thought" that the president was about to "officially . . . abandon Israel as a United States ally." Of course, Obama never did any such thing.

The negotiations led, on July 14, 2015, to the announcement of the Joint Comprehensive Plan of Action between Iran, the United States, Russia, China, France, Britain, Germany, and the European Union. In one of his many denunciations of the deal, on July 15, Limbaugh returned to one of his most common tribalizing tropes. He intoned that it was "rooted" in the deal "that he [Obama] doesn't think Iran's the bad guys. If anybody is, we are." The host then reminded his audience about the anti-American president's relationship with the anti-American Reverend Wright.

Syria and Iraq

Israel was far from the only foreign policy initiative where Limbaugh tribalized American politics through language designed to "other" the president. When criticizing Obama's policy toward war-torn Syria, for example, the host took the opportunity to race bait: "Bush had Shock and Awe? We're looking at shuck and jive here. That's what I'm gonna name this. The Obama operation in Syria, Operation Shuck and Jive." Shuck and Jive is a term that has racial connotations, and Salon editor-at-large Joan Walsh called Limbaugh out for hurling this slur. Others, including 2008 GOP vice-presidential nominee Sarah Palin and New York Democratic Governor Andrew Cuomo, had already been chided for aiming this term at Obama, and given Limbaugh's established history of race-baiting, it is more than reasonable to assume he knew exactly the dog whistle he was blowing for his audience.[9]

On September 4, 2015, Limbaugh blamed the Syrian crisis on the way Obama viewed America: "This is what happens when the United States abdicates its role as leader of the free world . . . when a bunch of leftist idealists and theorists get in power and think the United States is the problem in the world . . . the focus of evil in the world." Seven days later, after the United States announced that it would admit 10,000 Syrian refugees (compared to hundreds of thousands accepted by Germany, which has one quarter of our population, for example), Limbaugh characterized them as "the people who are behind 9/11. At least to people who lost family and friends, that's how it appears." Right after this, Limbaugh cited comments from former New York City Mayor Rudolph Giuliani—the political figure most directly associated with 9/11. The host's goal here was to get his audience to think that Barack Obama was letting 9/11 terrorists into America, without saying so directly—"that's how it appears."

Limbaugh also alleged that any of the 10,000 refugees could request to bring family members into the country, "so you can multiply these numbers by three, four maybe." He added: "none of these people are going to be vetted." PolitiFact reviewed the claim that the U.S. had "no ability to vet" the Syrian refugees and found it "mostly false."[10] President Trump's so-called "Muslim Travel Ban"—which sought to prevent anyone from Syria and a number of other Muslim countries from traveling to the United States—relied on these same kinds of lies about unvetted refugees.[11]

Race-baiting also featured in Limbaugh's attacks on Obama's Iraq policy. The host blamed the president for the pullout of U.S. troops from Iraq, even though the Bush Administration had previously negotiated an agreement that mandated all American troops leave the country by the end of 2011. When Obama tried to negotiate for a residual force of a few thousand troops to stay behind, the Iraqi Parliament made clear it would not approve the Status of Forces Agreement that would have provided the legal protections necessary to make the troops' stay feasible.[12] Limbaugh lied about this, saying on June 24, 2014, that "we had all the cards . . . Even a trained ape could have gotten a status of force agreement." The "ape" reference has obvious racial overtones. Additionally, on August 11, 2014, Limbaugh asserted that Iraqi Prime Minister Nouri al-Maliki had proffered the necessary agreement and "signed it. Obama rejected it." This was not true. The host then likened Obama's "rejection" to the way Al Sharpton and Jesse Jackson supposedly always rejected proposed solutions to problems relating to race because doing so was to their advantage.

Don't Forget Benghazi

On Libya, Limbaugh returned to one of his favorite tribalizing themes against Obama: that the president was an apologist for American values and power. On March 9, 2011, during the uprising that ultimately overthrew that country's longtime dictator, Muammar Khadafy, Limbaugh asked if there was "any evidence that he [Obama] has the slightest understanding or idea what's happening there or why or does he even care?" Eight days later, the host chastised Obama over having not yet decided on a military response to events in Libya, and stated that the root of the problem with administration policy was the president's "view of this country . . . [He] does not believe in American exceptionalism . . . apologize[s] for the United States . . . believes that the United States has achieved its superpower position illegitimately."

On March 22, after the United States and other allies had begun an air campaign in support of anti-Khadafy forces, Limbaugh brought up Louis Farrakhan as well as Reverend Wright, and went back again to Obama's allegedly negative view of American power, declaring that, "We are being led . . . by people who believe that the United States is the problem in the world, not the solution." When the president addressed the country about Libya on March 28, Limbaugh on the following day characterized Obama's embrace of multilateralism (i.e., working in coordination with our allies and operating by consensus rather than going it alone) as reflecting an "Obama Doctrine," according to which "our sovereignty, we're waving it good-bye." This charge fed a larger right-wing conspiracy theory that Obama wanted to undermine American sovereignty.[13]

When forces supported by the United States and NATO ultimately killed Khadafy, Limbaugh on October 20, 2011, offered sarcastic praise, before muddying the waters by again bringing up Wright and Farrakhan, both of whom the host said would likely be upset because they "loved" Khadafy. Limbaugh then played an extended audio clip of Farrakhan in which he called Obama an assassin, but also called him "my brother." Here, Limbaugh was reminding his audience of the connections between Obama and these two black radicals, each of whom had repeatedly uttered anti-American rhetoric.

The death of Khadafy did not, unfortunately, mean that Libya's problems were over. The country experienced continued bloodshed and civil war, as various factions struggled for power. One of them, a fundamentalist Islamist group called Ansar al-Sharia, carried out attacks on September 11, 2012, that targeted U.S. diplomatic sites in Benghazi. These attacks resulted in the death of Chris Stevens, the U.S. Ambassador to Libya, and three other Americans. Limbaugh went over the attack in great detail, excoriating the president and his administration with his typical racially-infused rhetoric. On September 12, Limbaugh said, "His [Obama's] instinct is to sympathize with the attackers, just like Reverend Wright said '9/11, America's chickens coming home to roost.' That's exactly it."

The following day, Limbaugh tied together his Benghazi criticisms by again accusing Obama of apologizing for America. This time, the host also brought Secretary of State Hillary Clinton into the mix. Limbaugh argued that U.S. foreign policy overall was "imploding." Why? Because the president and Secretary Clinton "have a politically correct conflict resolution 'United States is always at fault' worldview. That is how you get Obama apologizing all over the world shortly after he takes office. That's why Obama bows to all these foreign leaders . . . why he went to Cairo and made this speech." This was also why four Americans died in Benghazi, according to Limbaugh.

On October 11, 2012, Limbaugh accused the president and Secretary Clinton of "purposely lying" to Pat Smith, whose son Sean was one of the four Americans killed. The host continued by blackening Obama, implying that while he did not care about the Smith family, he did take care of what was important to him, namely, "a fundraiser with

Jay-Z. How about that fundraiser with Jay-Z? Boy, Obama, he's got that racial angle covered, doesn't he? That guy's smart." I would argue that it was Limbaugh who always had the racial angle covered when it came to Obama. As for the most serious specific charges leveled at the administration on Benghazi—that officials ignored intelligence reports about the possibility of an attack, attempted to cover up what happened, and lied for political reasons about the attackers' motivations—they have all been debunked.[14]

One of Limbaugh's most notorious slanders on Benghazi came on August 6, 2013, when he repeated a rumor that high-profile White House advisor Valerie Jarrett—whom he noted was "not in the chain of command" and had no military role whatsoever—had issued a directive ordering the military personnel in Benghazi to "stand down" and that as a result "four Americans died." Limbaugh described Jarrett as a "community organizer acolyte. I mean, she is Obama." (The host did not even have to identify Jarrett's race directly; by referring to her as a "community organizer" his audience would have known she was black.) He added that she "would not have to be given an order by Obama to know what he wanted. In fact, it may be that Valerie Jarrett often tells Obama what it is he wants." This accusation fit another tribalizing theme of Limbaugh's, that of undercutting Obama's masculinity by characterizing him as taking orders from women, in particular black women like Michelle Obama and Jarrett. This charge showed up on Fox News the next day, where Steve Doocy repeated it. When Doocy was asked whether the charge was true, he replied, "Rush was talking about it."[15]

This incident exemplifies how the right-wing echo chamber works. A media figure like Limbaugh says something false (also racially divisive in this case) that he has either made up or picked up from a non-journalistic source. Right-wing "news" outlets then report that Limbaugh has said it, so this piece of fake news spreads further and becomes a "fact" among conservatives. The mainstream media then starts talking about this "alternative fact" (to paraphrase Trump senior advisor Kellyanne Conway) as well—at the very least, asking whether it might be true, because it is being covered by a high-profile organization such as Fox News and they want to avoid being accused of "liberal media bias" for having ignored the story. In this case, no such stand down order was issued, by Jarrett or anyone else.[16]

More broadly, a University of Oxford study found that right-wing, Trump-supporting social media users were far more likely to spread "extremist, sensationalist, conspiratorial, masked commentary, fake news and other forms of junk news."[17] Many fake news consumers were primed for this kind of tribalizing propaganda by years of exposure to partisan media such as the Rush Limbaugh Show. This was another way that Limbaugh paved the way for Trump, who makes the host look like a piker when it comes to lying. For example, the *Washington Post* Fact Checker counted 7,645 "false or misleading claims" made by President Trump over his first 710 days in office.[18]

"The law-abiding people of this country and your guns, you are the problem."

While this chapter focuses mainly on how Limbaugh tried to "other" President Obama as anti-American and pro-Muslim through the lens of foreign policy, the host also used this theme when speaking about domestic terrorism.

On November 5, 2009, Nidal Hasan, a Muslim American army psychiatrist, murdered twelve soldiers and one civilian at Ford Hood, Texas. Four days later, in addressing what had happened, Limbaugh made an especially despicable effort to "other" Obama. He brought up Henry Louis Gates in order to remind his audience that the president allegedly always supported the non-white, "victimized minority" over the white American majority, even when the minority person was, as in the case of Hasan, a mass murderer. Limbaugh also pointed out that Hasan had gone to a mosque, where he heard a radical imam preach. The host then noted that Obama had attended Reverend Wright's church. Limbaugh's goal here was simple: to tie Obama, through Wright and Hasan, to murderous hatred of America.

Going further, Limbaugh offered a completely subjective, unfounded interpretation of the president's response to the Fort Hood killings: "He [Obama] didn't even make it a priority. He didn't even act like he was fazed by it." In truth, Obama's response to the killings began, "My immediate thoughts and prayers are with the wounded and with the families of the fallen and with those who live and serve at Fort Hood." It is difficult to see how that can be characterized as showing a lack of concern on the part of the president.[19]

Limbaugh brought up Wright and Obama together in discussing Hasan again the next day, and followed that up by saying that the president had blamed the United States for the attacks that killed 3,000 people on 9/11. The so-called evidence the host cited for this accusation was an article Obama had published eight days after the attacks. Limbaugh brought up the article again on July 28, 2011, claiming that "Obama, after 9/11, said he had empathy for the terrorists." Of course, these claims by Limbaugh were false. Here is what Obama actually wrote: "the essence of this tragedy . . . derives from a fundamental lack of empathy on the part of the attackers."[20] In other words, the truth was the complete opposite of what Limbaugh told his audience.

Another major domestic terrorism incident that Limbaugh used to "other" Obama was the Boston Marathon bombing. On April 15, 2013, two Muslim brothers originally from Chechnya, Dzhokhar and Tamerlan Tsarnaev, detonated bombs near the finish line of the Boston Marathon, killing three people and injuring dozens more. Seven days later, Limbaugh hit Obama over his reaction to the bombings. The host first brought up an old favorite, Reverend Wright and his "chickens have come home to roost" sermon. (That one never got old, as the host clucked about Wright's "chickens" seven times in reference to terrorism or U.S. foreign policy.[21]) Limbaugh then rebuked the president with one of his—and the right's—favorite criticisms, that "he can't bring himself to say 'Muslim terrorists.'" The real reason Obama did not use that or any similar term to characterize those who commit terrorist acts in the name of Islam was because he believed that doing so would harm national security. The president explained that the terrorists "try to portray themselves as religious leaders, holy warriors in defense of Islam. We must never accept the premise that they put forward because it is a lie. Nor should we grant these terrorists the religious legitimacy that they seek. They are not religious leaders. They are terrorists."[22] Reality aside, Limbaugh was only too happy to use this matter repeatedly as a wedge issue, in the process putting partisanship over national security.

Limbaugh also used domestic terrorism to tag Obama with a classic conservative attack, that the president was trying to take people's guns away from them. On December 2, 2015, Syed Rizwan Farook and Tashfeen Malik, a married Muslim couple, attacked an event for employees of the San Bernardino County Department of Public Health, where Farook worked. The couple murdered fourteen people before police killed them. Following the attack, Limbaugh went after the Obama Administration's counter-terrorism and anti-ISIS policy in familiar terms and, as before, threw out baseless accusations.

Particularly egregious, however, was the host's charge on December 7 that the president was "comfortable with a certain degree of violence because . . . what they really want to do is get your guns out of your hand . . . Not ISIS, not Islam—well, not Islam and not Muslims . . . The law-abiding people of this country and your guns, you are the problem."

Following the attacks at Pulse, an Orlando nightclub that catered to LGBT customers, Limbaugh continued this line of tribalization. On June 12, 2016, during the club's Latino Night, Omar Mateen, an American-born Muslim, murdered forty-nine people. After the president, in response, lamented that it was too easy for people who wished to do harm to acquire weapons, Limbaugh claimed on June 14 that this showed that Obama and his party believed "we conservatives, we Republicans, are their biggest enemy. They despise us more than they despise militant Islam," and believe "we . . . must be destroyed."

Limbaugh also used the Pulse attacks to bring things full circle and remind his audience that Obama was against America, and for Muslims, i.e. the terrorists. After the president used the killings to again defend his refusal to use a term such as "radical Islamist" to describe terrorists who were Muslim, Limbaugh explained that he repeatedly brought up this issue not because he believed that saying the words would impact the terrorists, but because "people have a legitimate question of whether or not Obama opposes them. Or, rather, if they're just the latest enemy of the day, that there's nothing unique about them . . . People are trying to decide . . . if our president is serious about this." Limbaugh claimed he was sincerely concerned about whether the president understood what he was dealing with. In reality, the host's criticisms were aimed at convincing people that Obama was soft on Islam and terrorism.

During the same broadcast Limbaugh revisited another of his

old standbys, that Obama was "really, really bothered out there about offending Islamists." He also claimed that the president did "not seem concerned about Christianity. He is a Christian. If he is [sic] get upset about attacks on Christianity, he never comes out defends [sic] Christianity."

Two days later, the host made another charge aimed at painting Obama as more concerned about Muslims than Americans, saying that the FBI and the federal government's "focus" was looking for those who "might be threatening or saying negative things about Muslims, targeting them, finding them, and exploring ways to punish them." Limbaugh continued: "Are you also looking out for threats against America by Muslims? Well, we presume so, but no . . . We're not allowed to!" He further argued that the FBI was unable to "investigate terror threats" because it was "hamstrung by" the administration's counter-terrorism strategy and the aforementioned "focus." The message was that Obama cared more about the feelings of Muslims than the safety of Americans. The purpose of the message was to tribalize American politics.

Chapter Five

"OBAMA'S ENTIRE ECONOMIC PROGRAM IS REPARATIONS!"

In addition to foreign policy and domestic terrorism, Limbaugh also deployed tribalizing rhetoric when criticizing President Obama on economic issues that, on the surface, were not directly connected to race or identity. The host falsely portrayed just about every one of Obama's economic policies as specifically aimed at hurting white Americans while benefitting Americans of color and, in a number of cases, "illegal aliens" as well. These included economic and budget issues such as the 2009 stimulus, the automobile industry bailout, welfare, tax policy, financial reform, and, above all, health care. In fact, to hear Limbaugh tell it, Obama's approach to every one of these matters flowed directly from his belief that America, i.e., white America (the two were essentially synonymous in the host's presentation) had committed grievous wrongs against African Americans that the government had to address. Or, as Limbaugh concisely put it: "Obama's entire economic program is reparations!"[1]

"It rewards people who don't work, who don't save."

Obama's first major economic initiative after getting elected was the stimulus package, known as the American Recovery and Reinvestment Act (ARRA), which was signed into law on February 17, 2009. Eight days later, among numerous attacks and other falsehoods he had leveled at the law, Limbaugh called the president's statement that the ARRA would give a tax cut to 95 percent of Americans a "lie" because the percentage of Americans who paid taxes was far lower than 95 percent. Approximately 40 percent, Limbaugh claimed, "don't pay taxes. They're going to get a tax cut. It's not a tax cut; they're going to get a welfare payment, and you're paying for it." This assertion was untrue on several levels. First of all, Limbaugh misquoted the president, who had actually said to a joint session of Congress that "95 percent of working households" would get a tax cut—a statement PolitiFact rated as true.[2] Furthermore, while approximately 40 percent of Americans do not pay federal income taxes, the host was incorrect to say that a large percentage of them "don't pay taxes," given that almost anyone who works pays payroll taxes. Most importantly for our purposes, Limbaugh again used welfare to blacken Obama by pitting "they"—the people he said were receiving "a welfare payment" from the president's stimulus package—against "you"—those who were going to be "paying for it."

On that final point, Limbaugh repeatedly lied by claiming that the ARRA removed the work requirement from welfare reform, or, as he did on March 17, 2009, that the bill required the states to spend the stimulus money on "new welfare cases . . . whatever else that the Obama administration determines." Similarly, on June 9, 2009, Limbaugh claimed that the president's push to require offsetting most types of new spending (known as "PAYGO" rules, which were signed into law on February 12, 2010) was merely an excuse to raise taxes and "redistribute" money to "the unions and . . . the civil rights coalitions . . . They've got nothing to give anybody without taking it from you first."

However, the specific stimulus item that most upset Limbaugh—judging by how often he brought it up—was the supposed "$4.19

billion for neighborhood stabilization or ACORN, community organizing voter fraud groups." After numerous mentions on January 27, 2009, Limbaugh repeated this claim on a half-dozen more broadcasts over the next two months—although the amount he cited had dropped to $2 billion by February 13.[3] Limbaugh was referring to neighborhood stabilization funds that were made available to local governments and non-profits to purchase and then rehabilitate vacant, foreclosed dwellings. ACORN, in theory, could have applied for these grants—but would have been in competition with hundreds of organizations. In response to the controversy, Bertha Lewis, a top official with ACORN, noted that, "We have not received neighborhood stabilization funds, have no plans to apply for such funds, and didn't weigh in on the pending rule changes."[4] PolitiFact also reviewed the issue, and found "no money designated for ACORN."[5] Nevertheless, Limbagh was still harping about ACORN getting stimulus money on May 24, 2011, (a year after the organization had gone under) adding, "I wonder if Reverend Sharpton's group, the National Action Network . . . got some of the stimulus money . . . I wonder if he got some of Obama's stash."

Limbaugh also stated on January 29, 2009, that the ARRA contained "tax credits of $500 to $1,000 for illegal aliens." This claim was based on an Associated Press story that said that the stimulus package under debate in Congress "could steer government checks to illegal immigrants, a top Republican congressional official asserted." The story was later corrected, the AP article was updated, and the claim was debunked.[6] Of course, Limbaugh's audience never heard about the new information. Limbaugh also thundered on the same show that the stimulus was "the most irresponsible confiscation of wealth and power, from you, the American people, in our nation's history . . . It rewards people who don't work, who don't save."

The "illegal alien" story is a typical example of how the conservative political and media infrastructure spreads falsehoods and disinformation. A single Republican politician makes an anonymous claim that something "could" happen. The claim gets reported by a mainstream organization like the AP, and then someone on the right like Limbaugh repeats it to his audience, saying that since he read about the claim in a place like the *New York Times* (the AP article was picked up by many newspapers), it must be true. In this case, Limbaugh was telling his listeners—confirmed by the liberal media no less—that Obama was giving tax credits to "illegal aliens", i.e., redistributing (white) taxpayers' hard-earned money to black and brown people.

The following month, on February 9, Limbaugh declared that "what's being done in the name of economic stimulus and jobs here is one of the biggest frauds perpetrated on the American people." The next day he characterized the stimulus as "not just a war on the achievers. It's an effort to buy votes to cement the power of the Democrat Party for generations." The host then played an exchange between the president and Julio Osegueda, a college student who also worked at McDonald's, in which Obama told him about the payroll tax break included in the stimulus. Limbaugh shared with his audience what Osegueda was supposedly really thinking: "I'm not talking about that. That means I have to keep working." The host essentially accused this student, who had a Latino-sounding name, of wanting to be given money without having to work. Limbaugh also cited Henrietta Hughes (see chapter 2), the woman who had purportedly asked the president for a car. The purpose of all this was to give the impression that the stimulus aimed to help people the host defined as freeloaders, who happened to be black and Latino.

The charge that the president was carrying out a "war on achievers" or otherwise punishing them was one Limbaugh hurled dozens of times during the debate over the stimulus and throughout 2009. On February 17, he said that Obama was waging war on behalf of the poor, and then added that, "He [Obama] believes that people in the lower socioeconomic groups are there because of oppressive tactics, selfishness, and the power of the people who have achieved. And his definition of people who have "achieved" is pretty low. Seventy-five grand, a hundred grand, you've achieved and you're facing a tax increase." Limbaugh then brought up Obama's "rage," along with Reverend Wright. This was a classic example of Limbaugh pitting the middle and even lower-middle classes against those who had less, whom he generally defined as members of racial minority groups.

The "F-word"

The economic stimulus was but one element of what Limbaugh described on February 10, 2009, as Obama's "all-out war on achievement in this country." The host also "othered" the president by using the "f-word," as he described the government's involvement with Chrysler and General Motors (GM)—the so-called auto bailout—as "fascism in a sense here with the government owning, operating, and advising the means of production in the case of the United Auto Workers (UAW), General Motors, Chrysler." If this was fascism, it was one that disappeared quickly and without violence, as the government had sold its shares in those companies by the end of 2013. According to the Center for Automotive Research, the U.S. would have lost almost 2 million jobs had GM disappeared, and over 4 million had the entire auto industry dissolved.[7] In addition to the fascism tag, on June 2, 2009, Limbaugh also said that the president was running the auto companies "the way a community organizer does it."

The auto bailout was not the only part of Obama's economic program that was fascist, in Limbaugh's view, nor was it the only piece he attacked by race-baiting. The host also termed the Dodd-Frank financial reform law "fascism" on April 14, 2010, and six days later criticized it by bringing up ACORN. Limbaugh tied that organization to the president, and falsely blamed it for the subprime mortgage crisis. Limbaugh did this again a week later, and again on July 28, 2010, a week after the legislation passed. In that day's segment condemning Dodd-Frank, he spoke of "ACORN at the front gate, a bunch of ragtag advocates for the poor threatening to burn down your bank," and, for good measure, mentioned the NAACP four times.

Obama's former pastor and "mentor" also came up in a discussion of financial industry reform. The host quoted Reverend Wright and reminded his listeners "this is what Obama believes." Additionally, Limbaugh charged the president with reviving the ideas behind the Community Reinvestment Act (see Chapter 1), which meant, in the host's explanation, making a renewed push to require banks to issue-more loans to lower income borrowers of color by threatening them with violating the CRA's anti-discrimination provisions: "He [Obama] is making banks go into minority neighborhoods. The subprime thing is being rerun. This time, not just loans to the poor. They have to open branches in poor and dangerous neighborhoods." During a different show, Limbaugh noted that Obama had once sued Citibank over "redlining," and had accused the banks of "snooker[ing] people into these mortgages." Limbaugh characterized this effort on behalf of poor borrowers as a "shakedown," and brought up the CRA and ACORN, as well as Jesse Jackson. The host also accused the Obama Administration of "replicating" the CRA, through provisions in the Dodd-Frank law.[8] At this point, Limbaugh's audience had heard repeatedly that the economy had crashed because poor black people and their Democratic allies had passed a law that forced banks to give them loans—subprime mortgages—that they could not repay. Now Limbaugh was telling his followers that the president wanted to do the same thing all over again.

Obama's Tax Proposals Will "Fundamentally Remove Capitalism as the US Primary Economic System."

The package of tax cuts passed in 2001 and 2003 under George W. Bush were scheduled to sunset on January 1, 2011, in which case income tax rates would have returned to Clinton-era levels. The debate over what to do occupied much of the president's and Congress's attention in the fall of 2010.

Limbaugh came out in favor of full extension of all the cuts and criticized Obama's proposal to allow tax rates to rise on high income earners. Part of that criticism included some of the host's favorite tribalizing lines, such as when he alleged that Obama would be "raising taxes on everybody, taking money out of the private sector and giving it to unions and giving it to government workers and giving it to himself and to ACORN." In another discussion of taxes, Limbaugh brought up "the SEIU (the Service Employees International Union—of which an article in *The Atlantic* said: "since the disbanding of ACORN, [it] is now the number-one boogeyman for the right."[9]) union [sic] thugs . . . community organizing groups, ACORN," as the Democrats' preferred recipients of tax revenues.[10] The host's criticisms also included calling Obama a "Marxist" as well as a "socialist" on three occasions.[11] In the lame duck congressional session after the 2010 mid-term elections, the president and Congress agreed to extend for two years all the Bush tax cuts as well as some measures contained in the stimulus that were also due to expire.

As the two-year extension began to draw to a close in 2012, Limbaugh again hammered Obama for wanting to raise taxes. The host predicted on November 16, 2012, that the president's plan would "fundamentally change the relationship of citizen to state . . . fundamentally remove capitalism as the US primary economic system." On November 29, he carried out a long harangue about the possibility, which had not come up in the actual negotiations, that the deal might include taxing 401(k) retirement accounts and pensions—"a lot of cash there, folks." As part of these blatant scare tactics, Limbaugh mentioned that Jesse Jackson had once advocated taxing private sector pensions (he brought up this point again on February 6, 2015). Limbaugh's message to his white audience was that black people were coming for the money they had worked hard all their lives to save. Limbaugh continued on this theme the following day, saying that Obama "wants to nationalize your 401(k), folks . . . pay you what it was worth on August of 2008, plus 600 bucks. He wants to take your IRA." Helaine Olen of Forbes thoroughly debunked this claim, which had originated with birther Jerome Corsi.[12] The final package was signed by the president on January 2, 2013, and contained no such provisions.

Limbaugh also used the frame of Obama as an anti-capitalist when discussing the 2011 federal budget. After a deal was reached, Limbaugh on April 13, 2011, criticized the budget priorities of the "Marxist president." He then added in some racial tribalization, blaming Democrats for the "irresponsible spending" they enacted in order to "buy votes," and adding that "they are exploiting a natural tendency of some people to be lazy and shiftless and sit out there and do nothing but collect a check." Lazy. Shiftless. As General Colin Powell once explained (referring to a similar comment made by someone else), there is a third word, a certain six letter noun that typically follows those two adjectives—one Limbaugh did not actually have to use, as his audience was conditioned to understand that he was talking about black people.[13] Just in case anyone who was listening to him did not get it, the next day Limbaugh said that Obama wanted to hand over hundreds of billions of dollars "to government unions and ACORN." The host repeated this claim a second time, for emphasis, about a minute later. As late as June 26, 2011—over a year after ACORN had ceased to exist—Limbaugh was still complaining about the group getting "federal taxpayer dollars."

The clash over federal spending levels reached a crisis point in the summer of 2011, when the Republican-led House of Representatives refused to approve an increase in the federal government's authority to borrow money, meaning that the government would be in default and unable to meet its obligations after borrowing reached the so-called debt ceiling. The government was projected to reach the debt ceiling on August 2. Given the importance of the U.S. government's guarantee that it would always meet its debts, a default might have had devastating consequences. In return for raising the debt ceiling, the Republicans demanded deficit reduction, and President Obama—himself interested in a comprehensive package including tax increases and spending cuts—began negotiating with House Speaker John Boehner.

Limbaugh followed the negotiations closely, using them as yet another opportunity to "other" the president. On July 11, 2011, the host snickered and said, "so Obama's out there pushing this magic August 2nd deadline to get this thing done. That's because Ramadan starts August 1st. (laughing) Well, it does. I looked it up." Later in the monologue, he added: "Somebody on the Republican side needs to sit there and say, 'We are not going to default on Ramadan.'" He made a similar Ramadan reference on six subsequent shows through August 1, and multiple times on that day.[14] Limbaugh's obvious goal here was to prompt his audience to connect Obama and Islam.

As the debt ceiling negotiations continued, so did the host's race-baiting and tribalizing. After the president made a speech about the need for "shared sacrifice" in order to avoid default, Limbaugh on July 25 responded that, "Obama's out there talking to La Raza. Is he gonna ask the illegal aliens to sacrifice, like pay taxes and follow our laws?" Putting aside the fact that undocumented immigrants do pay billions in federal, state, and local taxes, the host made sure his audience associated the country's largest Latino advocacy organization with illegal aliens. In discussing what would happen if a deal was not reached before August 2, i.e., whether Social Security checks would still go out, Limbaugh asserted that, "His [Obama's] union buddies are gonna get their money, and ACORN will get their money."

After the deal was finally announced, Limbaugh lamented on August 1 that "Obama will get his $2.4 trillion of walking-around money with no strings attached, a slush fund, spend it, give it to his union buddies just like he did the stimulus . . . Just another, potentially here, $2.4 trillion of money laundering." Walking-around money— aka "street money"—refers to funds paid by urban, often black politicians, to temporary employees involved in get-out-the-vote efforts. Limbaugh used this term to further blacken Obama. Following the deal's announcement, the credit rating agency Standard & Poor's downgraded the US's rating for the first time ever. In the wake of that action, Limbaugh alleged, "why wouldn't Obama be happy . . . Hasn't he always wanted to see America brought down a peg or two?" To drive his point home with a racial emphasis, the host added, "Jeremiah Wright just has to be as happy as he can be. 'America's chickens are coming home to roost.'"

"You lie."

No single policy issue defined the presidency of Barack Obama more than health care, so much so that both supporters and opponents alike ended up dubbing the Patient Protection and Affordable Care Act (ACA) passed in 2010 "Obamacare." Progressives had been trying to pass a national health care plan for a century before Obama took office, with conservatives largely opposing them.

Rush Limbaugh did not wait until the debate on health care legislation formally began to argue against reform, issuing his manifesto the day after Obama's inauguration: "But there's one thing we gotta stop is health care. I'm serious, now. If they get that, then that's the tipping point. Democracy as we know it is finished." Limbaugh repeated this point twice more over the next eight days.[15] "It's a job-killer," was one of the host's most cherished myths about the president's health care reform proposal. His audience heard many different versions of this theme, including on June 8, 2009, when Limbaugh averred that the plan, because of the (as-yet-unwritten) requirement that businesses provide health coverage, would lead companies to "fire people in order stay in business . . . anybody with a brain knows this." Given that, Limbaugh asked why the president wanted to "destroy the private sector economy," and answered that it was because Obama "want[ed] to return the nation's wealth to its 'rightful owners'" and thought "capitalism is unfair . . . unjust . . . immoral. And he's going to straighten that out." The first part of Limbaugh's answer was an attempt to divide Americans by race, while the statement as a whole served as the host's way of branding Obama as a Marxist.

As with so many other issues, Limbaugh attacked Obama on health care by attempting to blacken him. For example, he played a conversation between TV host Chris Matthews and South Carolina Democratic

Representative James Clyburn, whom Limbaugh identified as the "ex-chairman of the [B]lack [C]aucus." In the conversation, Matthews brought up the idea of reparations for slavery, and Clyburn responded that health care and other proposals were ways of "addressing inequities, disparities." Limbaugh summarized Clyburn's comments as saying that health care reform would aim to "return the nation's wealth to its rightful owners"—i.e., to take from whites and give to blacks. The host similarly declared that health care reform centered on "redistribution of wealth"—typically also including a mention of "rightful owners"—or "reparations" or "civil rights" three additional times in 2009, eight times in 2010, and six more after that.[16]

The topic of undocumented immigrants was also a major part of Limbaugh's attacks on health care reform. The host brought the issue up on June 15, 2009, claiming that large numbers of the uninsured in the United States were undocumented immigrants. He cited the conservative commentator George Will as having said (presumably in a TV appearance), who had written that 60 percent of the uninsured in San Francisco were undocumented. The next day, Limbaugh falsely applied that statistic nationally to argue that 60 percent of all the uninsured in America were "illegal aliens." The actual data from June 2009 showed that only 21 percent of the country's uninsured were immigrants—a figure that was not broken down into documented vs. undocumented.[17]

On August 20, Limbaugh told his audience that the courts would rule that undocumented immigrants would be eligible for benefits under health care reform because, he falsely claimed, they had already ruled that "illegal aliens have all citizen rights, and Obama knows this." The next day, referring to the League of United Latin-American Citizens and the National Council of La Raza, the host asked why Latino organizations were pushing so hard for Obamacare unless they thought "illegal immigrants" were going to benefit from it. Never mind that Hispanic American citizens as well as legal immigrants would benefit—Limbaugh wanted his audience to believe that those groups cared primarily about undocumented immigrants. (This tribalizing claim, expressed in a widely distributed email chain, earned a "pants on fire" lie designation from PolitiFact.[18]) In the end, undocumented immigrants were not covered under the ACA.

Few things got opponents of health care reform more riled up than the issue of the undocumented, which is why Limbaugh played it up so strongly. On September 9, 2009, when South Carolina Republican Representative Joe Wilson shouted out "you lie" at President Obama during a presidential address to a joint session of Congress—an unprecedented insult for which he later apologized—it was in response to the president's statement that his health care reform proposals "would not apply to those who are here illegally." Two days later, Limbaugh contended that "the media is slowly confirming that Joe Wilson was right." Was Limbaugh right? Not so much, according to PolitiFact, which assessed Wilson's declaration as "false."[19] Despite this, no matter how many times Obama reiterated that the undocumented would not be covered, Limbaugh kept saying the opposite. For example, on September 18, the host offered that "He's [Obama is] going to make the illegals legal! . . . That's how he's going to insure illegals."

"This is Mussolini-type Stuff . . ."

Opposition to health care reform reached a new level of intensity with the town hall meetings that members of Congress held during the summer of 2009. On his August 3 show, Limbaugh enthusiastically juxtaposed ACORN with the anti-Obamacare energy that dominated many of the meetings. He brought up the organization on multiple occasions in August, just about every time he talked about the town hall meetings, and overall, referred to ACORN while discussing health care reform or government's role in health care eleven times in the second half of 2009, three times in 2010, and once each in 2011 and 2013.[20] The purpose of this was to remind his audience of the contrast between ACORN—coded as representing black and poor Americans—and the mainly white anti-Obamacare protestors.

On August 6, after Florida Democratic Representative Kathy Castor held a town hall meeting that was turned into a "near riot" by anti-Obamacare protestors, Limbaugh contended that the president had sent "union thugs . . . to intimidate the genuine citizens out there who are upset about this. Those are paid activists . . . Obama . . . send[s] out his brownshirts [a reference to the SA, a Nazi paramilitary organization] to head up opposition to genuine American citizens."[21] A leaked memo revealed, however, that well-funded right-wing groups such as Americans for Prosperity, founded in 2004 and bankrolled by billionaire brothers Charles and David Koch, were coordinating the "genuine, heartfelt and pure"—in Limbaugh's words—Obamacare opposition that coalesced around the town hall meetings.[22] So, Limbaugh was accusing the president of doing something that conservatives were actually doing on a large scale. Additionally, as we have seen repeatedly, "thug" is a race-baiting word in the Limbaugh dictionary. And that is in addition to the connection the host made between Obama and Nazism. The contradiction between blackening Obama and calling him a Nazi did not bother Limbaugh, as ideological consistency was beside the point. The point was to tribalize our politics.

On August 7, Limbaugh told his listeners about a town hall meeting in St. Louis where "the union thugs, the SEIU people" attacked a conservative African American named Kenneth Gladney. Limbaugh further characterized the perpetrators as "Obama's army," and concluded: "This is Mussolini-type stuff . . . he's [Obama is] sending his union thugs out to physically assault . . . and . . . intimidate average Americans who just want some answers." Defending a black conservative victim provided Limbaugh with a sort of talisman against charges of racism. The "assault" on Gladney—Eric Boehlert of Media Matters called it a "charade"—became a huge story in the right-wing media, but ultimately the men charged with the crime were acquitted, after having testified that Gladney had initiated the violence.[23]

An array of familiar, racially themed attacks came together on August 10 when Limbaugh revisited the issue of the president pulling the strings behind not only the pro-reform voices at a town hall, but something much more sinister. Given that Obama could supposedly get large numbers of individuals to attend town hall meetings, Limbaugh asked, "what about voter fraud in 2010?" The host suggested that the president could tell any office-seeker, "'Well, I can find a way to get you reelected. Just call ACORN. We'll simply cheat.'" Four days later, Limbaugh brought up the president's former pastor while condemning the health care reform proposals. He first asserted "the race card is being played" to blunt those who opposed Obama, before saying that, "This is Jeremiah Wright . . . I said Obama was going to spark race problems when anybody disagreed with whatever his policy was."

"Oh, [the] Founders Did Not Intend what Obama Himself is Now Going to Do!"

As Congress debated health care reform throughout the fall of 2009, Limbaugh kept addressing the issue, now endlessly repeating the myth about so-called "death panels," where a government bureaucrat would decide whether someone would receive care or not. On October 28, he brought up the matter of the H1N1 swine flu raging at the time to craft a particularly raw example of race-baiting: "Apparently there are death panels in Chicago. Somebody's deciding who gets a [swine flu] vaccine there and who doesn't . . . We had that call from Chicago saying his kid couldn't get it because they weren't African-American or Native American or some other minority." That is what the Obamacare death panels would do, Limbaugh implied to his audience, let the white kids die and the dark-skinned people live. Concerns about non-whites receiving government resources while whites were excluded were common tribalizing themes of Limbaugh's.

During the 2016 campaign, Donald Trump echoed this kind of argument, often pitting racial groups against each other in a zero-sum game. For example, Trump often repeated the falsehood that "illegal immigrants are treated better in America than many of our vets," and likewise charged Obama and his 2016 opponent, Hillary Clinton, with showing more concern for the former than the latter. Trump also falsely stated that "illegal immigrant households receive far more in welfare benefits," and declared that "immigrants are taking our manufacturing jobs. They're taking our money. They're killing us."[24] Such statements—which were clearly meant to evoke images of non-white immigrants—appear to have had an impact, as Sides, Tesler, and Vavreck found that, in both the Republican primaries and the general election, "racialized perceptions of economic deservingness were . . . strongly related to support for Donald Trump."[25] In fact, Trump has a long history of using such divisive rhetoric, it is a well-known part of his brand. In a 1989 TV interview, he stated: "A well-educated black has a tremendous advantage over a well-educated white in terms of the job market."[26] Peer-reviewed field studies have demonstrated the opposite.[27]

After months of debate, on December 23, 2009, all sixty members of the Senate Democratic caucus voted to end a filibuster of the health care bill, thus bringing it to the floor for a final vote. The Senate approved the bill in a party-line vote on December 24. Limbaugh's next show was January 6, 2010, and the attacks on death panels and the overall bill resumed. The following day, Limbaugh offered his audience what could be best described as a "blackening" greatest hits, stating that those who voted for the president "believed Obama was going to buy 'em a new kitchen, they believed Obama's going to get 'em a new car, they believed Obama from his 'stash' is gonna get 'em a job, and Obama was going to give 'em their health care."

On January 19, 2010, Republican Scott Brown defeated heavily favored Democrat Martha Coakley in a special election to the U.S. Senate to fill the seat previously held by Senator Ted Kennedy, who had died in August 2009. Over the subsequent weeks, Democrats kept pushing to pass a health care reform law, and Limbaugh kept denouncing it. In case his listeners had forgotten, Limbaugh reminded them on February 22 of the racial stakes involved in health care reform: "This is returning the nation's wealth to its, quote, unquote, rightful owners. This is a civil rights bill. This is reparations."

By this point, Democrats were considering having the House pass the Senate bill as it stood, and then using the reconciliation process to make changes to the bill where possible, namely on budgetary or spending matters. Using reconciliation would avoid the Senate filibuster that, thanks to Brown's election, Republicans could now sustain with forty-one votes. On February 24, Limbaugh criticized this move, claiming that using reconciliation for a health care bill—as opposed to "budget bills"—was unprecedented and that Obama was violating basic American political principles: "Oh, [the] founders did not intend what Obama himself is now going to do!" Never mind the fact that the founders did not create the filibuster, it appears nowhere in the Constitution, and it was, according to testimony provided to the U.S. Senate by political science professor Sarah Binder, "created by mistake."[28] Limbaugh also ignored the fact that Republican Senate majorities had used reconciliation to pass non-budget bills, including not only the Bush tax cuts—which, in 2003, had passed only after Vice President Dick Cheney broke a 50-50 deadlock—but also wide-ranging health insurance reforms, including the COBRA law that allows people to continue buying health insurance through an employer after losing their jobs, the Children's Health Insurance Program, and others.[29]

As part of these discussions of constitutional principle, on March 4, Limbaugh slammed the process by which the health care bill was being considered as "really ugly." He continued by saying that "This is not how this stuff gets done . . . This is a total stab in the eye at the American public . . . They want no part of it, and so rules are being broken. Corners are being cut. The Chicago way: Whatever it takes to get this done." Limbaugh also included this criticism, ostensibly about the way the president denigrated physicians: "Obama uses doctors like Tiger Woods uses [P]ancake [H]ouse waitresses and pole dancers."

On March 12, after the story of Tiffany Owens—who had died after losing her job and then her health coverage—went national, Limbaugh informed his audience that Owens's mother, who had custody of her deceased daughter's children, had worked for "an ACORN offshoot." The host quickly corrected himself, however, noting it was not ACORN but rather the SEIU, before further correcting himself that the organization was merely "involved with" the SEIU. He then shared that "their basic stated mission [was] 'to achieve economic fairness in order to establish a Democratic society characterized by racial and social justice'—which just means redistribution of wealth." That show also included another bit about health care reform that was aimed at heightening racial and cultural anxiety: "What's up next? Immigration, amnesty and what does that mean? That means adding 25 million illegals to the health care rolls paid for by all of us." Thus, Limbaugh managed to cover both black and Hispanic people taking from whites in the same segment. In case that was not enough, he brought up the SEIU and ACORN again when railing against Obamacare five days later.

The House of Representatives passed the Senate health care bill on March 21, 2010, by a vote of 219 to 212, which ensured that the Patient Protection and Affordable Care Act would become law. The next day Limbaugh announced that "The will of the people was spat upon yesterday... You can't even say, loosely defined, we are much of a democracy." Obama signed the bill the following day, March 23, and "Obamacare" became the law of the land. After the administration issued new regulations—because that is how our system works in many cases, i.e., the law sets out parameters and the executive branch fills in the specifics—on July 15, 2010, Limbaugh complained that it had done so "by fiat," and referred to the new rules as "fatwas"—a reference to Islam. The rules required that certain services relating to preventive care be covered without co-payments or deductibles. The host commented that "Blood pressure, ahem, diabetes, ahem, cholesterol tests, ahem, cancer screenings. I mean, it sounds like union groups to me. The obese, the overweight, union members and some minorities thrown in."

"How Do You Say Free Riders in Spanish?"

The last obstacle to the ACA becoming fully operational was the judicial system, as opponents filed lawsuits to have the law declared unconstitutional. After a series of conflicting rulings from various lower courts, which Limbaugh discussed in detail as they were issued, the Supreme Court finally heard arguments in the case of *National Federation of Independent Business v. Sebelius.* Just a few weeks before the court rendered its decision, Limbaugh reflected on the meaning of the ACA, and, on May 25, 2012, connected it to the broader argument he had long been making about the anti-American radicalism of Obama. "It's his place in history . . . ." the host said, "He's out there saying America has never worked. He means capitalism has never worked . . . [Obamacare] gives him the slam-dunk opportunity to . . . remake this country, transform it into what it shoulda always been . . . This was his victory over America, folks."

The Supreme Court issued its ruling on Obamacare on June 28, 2012, striking down the requirement that all states expand Medicaid, but finding the rest of the law to be constitutional by a 5-4 vote. Limbaugh reacted that day. He harshly criticized the court, and the decision's author, Chief Justice John Roberts, who "was hell-bent to find a way to make this law applicable." Limbaugh also did not allow this historic moment to pass without accusing Obama of being racially divisive, opining that the president would have to change his approach to the upcoming 2012 election because, "I know Obama was gonna run against . . . four white guys and an Uncle Tom. He can't run against the Supreme Court now."

On July 2, Limbaugh played audio of then-House Minority Leader Nancy Pelosi defending the ACA's individual mandate fine—paid by those who could afford coverage but chose not to buy it—as "a penalty for free riders." He then argued that the Democrats were "the party that celebrates free riders," before shifting from free riders to "freeloaders" and citing "free handouts from the government," and "food stamps" being given to "food free riders." To make the connection even more explicit, Limbaugh asked, "How do you say free riders in Spanish?" After a break, Limbaugh gave the answer: "Aprovechados. That's somebody who takes advantage of the situation."

The story of a ten-year-old girl took center stage on Limbaugh's June 5, 2013 discussion of the Affordable Care Act. "I lit a cigar in honor of Sarah Palin right as the program began," he said. "Death panels. Just exactly what Sarah Palin said, exactly what we all knew. Obamacare establishes death panels, and right now [Health and Human Services Secretary Kathleen] Sebelius is it." Limbaugh was talking about Sarah Murnaghan, who suffered from cystic fibrosis and was initially unable to get on the waiting list for a lung transplant because the minimum age for a transplant was twelve. That same day, June 5, a judge ordered Sebelius to waive the rule. The next day Limbaugh declared that "Until the judge moved in, Kathleen Sebelius was the death panel . . . [She] was gonna determine whether or not—and she said, 'Some people live. Some people die.'" Sarah Murnaghan received a lung transplant on June 12, which failed. A second transplant surgery was done on June 15, which was, despite complications, a success. She is still alive as of this writing.

However, there was one major problem with Limbaugh's commentary—the entire situation had nothing to do with Obamacare. The age regulation for lung transplants, which includes the stipulation that the HHS Secretary can waive them, dates back to the 1990s. In addition to being wrong on the facts, Limbaugh also implied that Sebelius declined to waive the rule on partisan grounds, i.e., because of the party of the congressman who made the request on behalf of the Murnaghan family: "The congressman's a Republican. Of course Sebelius would refuse." Such a charge is ridiculous. Sebelius explained that not only was Murnaghan, at ten years old, below the minimum age of twelve, but added that there were approximately 40 other extremely sick patients age twelve or older who needed a lung transplant, including three additional children living near Murnaghan. According to Sebelius, "The decisions of the . . . transplant committee—which is not bureaucrats; it's transplant surgeons and health care providers who design the protocol—are based on their best medical judgment of the most appropriate way to decide allocation in an impossibly difficult situation."[30]

"Everything Is Identity Politics and Racial Politics."

In September 2013, conservatives, led by Texas Republican Senator Ted Cruz, pushed Congress to "defund Obamacare," and threatened to shutdown the federal government if the White House did not go along. Limbaugh strongly supported Cruz's efforts, which ultimately led to a government shut down on October 1. The same day, the Obamacare online healthcare exchanges went live. As part of the program, the federal government provided grants for so-called navigators, who were trained to assist people who needed help using the exchanges to purchase health insurance.

On his October 1 show, Limbaugh stated that the navigators in California, whom he incorrectly referred to as "the people running it [the exchange]," were none other than "people from" ACORN—which had dissolved three years earlier—SEIU, and Planned Parenthood. He also characterized the exchanges as "voter-registration outreach plans, essentially." In addition to mentioning ACORN five times during this segment, Limbaugh also reminded his audience of something he had mentioned on previous shows, namely that the NAACP also received funds relating to the health care exchanges.[31]

The president and congressional Republicans reached an agreement on October 15 to end the government shut down. Limbaugh was not pleased, and his show the next day centered on the old standby of presenting white conservatives as victims of the country's dominant racial discourse: "The Republicans have been hoodwinked . . . they are literally paralyzed because Obama is African-American . . . [Democrats] doubled down on that any criticism of Obama, 'cause now you're criticizing the first black president, that makes you a racist."

Even after the ACA was firmly in place, Limbaugh continued to bash the law and Obama. On February 6, 2014, the host falsely reported that the Congressional Budget Office had estimated that Obamacare would eliminate at least 2.5 million American jobs by 2017 (it was actually by 2021, as Limbaugh's audience heard Nancy Pelosi say shortly thereafter).[32] The CBO was not talking about jobs being lost. Instead, it explained that "The estimated reduction stems almost entirely from a net decline in the amount of labor that workers choose to supply, rather than from a net drop in businesses' demand for labor."[33] The CBO was referring to people who would, thanks to Obamacare, have the flexibility to leave jobs they were holding onto only because they had no other way of getting health coverage. Limbaugh used his usual racially-tinged language to criticize these people, saying they would be "eating . . . driving . . . watching TV . . . and making cell calls while not working. 'Cause somebody else is going to be paying for it."

This was not the case, however, as people who were in jobs because that was the only way they could get health insurance were not all going to stop working. Some might retire early if they could afford to, which would open up jobs for other Americans. Others might start a business and hire people, or take some other risk that would have been impossible prior to the passage of Obamacare. The *Washington Post* Fact Check assessed Limbaugh's claim, also made by the National Republican Congressional Committee, among others, and rated it three Pinocchios out of four.[34] Despite this, Limbaugh continued on in the same vein. Four days later, on February 10, at the end of a long rant about the CBO report, Limbaugh closed by talking about those who, unlike his audience, "need[ed] to be educated about the purpose of work." Who were such people? According to Limbaugh, they were "Obama stash ladies . . . the people in Detroit." The obvious implication was that black people would be the ones not working and would have "somebody else" pay for their insurance—all thanks to Obamacare.

Even as late as April 21, 2015, long after it had become clear that the ACA prohibited undocumented immigrants from receiving health coverage or other health benefits, Limbaugh kept circling back to that charge. First, he called the California Obamacare exchange "nothing more [sic] voter registration for illegals and money laundering for union operations," and continued that, "most favored nation status has been conferred to illegal aliens on a number of Obamacare policies." The host made clear that this aspect of Obamacare was explicitly about race-based redistribution, explaining the motivation behind the law as follows: "this is how we're gonna get even with all these powerful people in the majority who've given everything to themselves and left out these poor minorities." He lamented, without offering proof, that a "natural born American citizen" had to pay for health insurance premiums that "an illegal alien in the country can get for zilch." This grew into a longer rant that drew on familiar themes of white racial victimization:

> It's designed that way. The illegal alien or the welfare recipient or the poor person or whatever is the person with the grievance that must be addressed. There is no merit anymore. Everything is identity politics and racial politics. And if you are white, if you're in a majority, if you're wealthy, you have

benefited from unfairness tilted in your favor your whole life. Time to give up now, time to make even, time to pay back. Obama has come to balance the scales. Obama has come to take care of those who have been systematically left out by an evil, mean-spirited, extremist majority since the days of this country's founding.

Limbaugh's criticisms of the ACA continued throughout the rest of the Obama presidency. While the long-term history of the law remains to be written, the history Limbaugh told his audience was suffused with tribalization, and featured falsehoods and the worst kind of racial rhetoric. What we do know is that when President Obama signed the Affordable Care Act into law, 16 percent of Americans lacked health insurance coverage. According to official data from the United States Census Bureau, by the time he left office, that rate was down to 8.8 percent, an all-time low.[35]

Chapter Six

"ILLEGAL" IMMIGRANTS, AND THE PRESIDENT WHO LOVED THEM

George W. Bush won 40 percent of the Latino vote in 2004, in an election where he barely broke 50 percent overall. As president, he led an effort to pass comprehensive immigration reform, and supported the Comprehensive Immigration Reform Act of 2007 that included a path to citizenship for the undocumented, a push championed in the Senate by John McCain. By 2012, however, the Republican nominee, Mitt Romney, was calling for undocumented immigrants to deport themselves, an approach which, incredibly, Donald Trump criticized just weeks after Romney's loss as "crazy," "maniacal," and "mean-spirited," adding that "[Romney] lost everybody who is inspired to come into this country."[1] Four years later, Trump began his tribalizing 2016 White House campaign by characterizing Mexican immigrants as rapists who brought crime and drugs into the United States, before adding, charitably, "and some, I assume, are good people."[2] He also promised to build a wall between the United States and Mexico to keep immigrants from crossing illegally (and get Mexico to pay for it.)

As this timeline shows, by the end of the Obama Administration in early 2017, immigration had become a far more partisan issue for Republicans than it had been just a decade earlier. One of the chief catalysts for this change was Rush Limbaugh.

"An Invading Army of Illegal Aliens"

Limbaugh's fear-mongering and tribalizing around immigration started long before the 2016 campaign. Regarding Obama, it started not long after the president's first inauguration. In fact, it did not even take a month. On February 16, 2009, a caller to the Rush Limbaugh Show brought up the stimulus bill, and asked why it did not include money for what he called "the largest shovel-ready project in the country," i.e., the "fence trying to protect our borders between Mexico and the United States." Limbaugh answered that Obama had no interest in protecting the border, and then asked the caller why he thought that was the case. The caller responded that it was about winning Latino votes, and the host agreed that that was "a pretty good guess." Limbaugh then offered a prediction: "it isn't going to be long before we go back to amnesty." Amnesty refers to the granting of a path to citizenship for undocumented immigrants. Critics of immigration reform often use the word to imply that supporters want to offer blanket amnesty to all undocumented immigrants; in other words, to make them citizens either instantly or without any significant obstacles.

Limbaugh frequently used the concept of amnesty to go after Obama. For example, after the president spoke in favor of immigration reform, Limbaugh on March 19, 2009, referred to the 2007 bipartisan effort to pass comprehensive immigration reform as "amnesty," and "a total abrogation of US law." Obama, the host stated, would seek to enact some kind of amnesty "now." On April 10, Limbaugh explained to his audience that amnesty's purpose was "to expand the Democratic Party and kill the Republican Party" by giving citizenship, and thus the vote, to an overwhelmingly Latino population that would vote predominantly Democratic. To feed the cultural anxiety about demographic change that many of his listeners felt, Limbaugh added that the Democrats would "destroy the US culture in order get votes for power."

Similarly, the host warned on April 26, 2010, that whereas conservatives "want" immigrants "who want to assimilate and become Americans," the "results" of Democratic plans for immigration reform would be an "influx of people who are illegal and are not interested in assimilating." He also stated that this support for "amnesty for illegals is the greatest evidence" of Obama's supposed desire "to divide" Americans along racial and ethnic lines. Limbaugh also spoke of "an invading army of illegal aliens" who wanted to "come here and destroy what this is for everybody else," and asked whether it was "fair that we have to pay the cost of dealing with the crime caused by these illegals." In statements like these, we can clearly see the anti-immigration sentiments that Donald Trump would use to mobilize his supporters in 2016 and beyond.

On May 6, 2010, Limbaugh repeated a false statistic that Fox & Friends had shared with its audience, namely that "illegal aliens" killed 2,000 people in the U.S. each year. This number was derived by extrapolating from the murder rate in the home countries of undocumented immigrants, adjusted for an estimate of their age breakdown (young adults commit more murders). Thus, the number Limbaugh cited had absolutely no connection to actual people being murdered in the United States.[3]

This was by no means the only time Limbaugh spoke about crimes being committed by undocumented immigrants or people crossing the Mexican border illegally.[4] Here he again prefigured a theme Trump would employ prominently on the campaign trail and in the White House. For example, only four days after his inauguration, President Trump authorized the establishment of the VOICE (Victims of

Immigration Crime Engagement) Office, which, among other tasks, publicizes such crimes.[5] In truth, recent research shows that undocumented immigrants commit crimes at a lower rate than native-born Americans, and having more of the undocumented in a region correlates to lower overall rates of property crime and violent crime.[6] Of course, that was not something Limbaugh—or Trump—wanted their followers to hear.

"Cannot Ask Them for Their Papers."

If one state was the epicenter of the battle over immigration during the Obama presidency, it was Arizona. On April 23, 2010, Governor Jan Brewer signed a law, commonly known as SB 1070, that significantly challenged federal policy on immigration. Among the provisions aimed at cracking down on illegal immigration, the law mandated police officers who had already stopped someone for legitimate reasons to inquire about that person's immigration status, and made it a state crime for an "alien" to fail to carry documents showing that they had registered with the federal government as an alien, which federal law requires if they are over the age of thirteen.

The next Limbaugh show after SB 1070 became law was on April 26, and the host spent a great deal of time talking about Arizona. The show began with a caller from Tucson, who asked: "how do we stop paying welfare" for the undocumented? Limbaugh replied that "the only way . . . is to stop illegal immigration." He then went on to slam Democrats—and some Republicans—"who think to get the Hispanic vote you gotta give 'em welfare, you gotta give the illegals entry . . . they're going to continue to print money if they have to give them welfare . . . They see votes; they see welfare recipients; they see an increased percentage of the population dependent on government." The truth was that undocumented immigrants are not eligible to receive welfare payments, or Medicaid, or food stamps, or just about any form of benefits from the government. (On a related note, legal immigrants are likewise ineligible to get these benefits until they have lived in this country for five years.[7]) All residents, including the undocumented, are entitled to attend public school and receive emergency medical care, but that is far short of what Limbaugh claimed here.

The host then played audio of Obama criticizing Arizona's new immigration law, although he cut the tape mid-sentence before slamming the president for "ginning up a bunch of hate." Limbaugh was blaming the president for an act of vandalism in which someone had smeared refried beans in the shape of a Nazi swastika on windows in the state Capitol. The host went on to characterize "Barack Hussein Obama" as the leader of the push to "criminalize" law enforcement. He then referenced his frequently employed slander about Obama and 9/11: "It's like on 9/11. Obama seems to only have empathy here for the perps. He doesn't have any empathy or sympathy for the American people in Arizona." Later in the segment, Limbaugh stoked fear about supposedly lax border security leading to more crime as well as potential terrorist attacks waged by Muslims: "You got Hezbollah in Arizona, you got Mexican drug cartels operating in Arizona, you got a steady stream of illegals over the border and you've got people being killed."

Limbaugh further slammed the president for expressing concern that SB 1070 might lead to civil rights violations, and of seeking to create a coalition to oppose white Americans:

Civil rights violations . . . it's simple code words. Civil rights violations, you know who that's designed to stir up. And who's Obama stirring up anyway? We gotta reconnect young people,

African-Americans, Latinos, and women for 2010, in a video put out by the DNC over the weekend. This is the regime at its racist best. What's the regime doing? Asking blacks and Latinos to join him in a fight. What is a campaign if not a fight? He's asking young people, African-Americans, Latinos, and women to reconnect, to fight who? Who's this fight against? . . . We've never had a president like this who has purposely come to divide people . . . Freedom has no color, Mr. President. Freedom has no race.

Limbaugh also brought up Al Sharpton organizing protests in Arizona and Obama's opposition to SB 1070 in consecutive sentences. Limbaugh then played Obama's remarks again, followed quickly by five more mentions of Sharpton before playing audio of the reverend speaking about his plans to protest the Arizona law, followed by uttering his name three more times.

The host went right back to the same Obama remarks about reconnecting with groups the following day, this time breaking out one of his favorite blackening tools: Reverend Jeremiah Wright. Limbaugh twice played Wright's "Barack knows" clip (see chapter 1). Later on, he hit the president again over Arizona, and brought up not only Sharpton but also Jesse Jackson, playing audio of the reverend calling Arizona SB 1070 "a form of terrorism." Limbaugh then again connected the president and Jackson, and, for good measure, added that, "Obama and Sharpton are now inseparable."

On April 28, 2010, to make sure he had covered every base, Limbaugh attacked Obama on his immigration comments by tying him to ACORN. He also brought together immigration, voter fraud, and voter ID laws by accusing the president of "siding against us . . . the law-abiding citizens of this country . . . the legal immigrants . . . He goes to bat for the illegals . . . Because it is their votes he needs. And he can't get those votes if . . . voter photo ID is required at the polling place. That's what's undergirding all this." Limbaugh then criticized Obama and Attorney General Holder for considering a federal lawsuit against SB 1070. The host compared their eagerness to fight for Latino civil rights to the fact that they, in his words, "don't give a damn about the New Black Panthers intimidating voters and violating their civil rights in Philadelphia." The next day Limbaugh offered that Obama, in talking about immigration and Arizona, had been both "playing class warfare and dividing people on the basis of race." Thus, the host claimed, the president was "outdoing whatever Hitler and any Soviet commissar ever did." Limbaugh also warned that if Democrats "start giving them [illegal immigrants] the same goodies . . . that other minorities have, you have chaos."[8]

Limbaugh also went after the president on SB 1070 by bringing up the matter of sovereignty, through which the host argued that, under Obama, the United States had lost control of its borders, and thus its ability to determine who became an American. On May 19, Limbaugh played a clip of Obama saying, of the relationship between the United States and Mexico, that "we are defined not by our borders but by our bonds." The host pounced, twisting the president's words to suggest that he was not interested in protecting our border with Mexico: "With this regime in charge we are not defined by our borders—and without borders, we don't have sovereignty." Then, after playing audio of the president criticizing SB 1070 and talking about the civil rights of law-abiding Mexican citizens visiting the United States, Limbaugh similarly questioned where Obama's loyalties lay: "What country does Barack Obama believe himself to be the leader of? . . . He's siding against the American people, pandering to the president of Mexico . . . He is saying Arizona acted stupidly, just like he said of the cop in Cambridge." Mentioning the Henry Louis Gates arrest was another way to blacken Obama. The host closed by averring that the president had "turned" our country into "Mexico's doormat." Limbaugh also hit Obama for supposedly weakening our sovereignty on at least five other occasions.[9] Donald Trump, when talking about his border wall, has often connected it to sovereignty. For example, on December 20, 2018, he said that in pushing to build the wall he was "fighting for . . . the sovereignty of the United States."[10]

On May 21, 2010, Limbaugh criticized the administration's announcement that the U.S. Immigration and Customs Enforcement agency (ICE) had the authority to decide whether to deport or otherwise process anyone that Arizona authorities—or any other government agent, state or federal, for that matter—identified as an undocumented immigrant. The announcement was clearly a response to SB 1070. Limbaugh shot back, "Barack Obama has his boot on the throat of this country . . . and he's not going to let it up any time soon."

As talk of a Department of Justice lawsuit against SB 1070 was heating up, on July 1, Limbaugh played a clip of Obama talking earlier that day about the Arizona law in which he listed different immigrant groups that had faced discrimination throughout American history. Limbaugh rebuked the president for having played "the race card" because he mentioned "practically every race and ethnicity," but not "white guys . . . We are the victimizers." One small problem for the host: Obama had spoken about "immigrants from Ireland, Italy, Poland, other European countries." (And that was in the clip Limbaugh played.) The president also cited "Jewish people . . . being driven out of Eastern Europe." In fact, the only non-white immigrant ethnic group Obama mentioned as having suffered discrimination was Chinese Americans. Ignoring all this, Limbaugh launched into a familiar line of attack: "President Obama has now removed any doubt that the interests of foreign nationals takes [sic] priority over that of American citizens." Limbaugh did not tell his audience what the president, in his remarks, had demanded of the undocumented as part of any reform: "They must be required to admit that they broke the law. They should be required to register, pay their taxes, pay a fine, and learn English. They must get right with the law before they can get in line and earn their citizenship."[11]

Five days later, the DOJ filed suit against the Arizona law, and Limbaugh again accused the administration of "lying" about SB 1070. On July 28, U.S. District Judge Susan Bolton issued a preliminary injunction that prevented much of the law, including the elements that drew the most ire from opponents, from being implemented. Limbaugh condemned the "activist decision" and then went straight to fear-mongering, predicting that "Muslim terrorists are going to have a field day in Arizona . . . Cannot ask them for their papers. We can ask you for yours. Not them." Because Obama and Holder filed the lawsuit, they would be to blame for any attack, according to the host. Please note that through the end of the Obama presidency, no person, equipment, or material brought from Mexico was part of a terrorist attack that occurred in the United States.[12]

The legal challenges to Arizona SB 1070 came to a head when the Supreme Court issued its ruling in *Arizona v. United States* on June 25, 2012. The court struck down a number of the law's core elements, and essentially prevented the states from enforcing immigration law, which the decision declared fell under the purview of the federal government. The court did allow Arizona to continue asking those stopped lawfully to prove their immigration status. In discussing the ruling that day, Limbaugh called it "disheartening . . . mind-boggling." He also took the time to "other" Obama by bringing up the birther controversy: "If Obama . . . were arrested for driving without a license, say, in Kenya, would he object to them checking to see if he's a Kenyan citizen or not? . . . Obama, I am sure, has got relatives in Kenya before there was a Kenya."

Shortly after the ruling came down, the Obama administration announced that it was ending existing agreements with Arizona law enforcement institutions regarding immigration. This meant that, for the most part, the federal government would not act when state officials discovered, through a stop mandated by SB 1070, that someone was in the country illegally. Limbaugh responded that the White House had just told Arizona to "drop dead," and that this meant that Arizona was "an open border." According to the host, we now saw that Obama rejected "the rule of law" in favor of "the rule of man." Limbaugh added, crudely, that this was "a dictator's wet dream." He continued to characterize the president as a dictator who had no qualms about acting unconstitutionally, and asked, forebodingly: "What if Obama decides that the 22nd Amendment's no longer relevant, limiting presidents to two terms?"

Limbaugh continued to slam the administration's announcement the following day, when he accused Obama of siding "with people who are on the other side of the law," and of sending a message "to smugglers and traffickers and criminals of all kinds that Arizona is wide open. Come on in, gang!" These kinds of comments were another way, along with claims that the president sympathized with Black Lives Matter activists and, even worse, those who assassinated cops, that Limbaugh worked to tribalize American politics by presenting the president as standing on the side of black or brown criminals and of being anti-law and order.

The DREAM Act and DACA

Regarding federal legislation, during Obama's first two years in office, when Democrats held majorities in the House and Senate, the primary policy focus was the Development, Relief, and Education for Alien Minors (DREAM) Act. The bill would have provided temporary legal status and an eventual path to citizenship to undocumented immigrants who had arrived when they were under sixteen, and who had shown themselves to be "of good moral character," in other words, they had not been convicted of any serious crimes. On December 3, 2010, Limbaugh opined that the Act would not become law, and threw in a slanderous dig as well: "the DREAM Act . . . is just [Senate Majority Leader Harry] Reid thanking the Hispanics for stealing the election for him." Although the House of Representatives passed the bill on December 8, the Senate failed to overcome a filibuster, and the bill died on December 18, 2010.

After Republicans took over the majority in the House on January 3, 2011, Obama held a series of events that spring where he asked them to cooperate and pass comprehensive immigration reform. On May 10, he delivered a major address on the topic in El Paso, Texas. Limbaugh discussed the speech the next day, chiding Obama for not having introduced what he disparagingly called "an amnesty bill" when Democrats had majorities in both houses of Congress while "now proclaiming himself the leader of illegal immigrants and their quest for amnesty." Limbaugh accused the president of not caring enough about the issue to force his fellow Democrats to take a tough vote, and instead having "kicked it down the road" in order to use it as a campaign issue in 2012.

Moving into more direct scare tactics, the host said that Obama was mobilizing "the illegal aliens and his union goons to take to the streets to ram through amnesty."

In terms of immigration policy, the next major development occurred on June 15, 2012, when the White House issued an executive order authorizing Deferred Action for Childhood Arrivals (DACA), a very limited version of the DREAM Act according to which young people who arrived illegally under the age of sixteen and who were of good character would be eligible for protection from deportation, as well as a work permit that lasted for two years and which was renewable. (DACA did not, however, provide a path to citizenship or any kind of permanent legal status.) Furthermore, as an executive order, any future president could theoretically overturn it. President Trump aimed at doing exactly that on September 5, 2017, when his administration announced that the program would end in six months if Congress did not take legislative action to enshrine it in law. Lawsuits challenging the termination of DACA have not been resolved, and the program remains in effect as of this writing.

On his June 16, 2012 show, Limbaugh not only criticized DACA, he also brought out one of his old standards, namely the specter that the new policy would lead to undocumented immigrants voting. Furthermore, since DACA had been enacted by the executive branch alone, Limbaugh referred to it as reflecting Obama's "dictatorial" nature. The host also argued that "declaring amnesty for 800,000 illegals" through DACA—later in the show he forecast that the number would ultimately be much higher, although the initial estimate has proven remarkably accurate[13]—was worse than the crimes that led to the resignation of President Richard Nixon.

Limbaugh also contended that Obama had to implement DACA

because the number of undocumented immigrants from Mexico was falling (after peaking in 2007, the number steadily declined through 2015, the most recent year for which data is currently available).[14] This was a problem for Obama's party, the host averred, because they needed "a permanent underclass to keep the social safety net alive and kicking.. . And the Hispanic illegal aliens" were it. (To repeat, the undocumented cannot receive welfare or other "social safety net" benefits.) Limbaugh also noted that Democrats were "aborting themselves out of existence. So that has to be replaced." He was referring to the fact that women of color, who generally vote for Democrats, are disproportionately represented among those who have abortions. Connecting immigration policy to abortion was one of Limbaugh's most cynical accusations, and that is saying something.

Circling back to the president's motive in enacting DACA, the host offered that there were two goals: fortifying the Latino vote— which he claimed was "lagging"—and making it more "seductive" for the undocumented to stay in the United States.

"There will be amnesty in this country."

Shortly after Obama was reelected for a second term on November 6, 2012, Limbaugh prepared his audience for the political battle to come, one that, with hindsight, helped complete the Republican Party's transformation on immigration from what it had been under George W. Bush, to what it has become under Donald Trump. This was the fight over comprehensive immigration reform. Three days after the 2012 election, the host proclaimed: "There will be amnesty in this country. When you hear the phrase 'comprehensive immigration reform,' that's what it means."

The battle kicked into high gear on January 28, 2013, when a bipartisan group of four senators from each party, dubbed the "Gang of Eight," put out a compromise, comprehensive immigration proposal that included a path to citizenship for undocumented immigrants. The next day, Obama essentially endorsed the plan's principles in a speech at a Las Vegas high school. On his show that day, Limbaugh interviewed Florida Republican Senator Marco Rubio, perhaps the most important member of the Gang of Eight, given the hard-right stance he had long taken on immigration reform. (For example, during Rubio's 2010 Senate race he had opposed a path to any kind of legalization or citizenship for undocumented immigrants.[15]) The host praised Rubio, if not the Gang of Eight's proposal specifically, saying that, "you are meeting everybody honestly, forthrightly, halfway, you're seeking compromise."

Limbaugh's praise of Rubio's work as a member of the Gang of Eight began to weaken, however, as winter turned to spring. The eight senators formally introduced their bill on April 16, 2013. Two days later, the host all but suggested that Rubio was being used by Chuck Schumer and other Senate Democrats to help pass a bill that might not pass otherwise. Revealing his position more clearly, Limbaugh urged Republicans to completely oppose immigration reform, the way they had not, he claimed with apparent sincerity, opposed Obamacare. He then cited a poll that, he said, showed that only 4 percent of Americans "support immigration the way Obama wants" and that 96 percent opposed a "path to citizenship, amnesty."

This level of dishonesty was impressive, even for Limbaugh. Although the host did not specifically mention it, he was referring to a Gallup poll whose results had been published three days earlier, which asked an open-ended question: "What do you think is the most important problem facing this country today?" No single issue was named by more than 25 percent of respondents; "immigration/illegal aliens" got

4 percent. However, the notion that only 4 percent supported Obama's specific proposals on immigration reform—and therefore 96 percent opposed them—was an absurdly false representation of the poll's results. In fact, the Gallup article that presented the poll's results noted that, in a previous survey the organization had conducted two months earlier, more than 70 percent of Americans polled had favored a path to citizenship for the undocumented that, in broad terms, resembled the measures proposed by Obama and the Senate bipartisan group.[16]

The Senate Judiciary Committee held hearings, debated, and revised the immigration reform bill over the next month. On May 21, the committee voted 13 to 5 to send the bill to the Senate floor, with three of the eight Republicans voting yes. Regarding the bill's stipulation that the undocumented would have to follow a thirteen-year path to citizenship, Limbaugh warned one week later that it would be found unconstitutional because "all you need is one Obama judge . . . and, bammo, you've got instant citizenship, instant voting." On June 11, Limbaugh quoted from a *Washington Examiner* article that argued that the Senate bill would lead to businesses avoiding taxes mandated by Obamacare by hiring immigrants who had recently gained legal status, instead of U.S. citizens. The host claimed that because these newly legalized immigrants would not be eligible for Obamacare, employers could hire them, not give them health coverage, and not pay a fine. This was a complicated issue; FactCheck.org found that it would be very unlikely that any employer would end up taking such actions.[17] Limbaugh also reissued his warning that, if the Senate bill became law, Democrats would find a way "by hook or by crook" to get rid of its thirteen-year path to citizenship. On that day, the Senate voted 84 to 15 to proceed with debate, easily overcoming the sixty-vote threshold that was required.

The bipartisan support behind comprehensive immigration reform represented a real problem for its opponents, which was why Limbaugh pushed hard the idea that the president, rather than the Gang of Eight (which included four Republicans) were the ones who had crafted the bill. Two days later, when the Congressional Budget Office reported that the bill would have a positive impact both on the federal budget and the overall economy, the host called the findings "factually impossible." Additionally, embracing populist language, Limbaugh attacked "corporatists . . . crony capitalism . . . the association of major Big Business with government to the benefit of government and business . . . to the detriment of others," and added that the bill would "depress wages." Here Limbaugh was positioning himself, again presaging Trump, as an ostensible right-wing populist/economic nationalist on the side of workers being harmed by corporations who sold them out to maximize profits.

The bill ultimately passed the Senate by a vote of 68 to 32—with 14 Republicans in favor—on June 27. That day the host again played the faux populist Trump card, stating that, "In terms of illegal immigration. The corporatists and the crony capitalists want the cheap labor. To hell with anything else that happens as a result."

"You Are Losing Your Culture."

With Senate passage of the reform bill, attention now moved to the House. Limbaugh sounded the alarm to his audience—as well as fellow Republicans—on July 9, 2013, saying that if Speaker John Boehner brought the bill up for debate, it "might just pass" and become law. The host noted that although Boehner had promised not to do so, the House might still write a different immigration bill on its own and conference with the Senate to craft a compromise that would then be voted on by both chambers.

On August 12, Limbaugh continued to heighten fears about the effects of increased immigration, relating reports of "illegal immigrants from Mexico requesting asylum . . . overwhelming immigration agents in San Diego," as well as "Syrian refugees . . . now pouring into" the United States. The latter comment was aimed at raising concerns about terrorism. More recently, President Trump has also spoken repeatedly in similar terms about terrorists coming in to the U.S. through Mexico. For example, on January 4, 2019, he said that, "We have terrorists coming through the southern border because they find that's probably the easiest place to come through." The truth, according to Trump's own State Department, is that there is "no credible evidence indicating that international terrorist groups have established bases in Mexico, worked with Mexican drug cartels or sent operatives via Mexico into the United States."[18]

Limbaugh also talked in big picture terms, stating that "we're in the middle of one of the greatest demographic upheavals that this country has ever experienced . . . an identity transformation . . . sponsored and engineered by" President Obama. The host stated that the Democrats' "whole agenda has been to destroy what you and I call the distinct American culture," and lamented that "our elected officials . . . don't think that amnesty or immigration is a crisis."[19] Trump offered parallel sentiments on multiple occasions in 2018. For example, he contended that Europe made a "big mistake" letting in "millions . . . who have so strongly and violently changed their culture!"[20] He further called this decision a "shame" that "changed the fabric of Europe," before concluding that, "you are losing your culture."[21]

Another Limbaugh line of attack was to undercut Obama's credibility on border security. If the host could convince people that the president could not be trusted to enforce the law, it made it more likely they would not support a compromise that included a Democratic priority (a path to citizenship for the undocumented) and a Republican priority (enhanced border security measures), neither of which had enough support to pass on its own. On January 28, 2014, Limbaugh dismissed the administration's efforts on enforcement, saying that "There are no mass deportations taking place." In fact, criminal deportations actually went up in each of Obama's first four years in office, and in 2012 there were 200,000—double the number deported in 2008.[22] Three days later, the host offered another lie, that "illegal immigrants vote two to one Democrat." The truth is that non-citizens, even those here legally, are banned from voting in federal or state elections, and only a handful of places allow non-citizen voting in local elections. Thus, there is no evidence demonstrating that the undocumented are voting in any significant numbers.[23] Following that, as part of a discussion of a poll that showed Hispanic and Asian Americans holding liberal political positions, Limbaugh described today's immigrants—who belong mostly to those two groups—as representing an "infiltration to tear down the American culture."

In early February 2014, House Speaker Boehner echoed Limbaugh by saying he did not trust the president to enforce immigration laws, and therefore would not bring immigration reform legislation up for a vote. On February 6, the host played Boehner's comments, and praised the Speaker's statement as "helpful." Limbaugh returned to the matter the next day, saying that this showed that Obama "behave[s] outside the Constitution." Limbaugh also added a racially divisive remark, complaining that it was impossible to impeach Obama because he was black, "no matter how corrupt or how lawless." Limbaugh also offered a long, tribalizing rant on another show that May in which he argued that

Obama and "the left" supported "amnesty"—which would lead to more non-white voters—because they wanted, first, more people who would support affirmative action, and second, as part of their broader desire to punish white Americans and take America "down a couple pegs."[24]

Similarly, on June 13, 2014, Limbaugh played a clip of Obama saying, two days earlier, in Worcester, Massachusetts, that the "DREAM Act kids . . . [are] worried about whether, in fact, this country they love so deeply loves them back and understands that our future rests on their success." The host rebuked the president's remarks: "What president speaks this way? If you're gonna talk about the future of America, normally you talk about American kids." Limbaugh also contended that the remarks reflected the "mainstream leftist" view—to which Obama and his administration were "sympathetic"—that "American kids are the children of the white oppressors. The privileged, white oppressors!" By equating "American" and "white", Limbaugh was placing the president and the DREAM Act kids—and, by extension, undocumented immigrants in general—on one side, with white Americans on the other.

"So It Is an All-Out Assault, Folks, on What This Country Used to Be."

While supporters of comprehensive immigration reform continued to push the House to take up the issue, an immigration crisis played out in June and July 2014. There was a surge in the number of unaccompanied minors coming across the U.S.–Mexico border—most of them coming through Mexico from El Salvador, Guatemala, and Honduras after fleeing violence and/or poverty. According to a 2008 law signed by George W. Bush—whose role Limbaugh did mention—the federal government had significant responsibilities toward these children and could not simply send them back once they were taken into custody, as is done with most children whose country of origin is Mexico or Canada.

Limbaugh covered the story in great detail, absurdly suggesting on June 17 that the White House, despite its denials, was somehow responsible for this influx of unaccompanied minors: "if 90 percent are eligible for amnesty and get all these services by virtue of law, then how can their claim that they've got nothing to do with this possibly hold water?" Limbaugh then proclaimed, again heightening white anxiety about cultural change, "So it is an all-out assault, folks, on what this country used to be."

Ten days later, on June 27, Limbaugh accused Democrats of lying when they said they intended to send the children back to their country of origin, asserting instead, without evidence, that they really wanted to "make them citizens ASAP." In the same segment, Limbaugh also criticized the White House for stating that it would issue executive orders on immigration if Congress did not pass a reform bill, characterizing such a potential action as "authoritarian pretend dictatorial kind of power." Aiming at fears of Hispanics, the host continued: "Obama is basically telling Congress . . . 'You approve amnesty or I'm just gonna invite every person from Mexico to Argentina to El Salvador here to this country.'"[25]

Three days later Limbaugh called the influx of children "a great political opportunity" for Democrats, adding, "there's no way tens of thousands, and multiply that, of potential new Democrat voters is a crisis." Later in that show, the host acknowledged that the president had made clear his desire to send the children back home as soon as possible, and had requested that Congress authorize him to do so. However, Limbaugh then averred that Obama was confident the children would never be deported. Two days after that, he went further. "They're not being deported, and they're not gonna be deported," Limbaugh ranted, and referred to the unaccompanied minors as "an onslaught of 65,000." The next day he again charged the president with bearing responsibility, talking about Obama's "plans" and stating that, "55 or 60,000 kids don't just happen to coincidentally show up on the [s]outhern border." The host also said that "Obama want[ed]" the children to stay in the United States.[26]

On July 4, President Obama praised America's diversity and, regarding immigration, said that we should not "make it harder for the best and the brightest to come here." Limbaugh quoted this line three days later and shot back that "this invasion of 300,000 [undocumented immigrants] since April represents the best and the brightest—and if you oppose it, then you are, what? Well, racist and bigoted . . . Maybe it isn't an official invasion when the country's leaders invite the invaders in. That's what's happening here." Limbaugh was not only criticizing Obama through the specter of race, he was also telling his white audience that being called a "racist" meant that one was speaking the truth. This was how the host frequently undermined the credibility of anyone who pointed out how divisive his rhetoric was. Such an argument also ultimately benefited Trump by inoculating him, at least for many conservatives, against charges of racism.

The crisis of Central American minors remained a primary focus of Limbaugh's, as he talked about it on eleven consecutive shows between June 30 and July 15, 2014. On July 24, the host revisited the topic when he responded to the president's statement that the border was secure by citing a debunked claim from Texas Republican Governor Rick Perry that 203,000 undocumented immigrants over the previous five years had "ended up in jail," which included 3,000 cases of homicide and 8,000 of sexual assault. FactCheck.org later noted that Perry had "misused" the data. The numbers represented both people here legally and illegally, as well as those charged, but not convicted, of a crime. Limbaugh was more careful than Perry (who stated that, "illegal aliens" were "responsible for" these crimes), but the host still clearly implied the same thing by using the words "ended up in jail."[27]

Although the president asked Congress for funds to address the issue—Limbaugh on July 25 characterized this as seeking to create a "slush fund for Democrat reelection efforts"—Congress failed to pass legislation. Nevertheless, by early August, the pace of new arrivals had slowed significantly, and the federal government was able to close the three temporary shelters it had opened to house the increased numbers of children.

"2014 October Surprise"

By August 2014, more than a year after the Senate had passed comprehensive immigration reform, it had become evident that the House would not follow suit. The question then became what steps President Obama might take unilaterally, through executive action.

On August 4, Limbaugh said that executive action was "being bandied about" and that five to six million "illegals" would receive "blanket amnesty." He then pondered what type of executive action the president might take. Seeking to exacerbate white anxiety and depict Obama as anti-American, the host speculated that in order to reduce white Americans to a minority of the population, the president could simply "legalize any kind of foreign person he can get in here, any country, any group, whatever, just shake up the numbers, the balance . . . He knows he can't do this legislatively, but he wants to get it done because this is what America deserves." Limbaugh also characterized Obama's policies on immigration as "the cynical use of race" to alter the constitutional balance of powers between the three branches of the federal government. Finally, Limbaugh offered that the president wanted to destroy the Constitution because it "was ratified when we had slavery."

Three days later, Limbaugh warned his audience that, "He's [Obama is] now threatening the nuclear bomb executive amnesty." The host then went back to several old favorites, the "Obama phone woman" from Cleveland and the "people in Detroit and Obama's stash" and wondered how they would feel about sharing some of their government benefits with "newly made citizen illegal immigrants." This language not only further blackened Obama, but also reminded Limbaugh's followers about black and brown people receiving government benefits—a doubly effective statement in terms of heightening white racial resentment.

Limbaugh kept warning throughout August that the president would issue an "amnesty" covering five or six million undocumented immigrants, until the White House announced on September 6, 2014, that it would not take any executive action until after the November midterm elections. With any potential executive action by Obama temporarily on the back burner, Limbaugh needed other ways to scare his audience about the undocumented. After having spent multiple-shows in July and August citing the outbreak of the Ebola virus—which, counting only documented cases, killed over 11,000 Africans and one American—as a reason to "close the border,"[28] on September 8, the host pondered whether the enterovirus D68 outbreak that ultimately infected people in all but one state, and which may have killed fourteen (they tested positive but their deaths could not be definitively linked to EV-D68) was connected to the unaccompanied minors from Central America, and noted that "some people" believe it could be.

Limbaugh also wondered whether the White House was covering up such a connection.

In October, the Ebola story began to dominate the media. Republicans, including Limbaugh, hyped fears about the virus and used it to depict Obama as incompetent leading up to the midterm elections. More specifically, the host linked Ebola and immigration and/or border security on nine out of his first thirteen October broadcasts, and on two other occasions later in the month.[29] In addition, Limbaugh talked up the Ebola scare on six other occasions in October as well.[30] On October 16, Limbaugh revisited EV-D68 and the unaccompanied minors.

After Election Day, Ebola suddenly dropped off the radar screen for Limbaugh and the right in general, making clear the political nature of their previous focus on the issue. Journalist Elise Viebeck called it the "2014 October surprise."[31] Talking about Ebola and, in particular, connecting it to border security, had served its purpose, however, as Democrats lost thirteen House seats and, more importantly, nine Senate seats—which ended their eight-year run as the majority party in that chamber. However, the election did not change the fact that immigration reform remained a topic of great political importance.

In the final weeks leading up to the 2018 midterm elections, the right-wing media and Republican politicians, led by President Trump, coordinated to carry out a quite similar playbook, which James Poniewozik of the *New York Times* called a "reboot" of "a hit from 2014: 'Terror at the Border.'"[32] The 2018 version starred the refugee caravan travelling north, through Mexico, toward the United States.

Obama's Big Executive Action on Immigration: DAPA

President Obama had promised to act unilaterally after the midterm election, and he did. After the broad details of the president's plan became public, on November 13 Limbaugh interviewed Alabama Republican Senator Jeff Sessions, a staunch opponent of the bipartisan Senate comprehensive immigration reform bill who became, not coincidentally, the first senator to endorse Donald Trump for president, and then President Trump's first U.S. Attorney General. The host condemned what he knew of the plan—which centered on issuing temporary work permits to undocumented parents whose children were American citizens—in wildly exaggerated terms, saying that Obama was abrogating "all of our immigration laws with the stroke of his pen." Six days later, Limbaugh scoffed at the notion that the temporary work permits would not lead to full citizenship for the estimated four to five million recipients, arguing that if Obama could grant temporary work permits without Congress, he could grant citizenship as well, which the host predicted he would do in approximately six months. The following day Limbaugh declared that the president's plan would shoot the Constitution "full of holes."[33]

That same night, November 20, 2014, Obama announced his plan, known as Deferred Action for Parents of Americans (DAPA). To be eligible, one had to: 1) be the parent of a citizen or a green card holder, i.e. someone with legal permanent residence; 2) have arrived in the United States no later than 2010 and lived here since that time; and 3) not have committed any serious crimes. Those eligible would be protected from deportation and receive a work permit that would last three years, which could then be renewed as long as the program remained in place. The announcement also expanded DACA by removing the existing maximum age for eligibility, which had been previously set at thirty. The president based his authority to do all this on the discretion possessed by the executive branch on the matter of which crimes to prosecute. Given that approximately eleven million people were in the Unites States illegally, and prosecuting all of them was not feasible,

Obama argued that the actions he took were legitimate.

On the next day's show, Limbaugh offered that the president's speech reminded him of "a foreign invasion," and discussed Obama's "anger" and "rage" at America. The host described the president's motivation for introducing his plan, which he called "almost a punishment," as follows: "he [Obama] thinks we need to become a Third World country because, in his mind, we've created Third World countries. We have kept people in Third World countries. We've stolen from people in Third World countries. So it's about time we paid our dues." Limbaugh predicted that DAPA, aimed at 4.5 to 5 million people, was just a first step: "this is dipping a toe in the water . . . There's still seven million to go."

The host also revisited a theme he had spoken about previously, Obama's supposed desire to undo the results of the Mexican–American War by, one way or another, returning the lands the U.S. had taken to Mexican, or at least Latino, control. Limbaugh suggested this was the real "debt" that the president owed and would ultimately repay to Latinos by enacting even more far-ranging immigration measures down the road. In another example of race-baiting, three days later Limbaugh argued that the media's coverage of DAPA, as reflected in one particular *Washington Post* article, demonstrated both their ideological affinity for Obama as well as "race." Having already established this trope, Limbaugh here tribalized by reminding his listeners that the liberal media would not criticize a black president, and therefore should be considered a racial and ideological enemy.

For their part, Republicans in Congress did not take the White House executive actions lying down. On January 12, 2015, Limbaugh discussed their response, which was to use an upcoming bill funding the Department of Homeland Security (DHS)—the funding for which was scheduled to run out about six weeks later—as leverage to undo what he called "Obama's amnesty." The bill, which passed the House two days later, would have essentially undone DAPA and DACA.

Limbaugh kept the pressure on the GOP to hang tough. He told his audience that Republicans "hold the cards," but warned that GOP senators might be about to "fold a winning hand" and called their actions a "joke." Two days later he proclaimed: "illegals are being registered to vote" as a result of DAPA.[34]

While the host continued to press Senate Republicans, a Texas judge took the fate of DAPA into his own hands. On February 16, a preliminary injunction issued by Judge Andrew Hanen put a temporary halt to the November 2014 executive action that had created DAPA and expanded DACA, although it did not affect the initial, already existing DACA program. Twenty-six states had filed a lawsuit, *United States v. Texas*, to block the action two months earlier. Two days later, Limbaugh called the judge's ruling "brilliant." Eight day after that, on February 26, the host accused the president of preparing to "ignore the judge's order," as would a "king," and launched into another diatribe about Obama hating America. Finally, in response to the president's comment that immigration reform would eventually happen "because there's gonna be a President Rodriguez or a President Chin" someday, Limbaugh offered that these remarks showed that Obama believed that "a white president is illegitimate."[35]

Ultimately, Republicans in Congress backed down and passed a bill funding the DHS without any restrictions on DAPA or DACA. However, that mattered little because, fourteen months later, the Supreme Court deadlocked 4–4 on *United States v. Texas*, which meant the lower court's initial ruling blocking DAPA and the expansion of DACA remained in place. On September 5, 2017, President Trump rescinded the executive order on DAPA, putting any question of its implementation to rest for the foreseeable future.

"It Is About the American Way of Life."

On July 1, 2015, two weeks after Trump's infamous comments about Mexican immigrants being rapists and bringing drugs into the United States, a woman named Kathryn Steinle was shot and killed in San Francisco by Jose Inez Garcia Zarate, then known as Juan Francisco López-Sánchez. Zarate had initially entered the country illegally, been convicted of seven felonies, and deported five times, yet had come back again. The last time, he was imprisoned for illegal entry and, after serving his sentence, was released by local authorities despite the fact that federal law enforcement officials were prepared to deport him. The local and federal authorities each blamed the other for the failure of communication that led to his release, just two and a half months before Steinle's death. Zarate was ultimately acquitted of murder, as evidence showed that the bullet that killed Steinle had ricocheted off the ground before striking her. He was found guilty of being a felon in possession of a firearm.

On the campaign trail, Trump pounced, and Limbaugh followed suit a few days later. On July 7, in comments designed to inflame white racial resentment, the host claimed that Steinle's name would "never be as well known as Trayvon Martin," and that the president would not deliver the eulogy at her funeral, though Obama did not deliver a eulogy at the funeral of Martin or any other citizen killed by police. Obama did, however, speak at the memorial service for the five Dallas police officers murdered a year later (see chapter 3). Limbaugh speculated that the president did not care about Steinle's murder, and blamed it on the administration's immigration policies, which were "coming home to roost"—the phrase uttered by Reverend Wright that was discussed so often on Limbaugh's show. The host again talked about Obama hating America and wanting to alter its "composition" in order to change "the face of the country."

Limbaugh attacked the president over Steinle on three more shows over the next week.[36] On July 15, 2015, the host contrasted Obama not having contacted the Steinle family to his having written letters to forty-six felons whose sentences he commuted, and to his outreach to the family of Michael Brown in Ferguson. Limbaugh's point was to remind his listeners that Obama cared more about prisoners (read: black and Hispanic people) and black people killed by cops than a white woman who was murdered by someone here illegally. If there's one segment that both encapsulates Limbaugh's tribalizing history of the Obama presidency, and shows how his race-baiting rhetoric paved the way for the rise of Trump, this was it.

Limbaugh's tribalization of our politics did not end with the transition from President Obama to President Trump. The wall on our southern border, the one made out of concrete—or maybe steel, depending on which day Trump was speaking—that Mexico was supposed to pay for, remained a prominent issue into 2019. Two years had gone by after Trump's inauguration without any money appropriated, let alone spent, on the wall. After Trump appeared willing to sign off on another budget deal that included no funds to build the wall in order to keep the government running, Limbaugh demonstrated that he wanted more than just rhetoric from the president he had so enthusiastically introduced two months earlier at a pre-midterm rally in his Missouri hometown.

On December 19, 2018, Limbaugh condemned the agreement to fund the government that had already passed the Senate with overwhelming, bipartisan support, saying that it would mean "Trump gets nothing and the Democrats get everything." The next day, the host urged Trump to "Veto this thing and then head down to Mar-a-Lago."

Shortly thereafter, Limbaugh reported that Trump had reached out to assure him (and their mutual followers) that the White House would do as the host had demanded, and stick to a hard line on the wall and the shutdown. The wall, Limbaugh intoned, was "not just a campaign promise . . . It is about the American way of life."

At Trump's urging, the House rejected the Senate deal, and negotiations came to an end shortly thereafter. A number of federal departments ran out of funding and shut down at midnight the following night. They remained closed for thirty-five days. Retiring Tennessee Republican Senator Bob Corker, days before the end of his final term, lamented the influence Limbaugh (along with Ann Coulter) wielded, asking: "Do we succumb to [sic] tyranny of radio talk show hosts? We have two talk radio hosts who influenced the president – that's tyranny isn't it?"[37]

The government shutdown over the wall showed how the symbiotic relationship between Limbaugh and Trump had evolved over the years. In addition to helping seed the field prior to and during Trump's run for the White House, and maintaining his support for President Trump's tribalizing, bigoted policies, Limbaugh is, in a sense, standing to Trump's right, making sure that the president he helped elect stays on the prescribed path and does not moderate his positions. If Trump does waver, he risks invoking the wrath of the tribe he and Limbaugh helped create—an outcome the host himself broached, noting on December 19, 2018 that the wall "is why [Trump's] support base has not abandoned him." That is the problem with building a movement based to a significant degree on racial resentment and cultural anxiety: Angry, scared people expect the person they elect as leader to do whatever it takes to protect them from the things they have been taught to fear and hate, no matter the consequences for the rest of us.

Conclusion

LIMBAUGH (AND TRUMP) VS. OBAMA: WHOSE VERSION OF AMERICA WILL WE BE?

Us. Them. Taken alone, these words are mere descriptors. When, however, citizens of our society divide themselves into tribes, into "us" and "them"—in particular, when they do so along lines of race, culture, religion, or other characteristics that go to the core of how we identify ouselves—this threatens our country's future.

Some public figures recognize this danger. They work to reduce those divisions and invigorate ties among Americans across various boundaries. For example, in 2007, then-Senator Obama urged Americans to address "our empathy deficit—the ability to put ourselves in someone else's shoes; to see the world through those who are different from us—the child who's hungry, the laid-off steelworker, the immigrant woman cleaning your dorm room."[1] Other public figures take the opposite approach. In his final State of the Union Address in 2016, President Obama warned against following those "voices urging us to fall back into our respective tribes, to scapegoat fellow citizens who don't look like us, or pray like us, or vote like we do, or share the same background."[2]

This book has focused on one such voice.

Rush Limbaugh's depiction of the Obama presidency went far beyond substantive criticisms of policies proposed and actions taken.

Instead, a substantial portion of the host's words against the forty-fourth president were riddled with untruths. PolitiFact assessed thirty-seven of Limbaugh's statements, made from April 10, 2009, through November 22, 2016, and found two to be mostly true, five half true, nine mostly false, eleven false, and ten pants-on-fire lies. How many were rated simply true? Zero.[3] Limbaugh's lies about President Obama further eroded the belief that truth actually matters, and helped shatter the understanding most Americans once shared regarding the difference between real and fake news.

Most notably since the start of the 2016 presidential campaign, large numbers of Americans have accepted and spread fake news stories, including those that Vladimir Putin's Russia propagated in order to help elect Donald Trump. As we learned in the February 2018 indictment of thirteen Russian nationals issued by Robert Mueller, as well as from reports written for Senate Intelligence Committee that became public in December 2018, the Russian fake news campaign included a significant amount of racially polarizing material.[4] Some of it was aimed at suppressing support for Hillary Clinton among black voters, while other activity was geared toward heightening white racial resentment toward African Americans by, for example, suggesting that Black Lives Matter supporters were somehow behind various targeted killings of police officers. The latter is exactly the kind of inflammatory charge Limbaugh's audience heard on a regular basis throughout the Obama presidency. In How Democracies Die, their vitally important book published one year into the Trump presidency, Steven Levitsky and Daniel Ziblatt identified racialized partisanship, which they noted as having worsened over the past three decades, as "the greatest challenge to established forms of mutual toleration and forbearance since Reconstruction."[5]

In addition to promoting a narrative of deception, Limbaugh took every opportunity to paint President Obama as the "Other." The host did not merely disagree with Obama on policy; he also told his overwhelmingly white, conservative audience that the president was some kind of black nationalist radical who hated America and wanted to take their stuff in order to give it to lazy black and brown people, including "illegal immigrants." Most voters choose the candidate who they think cares most about them. They want someone who believes that they matter. According to Limbaugh, if you were white, you did not matter to President Obama.

White Anxiety Finds A Home

The numbers are clear: our country is becoming less white. A majority of children born today belong to a race or ethnicity other than non-Hispanic white, and sometime around 2050, people of color are projected to make up more than half the American population. The fear of demographic change—and the sense of white alienation that too often flows from it—is real and growing. One of the primary reasons for its growth is that Rush Limbaugh has spent years stoking it by warning that the browning of this nation will lead to the destruction of American culture. President Trump has spoken in these terms as well, as have others in the right-wing media. For example, in August 2018, after Fox News prime-time hosts Laura Ingraham and Tucker Carlson made similar kinds of comments, CNN posted an article with the headline, "White Anxiety Finds A Home At Fox News."[6]

Many white Americans, despite continuing, as an overall group, to enjoy a relative advantage over other ethnic groups, are watching their fortunes decline in absolute terms. The reduction in white life expectancy and the recent, drastic increase in the rate of so-called "deaths of despair" (those caused by drugs, alcohol, and suicide) among whites send a hugely important signal. We can see the political importance of this white anxiety in a 2016 study, which found that respondents expressed more support for the Tea Party after being told that the white percentage of the U.S. population or its collective income advantage over other racial groups was shrinking compared to those who were essentially told the opposite. Support for the Tea Party was also noticeably higher among those shown a photo manipulated to make President Obama appear darker versus those shown an accurate photo of a lighter-skinned Obama. This disparity demonstrates why Limbaugh put so much effort into rhetorically blackening the president. Overall, the study's authors concluded that pro-Tea Party sentiments at least partially resulted from "threats to the status of whites in America."[7]

Another study found that when those who strongly identify with their white identity are reminded about whites soon becoming a minority of the U.S. population, they more strongly back Trump as well as "anti-immigrant policies." Whites who did not strongly identify with their whiteness showed no such effect; in fact their level of support for Trump dropped.[8] Likewise, after examining survey data from the two most recent presidential elections, University of Pennsylvania political scientist Diana C. Mutz stated that, "Those who felt that the hierarchy was being upended—with whites discriminated against more than blacks, Christians discriminated against more than Muslims, and men discriminated against more than women—were most likely to support Trump."[9]

Similarly, a spring 2016 Pew survey of Republican voters found that, among those responding that a non-white majority would be "bad for the country," 63 percent expressed a "somewhat warm" or "very warm" feeling toward Trump, while only 26 percent expressed a "somewhat cold" or "very cold" feeling toward him. This compares to an almost even split—46 percent somewhat or very warm to 40 percent somewhat or very cold—among respondents who thought such demographic change would either be neutral or good for the U.S. Echoing studies mentioned in the introduction to this book, this study also found strong correlations between having more positive feelings toward Trump and holding negative opinions about Islam and immigration.[10] On a related note, a study conducted in July 2016 had whites read articles with different takes on the demographic future of America. One focused on increasing diversity, another on whites becoming a "minority" down the road, while a third emphasized "an enduring white majority based on intermarriage and inclusive white identity." The "white minority story" provoked significantly more responses of either anxiety or anger, particularly among Republican respondents.[11]

To many liberals, especially well-educated, cosmopolitan ones, multiculturalism and diversity appear to be self-evidently positive things that contain no downside whatsoever. Nevertheless, for those, especially the economically vulnerable (or those who perceive themselves to be) who grew accustomed to living for decades among others who were culturally and linguistically similar to themselves, such demographic changes are often disruptive, rather than stimulating. Such people fear waking up one day to discover that they are now outsiders who no longer understand how to navigate the society into which they were born.

Their fears can be exacerbated by something as straightforward as being unable to comprehend an accent when they call with a question about a bill or a product they bought. Yes, they may have reached an overseas call center staffed by non-Americans, but all they know is that, back when America was great, the phone was always answered by someone they understood. This situation can lead them to become afraid of something similar happening in a true emergency, and that fear, however unfounded, often leads to anger. Anxious, angry people are more likely to embrace and act on prejudices they have been exposed to, which, when they are feeling more secure about their own situation, they may be better able to resist.

This reality is why it is so foolish for Democrats to write off, for example, large swaths of Trump voters as incorrigible racists. Many voters are certainly drawn to Trump by an aspect of white identity politics, but for a good number, that does not define the totality of their belief system. Most people are not either "racist" or "not racist," but rather have prejudices that they might or might not act on in a given moment, depending on the circumstances. In political terms, it is unhelpful for progressives to measure success in terms of turning people from "racist" to "not racist." Instead, success means helping a percentage of people to see beyond whatever racial prejudices or resentments they have more often than they currently do. The worse things get for them, the more many white Americans defensively embrace their white identity. Limbaugh has long understood this, and the goal of his rhetoric on Obama was to reinforce and heighten the racial identity of white Americans, in order to increase support for the Republican Party, and candidates like Trump.

Therefore, Democratic campaigns should do the opposite of Limbaugh by employing rhetoric that encourages whites to prioritize other, non-racial aspects of their identity, rhetoric that centers on an inclusive yet strongly unified conception of American national identity. To clarify, in no way does this mean Democratic candidates should avoid talking about racial inequality or injustice and talk only about economic issues—although not talking about economic issues enough during the 2016 general election campaign was one of Hillary Clinton's major mistakes. Lynn Vavreck found that only 9 percent of Clinton's television ads that ran from June until the election contained an economic message. Going back to the 1952 presidential campaign, the average was around 28 percent.[12]

One thing Democrats should do is highlight how the Republicans' tribalization strategy aims at getting working-class whites to vote against their real economic interests. The authors of a recent, in-person survey of Minnesota voters found that emphasizing the "foundational link between economic and racial injustice" results in more white working-class voters pinpointing exactly who is responsible for their plight (i.e., the economic elites), and simultaneously excites non-white voters looking to elect someone who will stand up to big corporations and the wealthy, but who also prioritizes civil rights and equality.[13] The project's authors offered the following conclusion:

> The race-class message describes racism as a strategy that the reactionary rich are using against all people. By moving away from conversations about racial prejudice that implicitly pit whites against others, the race-class message makes clear how strategic racism hurts everyone, of every race. It signals to whites that they have more to gain from coming together across racial lines to tackle racial and economic injustice than from siding with politicians who distract the country with racial broadsides.[14]

This cannot be the whole of the Democratic message in every campaign, but it appears to be one that has significant appeal across racial lines.

In order to win elections and implement their ideas, progressives need white Americans and Americans of color to feel connected to one another as members of one national community, one people, or, as Barack Obama so often put it, one American family. Conservatives like Rush Limbaugh (and Donald Trump), on the other hand, need whites and non-whites to feel separate from one another, isolated from one another, even to see one another as enemies. The data on the growing correlation between white racial resentment and voting Republican over the past thirty years suggests that the host's efforts have had a profound impact.

White racial identity has been the foundation of the single most destructive form of identity politics over the course of American history. In colonial times, slave-owners raised the status of white indentured servants—many of whom had developed close relationships with the enslaved African Americans alongside whom they worked—transforming these "plain white folks" into equal citizens and telling them that they were superior to blacks, who were thus undeserving of freedom.[15] Why did they do this? Because the slave-owning elites had one fear above all: a white-black coalition of the masses that would unite to overthrow them. Similarly, after emancipation, the Southern economic elites made sure to bind poor whites to them through the race-based advantages conferred by Jim Crow, all in the name of thwarting that same white-black, class-based political partnership.[16]

In this century, some working- and even middle-class whites, especially those without a college degree, have been drowning economically in a way they have not since the Great Depression.[17] For those people, whatever privilege comes with being white is not enough to keep them afloat. They are angry, afraid, and looking for a scapegoat. Rush Limbaugh has been only too happy to oblige. He has absolutely no interest in helping the country figure out how to deal in a productive way with the white anxiety that arises from demographic change. He is interested in one thing, and one thing only: exacerbating this phenomenon in order to keep separate whites and Americans of color who do share common economic interests. That is how Republicans win elections.[18]

Limbaugh's divisive approach, in that specific regard, is a carbon copy of the approach taken by the nineteenth century Southern white elites. The more he can get working-and middle-class whites to identify with their racial identity—their tribe—above their economic interests, the better he will be able to prevent the multiracial, progressive coalition assembled by President Obama from growing strong enough to defeat Limbaugh/Trump-style conservatism once and for all. Ultimately, the right-wing needs white racial anxiety. In fact, it cannot survive without it.

ACKNOWLEDGMENTS

Few people write a book without help. I am not one of them. My academic home, Empire State College of the State University of New York, helped make this book possible by granting me a sabbatical leave to research and write it, as well as funding for the vital developmental editing this book has undergone. I am especially grateful to Michael Spitzer, who as dean at the time championed my sabbatical proposal and shepherded it through the process. Among my Empire State College faculty colleagues, I received invaluable support from two in particular: Melinda Blitzer and Donna Gaines, each of whom offered encouragement at crucial moments and were always willing to take a look at something I had written.

Aviel Roshwald and Steven Beller are two scholars who have guided my research and writing over the past two-plus decades, and I want to thank both of them for their feedback on this manuscript. They have been hearing about this project from the start.. I described it to Aviel at a diner near Columbia University during the Association for the Study of Nationalities Conference, and I remember him looking at me for a few seconds, and then asking, with a smile, whether I might consider a different title.

I also want to thank John K. Wilson, who read an early version of the manuscript and offered incredibly detailed feedback, as well as generous advice and guidance as I worked on getting the book published. I am very grateful to Hilary Claggett, who was the editor of my previous book, and who helped open my mind to taking this book in a slightly different and ultimately more fruitful direction than I had planned.

My developmental editor, Karen Adams, devoted countless hours to helping me get this book into shape, offering advice with not only edits but chapter structure and big picture, conceptual questions. She has been with me for the more than three years it has taken to get this project from my head to the printed page, and there have been few times where I have gone more than a week without emailing her.

To Markos Moulitsas, thank you so much for reading this manuscript and writing the Foreword, and thanks also for providing, in Daily Kos, a terrific platform for my writing. And a heartfelt thank you to Robert Lasner, my editor at Ig Publishing, for believing in this book, and for all his hard work and expertise in bringing it to print.

Last, but certainly not least, is my family. My wife, Jane, has not only given me her love and steadfast support, she has also read (or heard me read aloud) every page of this book, many of them more than once. Sometimes I asked for her help when she was trying to do other things, or just plain tired after a hard day's work of her own. She never said no, and always gave her full attention to whatever I had to show her. The words "thank you" do not cover the gratitude and appreciation I feel. It's a start.

I also want to thank my daughters, Lauren and Kate. Too many times over the past couple of years I have asked them to wait a minute, or a while, for my attention while I was trying to nail down a particular thought, or finish reading some piece of material. I hope they understand that, in this work and in all the work I do, I am trying to make them proud. Thanks also to the members of my family who have always cheered me on: my in-laws, Judy and Bill Kaufman, as well as my uncle Leslie Schuster—a professor of political science who has shown me for many years how rewarding a life in academia can be—and my aunt Genie Schuster, and to Mike Mazur, with whom I have had so many fruitful and interesting conversations about contemporary politics.

Finally, there is one more cheerleader I want to thank. My mother, Helaine Reifowitz Mazur, has been my longest-serving supporter. As excited as I was to learn this book would be published, I think she was even more so. My mother's optimism, love, and strength have buoyed me not just in writing this book, but throughout the whole of my life. I am proud to dedicate this book to her.

NOTES

PREFACE

1. For a detailed discussion of this concept in the academic literature, see Michael Tesler, "Racial Priming with Implicit and Explicit Messages," *Oxford Research Encyclopedia of Politics*, May 2017, http://politics. oxfordre.com/view/10.1093/acrefore/9780190228637.001.0001/ acrefore-9780190228637-e-49.

2. Rush Limbaugh Show Transcripts, *RushLimbaugh.com*, January 16, 2009, https://www.rushlimbaugh.com/archives/. Unless otherwise specified, all quotations are from the *Rush Limbaugh Show*. I found that a small percentage of segments from older shows were not transferred when Limbaugh updated his website at the end of 2016. As an alternative to *RushLimbaugh. com*, transcripts that appear to be complete are available at the Internet Archive Wayback Machine's Limbaugh site. You can search for any date by starting at http://web.archive.org/web/20120305065111/http://www.rushlimbaugh. com:80/.

3. A war of words erupted between Limbaugh and Republican National Committee chair Michael Steele, who claimed that he was the "de facto leader of the Republican Party," not Limbaugh. Shortly afterwards, the chairman apologized to the host, clearing up any question about who wielded greater authority. Adam Nagourney, "R.N.C. Chairman Apologizes to Limbaugh in Flap Over His Role," *New York Times*, March 2, 2009, https://thecaucus.blogs.nytimes.com/2009/03/02/ rnc-chairman-apologizes-to-limbaugh-in-flap-over-his-role/?_r=0.

4. Terry Mancour, "Obama v Limbaugh," *The Guardian*, January 27, 2009,

https://www.theguardian.com/commentisfree/cifamerica/2009/jan/27/barack-obama-rush-limbaugh.

5. Ta-Nehisi Coates, "Better Is Good: Obama on Reparations, Civil Rights, and the Art of the Possible," *The Atlantic*, December 21, 2016, https://www.theatlantic.com/politics/archive/2016/12/ta-nehisi-coates-obama-transcript-ii/511133/.

6. "Limbaugh Holds on to His Niche—Conservative Men," *Pew Research Center*, February 3, 2009, http://www.pewresearch.org/2009/02/03/limbaugh-holds-onto-his-niche-conservative-men/. A 2012 Pew Research survey found his audience to be 59 percent percent male; see "In Changing News Landscape, Even Television Is Vulnerable," *Pew Research Center*, September 27, 2012, section 4, http://www.people-press.org/2012/09/27/section-4-demographics-and-political-views-of-news-audiences/.

7. Michael Tesler, *Post-Racial or Most-Racial? Race and Politics in the Obama Era* (Chicago: University of Chicago Press, 2016), 148–49.

8. Ibid., 195. Emphasis in original.

9. Michael Tesler, "Economic Anxiety Isn't Driving Racial Resentment. Racial Resentment Is Driving Economic Anxiety," *Washington Post*, August 22, 2016, https://www.washingtonpost.com/news/monkey-cage/wp/2016/08/22/economic-anxiety-isnt-driving-racial-resentment-racial-resentment-is-driving-economic-anxiety/?utm_term=.cf45505117bb.

10. Michael Tesler, "The Spillover of Racialization into Evaluations of Bo Obama," *Yougov.com*, April 10, 2012, https://today.yougov.com/news/2012/04/10/spillover-racialization-evaluations-bo-obama/.

11. Adam M. Enders and Jamil S. Scott, "White Racial Resentment Has Been Gaining Political Power for Decades," *Washington Post*, January 15, 2018, https://www.washingtonpost.com/news/monkey-cage/wp/2018/01/15/white-racial-resentment-has-been-gaining-political-power-for-decades/?utm_term=.da60556f2aa6.

12. Marc Hetherington and Drew Engelhardt, "Donald Trump's Surprising Success with Southern Evangelicals," *The Cook Political Report*, February 26, 2016, http://webcache.googleusercontent.com/search?q=cache:2OCGOSk-MddoJ:cookpolitical.com/story.pdf/9309+&cd=2&hl=en&ct=clnk&gl=us.

13. Lee Drutman, "How Race and Identity Became the Central Dividing Line in American Politics," *Vox*, August 30, 2016, https://www.vox.com/polyarchy/2016/8/30/12697920/race-dividing-american-politics.

14. Hertherington and Engelhardt, "Donald Trump's Surprising Success with Southern Evangelicals."

15. John Sides, "Race, Religion, and Immigration in 2016," *Voter Study Group*,

June 2017, https://www.voterstudygroup.org/reports/2016-elections/race-religion-immigration-2016.

16. Michael Tesler, "Trump is the First Modern Republican to Win the Nomination Based on Racial Prejudice," *Washington Post*, August 1, 2016, https://www.washingtonpost.com/news/monkey-cage/wp/2016/08/01/trump-is-the-first-republican-in-modern-times-to-win-the-partys-nomination-on-anti-minority-sentiments/?utm_term=.0acd722be22a.

17. See John Sides, Michael Tesler, Lynn Vavreck, *Identity Crisis: The 2016 Presidential Campaign and the Battle for the Meaning of America* (Princeton: Princeton University Press, 2018), pp. 89-90. See also Thomas B. Edsall, "Donald Trump's Identity Politics," *New York Times*, August 24, 2017, https://www.nytimes.com/2017/08/24/opinion/donald-trump-identity-politics.html?smprod=nytcore-iphone&smid=nytcore-iphone-share&_r=0. Edsall's article quoted from the book by Sides, et. al., which had not yet been published.

18. Sides, Tesler, Vavreck, *Identity Crisis*, pp. 163–69.

19. See Mehdi Hasan, "Top Democrats Are Wrong: Trump Supporters Were More Motivated by Racism Than Economic Interests," *The Intercept*, April 6, 2017, https://theintercept.com/2017/04/06/top-democrats-are-wrong-trump-supporters-were-more-motivated-by-racism-than-economic-issues/. Hasan interviewed Klinkner in writing this article.

20. Michael Tesler, "Views about Race Mattered More in Electing Trump Than in Electing Obama," *Washington Post*, November 22, 2016, https://www.washingtonpost.com/news/monkey-cage/wp/2016/11/22/peoples-views-about-race-mattered-more-in-electing-trump-than-in-electing-obama/.

21. Brian F. Schaffner, Matthew MacWilliams, Tatishe Nteta, "Explaining White Polarization in the 2016 Vote for President: The Sobering Role of Racism and Sexism," Paper prepared for presentation at the Conference on The U.S. Elections of 2016: Domestic and International Aspects. January 8-9, 2017, IDC Herzliya Campus, http://people.umass.edu/schaffne/schaffner_et_al_IDC_conference.pdf.

CHAPTER ONE

1. Richard Gehr, "Mouth at Work," Newsday, October 8, 1990.

2. Limbaugh Transcripts, December 8, 2004, January 19, 2007.

3. Gehr, "Mouth at Work."

4. Michael D. Shear, "'I'm Not a Racist,' Trump Says in Denying Vulgar Comment," *New York Times*, January 14, 2018, https://www.nytimes.

com/2018/01/14/us/politics/trump-im-not-a-racist.html. See also Marc Fisher, "Donald Trump: I Am the Least Racist Person," *Washington Post*, June 10, 2016, https://www.washingtonpost.com/politics/donald-trump-i-am-the-least-racist-person/2016/06/10/eac7874c-2f3a-11e6-9de3-6e6e7a14000c_story.html?utm_term=.c0c516e27b36.

5. Michael Gerson, "The Party of Lincoln is Dying," *Washington Post*, June 9, 2016, https://www.washingtonpost.com/opinions/the-party-of-lincoln-is-dying/2016/06/09/e669380a-2e6b-11e6-9de3-6e6e7a14000c_story.html?utm_term=.eafcd3cda123.

6. Ezra Klein, "The Hard Question Isn't Why Clinton Lost—It's Why Trump Won," *Vox*, November 11, 2016, http://www.vox.com/policy-and-politics/2016/11/11/13578618/why-did-trump-win. See also Tali Mendenberg, *The Race Card: Campaign Strategy, Implicit Messages, and the Norm of Equality* (Princeton: Princeton University Press, 2001), which remains the most important book on the topic.

7. "Top Talk Audiences (December 2018)," *Talkers*, http://www.talkers.com/top-talk-audiences/.

8. Paul Farhi, "Limbaugh's Audience Size? It's Largely Up in the Air," *Washington Post*, March 7, 2009, http://www.washingtonpost.com/wp-dyn/content/article/2009/03/06/AR2009030603435.html; Ethan Epstein, "Is Rush Limbaugh in Trouble?" *Politico*, May 24, 2016, http://www.politico.com/magazine/story/2016/05/is-rush-limbaugh-in-trouble-talk-radio-213914.

9. Kathleen Hall Jamieson and Joseph N. Capella, *Echo Chamber: Rush Limbaugh and the Conservative Media Establishment* (Oxford: Oxford University Press, 2010), ix. See xiii–xiv for an overview of the book's larger analysis of Limbaugh's impact during these years.

10. Limbaugh Transcripts, March 16, 2012, July 22, 2015.

11. Hatewatch Staff, "Getting Cucky: A Brief Primer On The Radical Right's Newest 'Cuckservative' Meme," *Southern Poverty Law Center*, August 7, 2015, https://www.splcenter.org/hatewatch/2015/08/07/getting-cucky-brief-primer-radical-rights-newest-cuckservative-meme.

12. Jeet Heer, "Conservatives Are Holding A Conversation About Race," *New Republic*, July 26, 2015, https://newrepublic.com/article/122372/conservatives-are-holding-conversation-about-race?utm_content=bufferb777c&utm_medium=social&utm_source=twitter.com&utm_campaign=buffer.

13. Limbaugh Transcripts, May 26, 2010, August 29, 2011.

14. Ibid., July 17, 2013, July 25, 2013.

15. Ibid., July 30, 2009.

16. Limbaugh Transcripts, May 7, 2015, July 12, 2016.

17. Richard Wolffe, *Renegade: The Making of a President* (New York: Crown Publishers, 2009), 324.

18. Limbaugh Transcripts, February 10, 2010, March 23, 2010, July 12, 2010, August 11, 2010, October 7, 2010, October 12, 2010, October 18, 2010, October 26, 2010, October 27, 2010, September 28, 2011, July 17, 2013, July 25, 2013, February 28, 2014, April 9, 2014, July 23, 2014, August 25, 2014, October 31, 2014, July 10, 2015, August 15, 2015, September 21, 2016.

19. Limbaugh Transcripts, July 1, 2010, July 2, 2010.

20. Chris Usher, "No Proof in New Black Panther Case: Official," *CBS News*, July 25, 2010, http://www.cbsnews.com/news/no-proof-in-new-black-panther-case-official/.

21. Here is a full list of all shows that contain at least one NBPP mention, Limbaugh Transcripts, June 1, 2009, June 12, 2009, August 13, 2009, November 2, 2009, January 18, 2010, March 4, 2010, March 25, 2010, April 16, 2010, July 7, 2010, July 13, 2010, July 14, 2010, July 20, 2010, July 21, 2010, September 29, 2010, March 2, 2011, May 11, 2011, May 23, 2011, August 11, 2011, October 3, 2011, October 14, 2011, March 28, 2012, April 11, 2012, May 30, 2012, March 18, 2013, June 25, 2013, April 9, 2014, May 13, 2014, August 15, 2014, August 19, 2014, August 20, 2014, November 25, 2014, December 22, 2014, July 8, 2016, July 11, 2016, July 13, 2016, July 18, 2016, July 19, 2016.

22. Clark Hoyt, "The ACORN Sting Revisited," *New York Times*, March 20, 2010, http://www.nytimes.com/2010/03/21/opinion/21pubed.html.

23. Limbaugh Transcripts, September 4, 2008, September 22, 2008.

24. Limbaugh Transcripts, June 18, 2009, February 12, 2010, March 23, 2010, May 5, 2010, May 13, 2010.

25. Jamelle Bouie, "Richard Sherman Is Right: Thug Is the New N-World [sic]," *Daily Beast*, January 21, 2014, http://www.thedailybeast.com/articles/2014/01/27/richard-sherman-is-right-thug-is-the-new-n-world.html.

26. Rubén Hernández-Murillo, Andra C. Ghent, and Michael T. Owyang, "Did Affordable Housing Legislation Contribute to the Subprime Securities Boom?" *Federal Reserve Bank of St. Louis, Working Papers Series*, March 2012 (revised December 2014), https://research.stlouisfed.org/wp/2012/2012-005.pdf.

27. See Eric Schnurer, "Just How Wrong Is Conventional Wisdom about Government Fraud?" *The Atlantic*, August 15, 2013, http://www.theatlantic.com/politics/archive/2013/08/just-how-wrong-is-conventional-wisdom-about-government-fraud/278690/. See also Kim Severson, "Food Stamp

Fraud, Rare but Troubling," *New York Times*, December 18, 2013, http://www.nytimes.com/2013/12/19/us/food-stamp-fraud-in-the-underground-economy.html.

28. Ibid., September 17, 2009. "Heartland Democratic Presidential Forum," *C-SPAN.org*, December 1, 2007, https://www.c-span.org/video/?202631-1/heartland-democratic-presidential-forum.

29. Limbaugh Transcripts, January 23, 2013, February 15, 2013, February 11, 2014, February 12, 2014, March 6, 2015, November 4, 2015.

30. Ibid., February 25, 2009, March 16, 2009, March 25, 2009, April 2, 2009, April 10, 2009, July 23, 2009, October 7, 2009, May 5, 2010, June 1, 2010, June 22, 2010, October 14, 2010, December 8, 2010, January 10, 2011, March 28, 2011, March 29, 2011, May 23, 2011, May 27, 2011, June 12, 2011, June 29, 2011, May 18, 2012, July 26, 2012, August 12, 2012, July 10, 2013, August 6, 2013, January 29, 2014, March 3, 2014, July 16, 2014, July 21, 2014, October 22, 2014, November 25, 2014, December 1, 2014, March 3, 2015, May 1, 2015, November 10, 2015, May 2, 2016, July 8, 2016, July 18, 2016, September 21, 2016, November 17, 2016.

31. Ibid., February 25, 2009, January 10, 2011, March 11, 2011, November 17, 2016.

32. Ibid., January 27, 2009, June 2, 2009.

33. Ibid., October 16, 2009.

34. Ibid., April 22, 2009, June 2, 2009, June 28, 2009, June 29, 2009, August 11, 2009, August 21, 2009, September 22, 2009, October 2, 2009, October 16, 2009, November 2, 2009, November 3, 2009, July 10, 2010, August 23, 2010.

35. "Republicans Not Handling Election Results Well," *Public Policy Polling*, December 4, 2012, http://www.publicpolicypolling.com/main/2012/12/republicans-not-handling-election-results-well.html.

36. Limbaugh Transcripts, March 21, 2012, April 6, 2012, October 22, 2014.

37. Sami Edge, "A Review of Key States with Voter ID Laws Found No Voter Impersonation Fraud," *Center for Public Integrity*, August 21, 2016, https://www.publicintegrity.org/2016/08/21/20078/review-key-states-voter-id-laws-found-no-voter-impersonation-fraud.

38. Justin Levitt, "A Comprehensive Investigation of Voter Impersonation Finds 31 Credible Incidents out of One Billion Ballots Cast," *Washington Post*, August 6, 2014, https://www.washingtonpost.com/news/wonk/wp/2014/08/06/a-comprehensive-investigation-of-voter-imper-sonation-finds-31-credible-incidents-out-of-one-billion-ballots-cast/?utm_

term=.bbafa6c3db6f.

39. Keith Gunnar Bentele and Erin E. O'Brien, "Jim Crow 2.0?: Why States Consider and Adopt Restrictive Voter Access Policies," *Perspectives on Politics* 11, no. 4 (2013): 1088, http://forum.lwv.org/document/jim-crow-20-why-states-consider-and-adopt-restrictive-voter-access-policies.

40. *North Carolina State Conference of the NAACP, et. al., v. McCrory*, U.S. Court of Appeals for the Fourth Circuit, 11, https://www.ca4.uscourts.gov/Opinions/Published/161468.P.pdf.

41. Michael Wines, "How Charges of Voter Fraud Became a Political Strategy," *New York Times*, October 21, 2016, http://www.nytimes.com/2016/10/22/us/how-charges-of-voter-fraud-became-a-political-strategy.html?smprod=nytcore-iphone&smid=nytcore-iphone-share&_r=0.

42. Paul Waldman, "Trump's Talk of a Rigged Election? Republicans Built That," *Washington Post*, October 17, 2016, https://www.washingtonpost.com/blogs/plum-line/wp/2016/10/17/trumps-talk-of-a-rigged-election-republicans-built-that/?utm_term=.565f47f30821.

43. Roland Martin, "The Full Story Behind Wright's 'God Damn America' Sermon," *CNN.com*, March 21, 2008, http://ac360.blogs.cnn.com/2008/03/21/the-full-story-behind-wright%E2%80%99s-%E2%80%9Cgod-damn-america%E2%80%9D-sermon/.

44. See also Ian Reifowitz, *Obama's America: A Transformative Vision of Our National Identity* (Washington, D.C.: Potomac Books, 2012), pp. 94–103.

45. Linbaugh Transcripts, January 28, 2009, February 17, 2009, September 8, 20009, March 20, 2009, March 30, 2009.

46. Ibid., February 18, 2009, March 20, 2009, May 5, 2009, June 4, 2009, July 23, 2009, August 4, 2009, September 11, 2009, September 16, 2009, October 2, 2009, October 6, 2009, October 8, 2009, January 12, 2010, January 13, 2010, July 8, 2010, October 26, 2010, October 28, 2010, December 8, 2010, December 14, 2010, April 21, 2011, May 11, 2011, September 1, 2011, October 14, 2011, November 22, 2011, December 15, 2011, April 11, 2012, March 4, 2013, April 9, 2014, May 5, 2014, August 5, 2014, July 16, 2014, December 8, 2014, December 18, 2014, February 20, 2015, May 5, 2015, May 6, 2015, May 7, 2015, May 11, 2015, May 13, 2015, November 13, 2015, March 30, 2016, December 13, 2016.

47. Ibid, February 18, 2009.

48. Ibid., June 11, 2009, September 18, 2015.

49. Ibid., February 17, 2009, March 5, 2009, March 6, 2009, April 14, 2009, April 16, 2009, May 4, 2009, May 14, 2009, June 3, 2009, June 5, 2009, June

11, 2009, June 17, 2009, June 30, 2009, July 24, 2009, July 30, 2009, August 6, 2009, August 12, 2009, August 14, 2009, August 20, 2009, August 27, 2009, September 10, 2009, September 11, 2009, September 21, 2009, September 25, 2009, September 30, 2009, , October 1, 2009, November 9, 2009, November 10, 2009, November 13, 2009, November 23, 2009, December 8, 2009, December 10, 2009, December 21, 2009, January 11, 2010, January 18, 2010, February 18, 2010, April 2, 2010, April 5, 2010, April 19, 2010, April 22, 2010, April 30, 2010, May 3, 2010, May 10, 2010, June 2, 2010, July 8, 2010, August 13, 2010, August 23, 2010, September 7, 2010, September 30, 2010, October 19, 2010, October 20, 2010, October 28, 2010, November 8, 2010, November 15, 2010, November 22, 2010, December 8, 2010, December 17, 2010, December 20, 2010, January 12, 2011, March 2, 2011, March 9, 2011, March 17, 2011, March 22, 2011, March 24, 2011, April 7, 2011, April 14, 2011, April 25, 2011, May 5, 2011, May 11, 2011, June 10, 2011, August 2, 2011, August 12, 2011, August 31, 2011, September 2, 2011, September 22, 2011, September 27, 2011, October 3, 2011, October 12, 2011, October 13, 2011, October 25, 2011, December 12, 2011, May 18, 2012, May 30, 2012, June 7, 2012, June 12, 2012, August 13, 2012, September 12, 2012, September 25, 2012, October 11, 2012, January 24, 2013, April 1, 2013, April 22, 2013, August 27, 2013, August 30, 2013, December 4, 2013, January 13, 2014, March 27, 2014, March 28, 2014, May 1, 2014, May 23, 2014, June 7, 2014, November 7, 2014, January 17, 2015, February 23, 2015, May 11, 2015, June 17, 2015, July 15, 2015, November 3, 2015, December 17, 2015, February 4, 2016, February 14, 2016, May 2, 2016, August 15, 2016.

50. Ibid, April 14, 2009, July 22, 2009, January 18, 2010, February 11, 2010, March 17, 2010, May 18, 2010, October 27, 2010, April 6, 2011, March 28, 2012, April 11, 2012, May 30, 2012, July 10, 2013, April 9, 2014, July 14, 2014, August 19, 2014, September 25, 2014, October 22, 2014, October 31, 2014, November 25, 2014, November 26, 2014, December 1, 2014, December 19, 2014, December 22, 2014, December 23, 2014, February 27, 2015, March 12, 2015, March 24, 2015, April 30, 2015, May 1, 2015, May 28, 2015, June 15, 2015, July 13, 2015, April 5, 2016, July 18, 2016, September 21, 2016.

51. Ibid., March 24, 2008.

52. Ibid., February 19, 2010.

53. "Louis Farrakhan," *Southern Poverty Law Center*, https://www.splcenter.org/fighting-hate/extremist-files/individual/louis-farrakhan.

54. Hank DeZutter, "What Makes Obama Run," *Chicago Reader*, December 8, 1995, https://www.chicagoreader.com/chicago/what-makes-obama-run/

Content?oid=889221. In addition to these, Limbaugh also linked Obama to Farrakhan twice; see Limbaugh Transcripts, August 23, 2010, July 13, 2016.

55. Limbaugh Transcripts, March 3, 2010, September 13, 2010, July 18, 2016.

56. The reference is to the 1962 film (remade in 2004), in which the Soviet Union seeks to plant someone it controls into the presidency of the United States. The original is a classic in every sense of the word, and I will always be grateful to my father, Jerry Reifowitz, for introducing it to me. Limbaugh's use of the phrase is especially galling given his support for Trump, who, the U.S. intelligence community concluded, received significant assistance from the Russian government during his White House bid.

57. Limbaugh Transcripts, August 19, 2010, April 20, 2011, January 12, 2015, May 28, 2015, February 4, 2016.

58. Ibid., May 4, 2011, March 28, 2011.

59. Michael Tesler, *Post-Racial or Most-Racial?*, 47.

60. For a few examples, see Limbaugh Transcripts, February 10, 2010, March 29, 2011, November 30, 2011, July 17, 2015.

61. Ibid., September 29, 2010, October 21, 2010, March 28, 2011.

62. Ibid., August 17, 2010, August 19, 2010, August 20, 2010, September 9, 2010, October 28, 2010.

63. Ibid., February 5, 2015. The others were April 4, 2011, February 6, 2015, February 4, 2016, June 14, 2016.

64. "Trump Supporters Think Obama Is A Muslim Born in Another Country," *Public Policy Polling*, September 1, 2015, http://www.publicpolicypolling.com/main/2015/08/trump-supporters-think-obama-is-a-muslim-born-in-another-country.html.

65. Jennifer Agiesta, "Misperceptions Persist about Obama's Faith, But Aren't as Widespread," *CNN.com*, September 14, 2015, http://www.cnn.com/2015/09/13/politics/barack-obama-religion-christian-misperceptions/

66. Philip Klinkner, "The Easiest Way to Guess if Someone Supports Trump? Ask if Obama Is a Muslim," *Vox*, June 2, 2016, http://www.vox.com/2016/6/2/11833548/donald-trump-support-race-religion-economy.

67. Adam Serwer, "The Nationalist's Delusion," November 20, 2017, *The Atlantic*, https://www.theatlantic.com/politics/archive/2017/11/the-nationalists-delusion/546356/

68. Glenn Thrush and Maggie Haberman, "Trump Gives White Supremacists an Unequivocal Boost," *New York Times*, August 15, 2007, https://www.nytimes.com/2017/08/15/us/politics/

trump-charlottesville-white-nationalists.html.

69. Eugene Robinson, "President Trump Is The Master of Abhorrent Identity Politics," *Washington Post*, November 2, 2017, https://www.washingtonpost.com/opinions/president-trump-is-the-master-of-abhorrent-identity-politics/2017/11/02/e675bca8-c003-11e7-959c-fe2b598d8c00_story.html?utm_term=.0baf28ef03db. See also Perry Bacon Jr., "The Identity Politics of the Trump Administration," *Five Thirty Eight*, May 4, 2017, https://fivethirtyeight.com/features/the-identity-politics-of-the-trump-administration/; and Thomas B. Edsall, "Donald Trump's Identity Politics," *New York Times*, August 24, 2017, https://www.nytimes.com/2017/08/24/opinion/donald-trump-identity-politics.html?_r=0.

70. Arie Perliger, "Homegrown Terrorism and Why the Threat of Right-Wing Extremism Is Rising in America," *Newsweek*, June 4, 2017, http://www.newsweek.com/homegrown-terrorism-rising-threat-right-wing-extremism-619724.

71. Wesley Lowery, Kimberly Kindy, and Andrew Ba Tran, "In the United States, Right-Wing Violence Is on the Rise," *Washington Post*, November 25, 2018, https://www.washingtonpost.com/national/in-the-united-states-right-wing-violence-is-on-the-rise/2018/11/25/61f7f24a-deb4-11e8-85df-7a6b4d-25cfbb_story.html?noredirect=on&utm_term=.4984bb2eb05b.

72. U.S. Department of Homeland Security, "Rightwing Extremism: Current Economic and Political Climate Fueling Resurgence in Radicalization and Recruitment," April 7, 2009, https://webcache.googleusercontent.com/search?q=cache:mRmkS77Lmp0J:https://fas.org/irp/eprint/rightwing.pdf+&cd=1&hl=en&ct=clnk&gl=us.

CHAPTER TWO

1. Transcript available at: "Barack Obama's Speech in Independence, MO," June 30, 2008, http://www.nytimes.com/2008/06/30/us/politics/30text-obama.html?mcubz=0.

2. Limbaugh Transcripts, July 3, 2009, December 15, 2009, December 15, 2011.

3. Ibid., November 30, 2011, August 22, 2012, October 31, 2011.

4. Ibid., August 16, 2010, September 30, 2010, October 13, 2010, October 28, 2010.

5. Ibid., March 23, 2011.

6. See, for example, Ibid., April 10, 2018, May 2, 2018, May 17, 2018.

7. See, for example, Ibid., July 12, 2017.

8. Ibid., December 8, 2010, November 22, 2011.

9. Ibid., January 11, 2012.

10. Ibid., April 25, 2011, January 17, 2013, June 16, 2014, June 27, 2014, August 5, 2014.

11. Sandra Sobieraj Westfall, "The Obamas: How We Deal with Our Own Racist Experiences," *People*, December 17, 2014, http://people.com/celebrity/the-obamas-how-we-deal-with-our-own-racist-experiences/. Although the full interview appeared in print on December 19, that quotation appeared in an excerpt released on December 17, and thus was available before Limbaugh made his comments.

12. Limbaugh Transcripts, May 7, 2015.

13. Ibid., December 21, 2015, January 12, 2016.

14. Ibid., May 16, 2011, September 1, 2011, December 7, 2011.

15. Adam Serwer, "The Nationalist's Delusion," *The Atlantic*, November 20, 2017, https://www.theatlantic.com/politics/archive/2017/11/the-nationalists-delusion/546356/.

16. Rush Limbaugh Show Transcripts, RushLimbaugh.com, April 7, 2009, April 8, 2009, June 10, 2009, https://www.rushlimbaugh.com/archives/.

17. Amy Hollyfield, "Obama's Birth Certificate: Final Chapter," *PolitiFact.com*, June 27, 2008, http://www.politifact.com/truth-o-meter/article/2008/jun/27/obamas-birth-certificate-part-ii/.

18. Limbaugh Transcripts, November 9, 2010, January 21, 2011, February 24, 2011, March 17, 2011, March 24, 2011, May 18. 2012.

19. Michael D. Shear, "With Document, Obama Seeks to End 'Birther' Issue," *New York Times*, April 28, 2011, http://www.nytimes.com/2011/04/28/us/politics/28obama.html.

20. The quotations are compiled in Gregory Krieg, "14 of Trump's Most Outrageous 'Birther' claims—Half From After 2011," CNN.com, September 16, 2016, https://www.cnn.com/2016/09/09/politics/donald-trump-birther/index.html.

21. Ibid.

22. Maggie Haberman and Alan Rappeport, "Trump Drops False 'Birther' Theory, but Floats a New One: Clinton Started It," *New York Times*, September 16, 2016, https://www.nytimes.com/2016/09/17/us/politics/donald-trump-birther-obama.html.

23. Maggie Haberman and Jonathan Martin, "Trump Once Said the 'Access Hollywood' Tape Was Real. Now He's Not Sure," *New York Times*, November 28, 2017, https://www.nytimes.com/2017/11/28/us/politics/trump-access-hollywood-tape.html?_r=0.

24. Associated Press, "National Enquirer Hid Trump Secrets in a Safe,

Removed Them Before Inauguration," August 23, 2018, *NBCNews.com*, https://www.nbcnews.com/politics/donald-trump/national-enquirer-hid-trump-secrets-safe-removed-them-inauguration-n903356.

25. Michelle Obama, *Becoming* (New York: Crown, 2018), p. 353.

26. Francis Wilkinson, "Conservatives Fear Discrimination Against Whites," *Bloomberg.com*, March 21, 2014, https://www.bloomberg.com/view/articles/2014-03-21/conservatives-fear-discrimination-against-whites. Poll conducted by Latino Decisions for the Center for American Progress and Policy Link, "Building an All-In Nation," October 2013, https://www.americanprogress.org/wp-content/uploads/2013/10/AllInNation-1.pdf.

27. Limbaugh Transcripts, July 22, 2010, August 10, 2010, January 28, 2010, September 16, 2010.

28. Ibid., October 11, 2010.

29. Ibid., January 16, 2014, June 16, 2014. See also May 25, 2011, May 18, 2012, August 2, 2012, July 16, 2014, December 8, 2014, along with other times he mentioned affirmative action without also talking about Obama.

30. For a thorough discussion of this and other uses of racial dog whistles in American politics, see Ian Haney López, *Dog Whistle Politics: How Coded Racial Appeals Have Reinvented Racism and Wrecked the Middle Class* (Oxford: Oxford University Press, 2014). See also Martin Gilens, *Why Americans Hate Welfare: Race, Media and the Politics of Anti-Poverty Policy* (Chicago: University of Chicago Press, 1999).

31. Limbaugh Transcripts, May 28, 2009.

32. Ibid., June 15, 2012, July 20, 2015, August 4, 2011, August 5, 2011, June 26, 2009. On reparations, see also July 21, 2010, December 1, 2010, August 17, 2011, July 16, 2014.

33. Ibid., January 12, 2010. See also June 30, 2009, July 22, 2009, September 10, 2009, September 15, 2009, October 6, 2009, January 14, 2010 (along with mentions of Saul Alinsky and ACORN), July 8, 2010, July 21, 2010, January 20, 2014, May 13, 2015.

34. Michael Tesler, *Post-Racial or Most-Racial?*, 108.

35. "Free Money From Obama's Stash," *American Renaissance*, October 8, 2009, http://www.amren.com/news/2009/10/free_money_from/.

36. Ed Hornick, "Homeless Woman's Plea to Obama Draws Flood of Support," *CNN.com*, February 12, 2009, http://www.cnn.com/2009/POLITICS/02/11/henrietta.hughes/index.html.

37. John K. Wilson, "Racist Rant and Fake Quotes," April 26, 2011, http://limbaughbook.blogspot.com/2011_04_01_archive.html. See also his book

The Most Dangerous Man In America: Rush Limbaugh's Assault on Reason (New York: Thomas Dunne Books, 2011).

38. Tony Romm, "FEMA to GOP: We Never Gave Grant to ACORN," The Hill, October 7, 2009, http://thehill.com/blogs/blog-briefing-room/news/62021-fema-halts-acorn-grant-gop-lawmaker-praises-decision. See also "ACORN Plans Independent Investigation," NBCNews. com, September 16, 2009, http://www.nbcnews.com/id/32880434/ns/politics-more_politics/#storyContinued.

39. Limbaugh Transcripts, February 25, 2009 (Florida), November 12, 2009 (Detroit), December 2, 2009 (Detroit), January 28, 2010 (Florida, although he erroneously said that the town hall was in Tampa), March 23, 2010 (Florida, but he put it in Atlanta), April 22, 2011 (Florida, but again he put it in Tampa), May 5, 2011 (Detroit), August 17, 2011 (both Detroit and Florida), February 9, 2012 (Florida), April 4, 2012 (Detroit), May 30, 2012 (Florida, this time "Naples or Tampa, wherever it was"), February 10, 2014 (Detroit), November 13, 2015 (Florida).

40. Ibid., February 9, 2012, December 12, 2012, September 13, 2013.

41. Ibid., July 26, 2012. See Stanley Kurtz, *Spreading the Wealth: How Obama is Robbing the Suburbs to Pay for the Cities* (New York: Penguin Group, 2012).

42. Ibid., July 17, 2012, August 2, 2012, August 9, 2013, September12, 2013, July 15, 2014, July 13, 2015, October 13, 2015.

43. Haney López, *Dog Whistle Politics*, 4.

44. López's remarks appear in: *The Root* Staff, "8 Sneaky Racial Code Words and Why Politicians Love Them," The Root, March 15, 2014, https://www.theroot.com/8-sneaky-racial-code-words-and-why-politicians-love-the-1790874941.

45. See Reifowitz, *Obama's America*, pp. 87-88.

46. Limbaugh Transcripts, December 5, 2012, December 12, 2013, November 6, 2015.

47. See, for example, Katherine Bradley and Robert Rector, "Stimulus Bill Abolishes Welfare Reform and Adds New Welfare Spending," The Heritage Foundation, February 11, 2009, http://www.heritage.org/welfare/report/stimulus-bill-abolishes-welfare-reform-and-adds-new-welfare-spending#_ftnref3.

48. On Chicago, see Eric Klinenberg, *Heat Wave: A Social Autopsy of Disaster in Chicago* (Chicago: Chicago University Press, 2002).

49. Paul Steinhauser, "Romney Attacks Obama over Welfare in

Third Campaign Commercial," *CNN.com*, August 20, 2012, http://politicalticker.blogs.cnn.com/2012/08/20/romney-attacks-obama-over-welfare-in-third-campaign-commercial/.

50. Molly Morehead, "Mitt Romney Says Barack Obama's Plan for Welfare Reform: 'They Just Send You Your Check,'"*PolitiFact.com*, August 7, 2012, http://www.politifact.com/truth-o-meter/statements/2012/aug/07/mitt-romney/mitt-romney-says-barack-obamas-plan-abandons-tenet/; Eugene Kiely, "Does Obama's Plan "Gut Welfare Reform"?" *FactCheck.org*, August 9, 2012, http://www.factcheck.org/2012/08/does-obamas-plan-gut-welfare-reform/; Tom Foreman and Eric Marrapodi, "FactCheck: Romney's Welfare Claims Wrong," *CNN.com*, August 30, 2012, http://www.cnn.com/2012/08/23/politics/fact-check-welfare/; Glenn Kessler, "Spin and Counter-Spin in the Welfare Debate," *Washington Post*, August 8, 2012, https://www.washingtonpost.com/blogs/fact-checker/post/spin-and-counterspin-in-the-welfare-debate/2012/08/07/61bf03b6-e0e3-11e1-8fc5-a7d-cf1fc161d_blog.html?tid=a_inl.

51. Greg Marx, "Romney's Welfare Ads: Whom Do They Affect?" *Columbia Journalism Review*, September 17, 2012, http://www.cjr.org/united_states_project/romneys_welfare_ads_whom_do_th.php.

52. See also Limbaugh Transcripts, July 13, 2015, May 2, 2016.

53. Sarah Jones, "Trump Will Always Find a Way to Punish the Poor," *New York Magazine*, December 20, 2018, http://nymag.com/intelligencer/2018/12/trump-proposes-stricter-work-requirements-for-food-stamps.html.

54. Jill Colvin, "Trump Signs Executive Order Pushing Work for Welfare," *U.S. News & World Report*, April, 10, 2018, https://www.usnews.com/news/politics/articles/2018-04-10/trump-signs-executive-order-targeting-public-aid-programs.

55. Jamelle Bouie, "How Trump Happened," *Slate.com*, March 13, 2016, http://www.slate.com/articles/news_and_politics/cover_story/2016/03/how_donald_trump_happened_racism_against_barack_obama.html.

56. Limbaugh Transcripts, September 8, 2009. This is one of many examples of Limbaugh equating the beliefs of Obama and Jones.

CHAPTER THREE

1. Touré, "When Calling 911 Makes the Emergency," *The Daily Beast*, May 12, 2018, https://www.thedailybeast.com/when-calling-911-makes-the-emergency?ref=scroll.

2. The last four were in connection to either the unrest in Ferguson or the assassinations of police officers in New York City and Dallas, all of which are discussed later in this chapter. See Limbaugh Transcripts, September 15, 2009, November 10, 2009, August 19, 2014 (Ferguson), December 22, 2014 (the two NYPD officers who were murdered), July 11, 2016 (the officers murdered in Dallas), and July 12, 2016 (Dallas), https://www.rushlimbaugh.com/archives/.

3. CNN Wire Staff, "NAACP 'Snookered' over Video of Former USDA Employee," *CNN.com*, July 21, 2010, http://edition.cnn.com/2010/POLITICS/07/20/agriculture.employee.naacp/#fbid=X40jhuCTauq.

4. Michael Tesler, *Post-Racial or Most-Racial?*, p. 35. See also p. 100, p. 117. Tesler also cited Nicholas Winter, *Dangerous Frames: How Ideas about Race and Gender Shape Public Opinion* (Chicago: University of Chicago Press, 2008), p. 149.

5. Brett LoGiurato, "Drudge Report Leads With A Story Questioning Obama's Hoodie Sale, And The Obama Campaign Says It's Ridiculous," *Business Insider*, March 27, 2012, http://www.businessinsider.com/obama-hoodie-sale-leads-to-questioning-2012-3.

6. Jake Miller, "Obama Calls for Calm in Wake of George Zimmerman Verdict," *CBS News*, July 15, 2013, http://www.cbsnews.com/news/obama-calls-for-calm-in-wake-of-george-zimmerman-verdict/.

7. A more recently released section of the video has raised more questions about what exactly went on in the store. See, for example, Mitch Smith, "New Ferguson Video Adds Wrinkle to Michael Brown Case," *New York Times*, March 11, 2017, https://www.nytimes.com/2017/03/11/us/michael-brown-ferguson-police-shooting-video.html?_r=0.

8. Sides, Tesler, Vavreck, *Identity Crisis*, pp. 165-67.

9. Zack Beauchamp, "A New Study Reveals the Real Reason Obama Voters Switched to Trump," *Vox*, October 16, 2018, https://www.vox.com/policy-and-politics/2018/10/16/17980820/trump-obama-2016-race-racism-class-economy-2018-midterm.

10. Dylan Matthews, "Donald Trump Has Every Reason to Keep White People Thinking About Race," *Vox*, November 30, 2016, http://www.vox.com/policy-and-politics/2016/11/30/13765248/donald-trump-race-priming-political-science.

11. Limbaugh Transcripts, April 4, 2017.

12. Mike Allen, "Holder's Parting Shot: It's Too Hard to Bring Civil Rights Cases," *Politico*, February 27, 2015, http://www.politico.com/story/2015/02/eric-holder-civil-rights-interview-mike-allen-115575. Allen offered that

Holder's proposal "aimed partly at preparing the country for the possibility that no federal charges would be brought in the death of Michael Brown."

13. Ibid., May 22, 2015, May 26, 2015, May 28, 2015, and June 15, 2015.

14. Emily Atkin, "Donald Trump On Black Lives Matter: 'We Have To Give Power Back To The Police,'" *ThinkProgress*, August 2, 2015, https://thinkprogress.org/donald-trump-on-black-lives-matter-we-have-to-give-power-back-to-the-police-6769b42e96fb/.

15. Justin Fox, "Pssst: Crime May Be Near an All-Time Low," *Bloomberg. com*, February 12, 2018, https://www.bloomberg.com/opinion/articles/2018-02-12/pssst-crime-may-be-near-an-all-time-low.

16. Nick Wing, "Donald Trump Says 'Police Are The Most Mistreated People' In America," *HuffPost*, January 14, 2016, https://www.huffingtonpost.com/entry/donald-trump-police_us_569869d1e4b0b4eb759df9b8.

17. Fox News Transcript, "Donald Trump: 'We Have to Demand Law and Order,'" July 19, 2016, https://www.foxnews.com/transcript/donald-trump-we-have-to-demand-law-and-order.

18. Matt DeLong and Dave Braunger, "Breaking Down the Dashcam: The Philando Castile Shooting Timeline," *Star-Tribune*, July 3, 2017, http://www.startribune.com/castile-shooting-timeline/429678313/.

19. Louis Nelson, "Trump: 'I Am the Law and Order Candidate,'" *Politico*, July 11, 2016, https://www.politico.com/story/2016/07/trump-law-order-candidate-225372.

20. Jaweed Kaleem, "South Carolina Lutheran Pastor: Dylann Roof Was Church Member, His Family Prays For Victims," *Huffington Post*, June 19, 2015, https://www.huffingtonpost.com/2015/06/19/dylann-roof-religion-church-lutheran_n_7623990.html.

CHAPTER FOUR

1. Limbaugh Transcripts, November 16, 2015, March 24, 2016.

2. Here's the full list: Ibid., March 27, 2009, April 1, 2009, April 7, 2009, April 8, 2009, April 14, 2009, April 20, 2009, April 21, 2009, April 22, 2009, May 11, 2009, May 13, 2009, May 14, 2009, May 19, 2009, May 21, 2009 (Limbaugh accused Obama of making "essentially an apology to terrorists."), June 2, 2009, June 3, 2009, June 4, 2009, June 8, 2009, June 17, 2009, July 3, 2009, August 25, 2009, September 23, 2009, September 28, 2009, September 30, 2009, October 2, 2009, October 6, 2009, November 10, 2009, November 13, 2009, November 17, 2009, November 19, 2009, December 1, 2009,

December 2, 2009, December 18, 2009. Attacking the president over supposedly apologizing for America had become so common for Limbaugh that on May 27, 2016, he rebuked Obama for undertaking "yet another apology tour."

3. Ibid., June 10, 2013, February 25, 2014.

4. "Obama Gitmo Closure, Torture Ban," *Democracy Now*, January 23, 2009, https://www.democracynow.org/2009/1/23/headlines.

5. Robert Farley, "Republican National Committee Claims Obama Administration Offered $900 Million to Hamas to Rebuild Gaza," *PolitiFact.com*, July 14, 2009, http://www.politifact.com/truth-o-meter/statements/2009/jul/14/republican-national-committee-republican/RNC-poll-Hamas-Gaza/.

6. "Obama's Speech in Cairo," *New York Times*, June 4, 2009, http://www.nytimes.com/2009/06/04/us/politics/04obama.text.html.

7. Limbaugh Transcripts, August 14, 2009.

8. Jon Greenberg, "Blog Claims U.S. Funded anti-Netanyahu Election Effort in Israel," *PolitiFact.com*, March 25, 2015, http://www.PolitiFact.com/punditfact/statements/2015/mar/25/blog-posting/blog-claims-us-funded-anti-netanyahu-election-effo/.

9. Hadas Gold, "Joan Walsh: Limbaugh a 'Racist Troll,'" *Politico*, September 9, 2013, http://www.politico.com/blogs/media/2013/09/joan-walsh-limbaugh-a-racist-troll-172182.

10. Linda Qiu, "Ben Carson: 'There Is Currently No Ability to Vet' Syrian Refugees," *PolitiFact.com*, November 19, 2015, http://www.PolitiFact.com/truth-o-meter/statements/2015/nov/19/ben-carson/ben-carson-there-currently-no-ability-vet-syrian-r/.

11. Glenn Thrush, "Trump's New Travel Ban Blocks Migrants From Six Nations, Sparing Iraq," *New York Times*, March 6, 2017, https://www.nytimes.com/2017/03/06/us/politics/travel-ban-muslim-trump.html. John Kelly, Trump's Secretary of Homeland Security, stated that "unregulated, unvetted travel is not a universal privilege, especially when national security is at stake."

12. Colin H. Kahl, "No, Obama Didn't Lose Iraq," *Politico*, June 15, 2014, http://www.politico.com/magazine/story/2014/06/no-obama-didnt-lose-iraq-107874#.U6BHs41dU00.

13. See, for example, Victor Thorn, "Obama, Clinton, Selling Out U.S. Sovereignty in Secret," *American Free Press*, May 21, 2012, https://americanfreepress.net/selling-out-to-the-nwo/. For more analysis see Kurt Eichenwald, "The Plots to Destroy America," *Newsweek*, May 15, 2014, http://www.newsweek.com/2014/05/23/plots-destroy-america-251123.html.

14. Eugene Kiely, "PAC Attack on Clinton's Benghazi Record," *FactCheck.*

org, November 3, 2016, http://www.factcheck.org/2016/11/pac-attack-on-clintons-benghazi-record/. See also Brennan Suel and Olivia Kittel, "A Comprehensive Guide to Benghazi Myths and Facts," *MediaMatters.org*, June 28, 2016, http://www.mediamatters.org/research/2016/06/28/comprehensive-guide-benghazi-myths-and-facts/211240#Coverpercent20Up.

15. Media Matters Staff, "Fox's Doocy Floats Evidence-Free Conspiracy Theory From Limbaugh About Valerie Jarrett And Benghazi," *MediaMatters.org*, August 7, 2013, http://mediamatters.org/video/2013/08/07/foxs-doocy-floats-evidence-free-conspiracy-theo/195275.

16. Erik Wemple, "Benghazi: More 'Stand Down' Fallout for *Fox News*," *Washington Post*, January 16, 2014, https://www.washingtonpost.com/blogs/erik-wemple/wp/2014/01/16/benghazi-more-stand-down-fallout-for-fox-news/.

17. Vidya Narayanan, Vlad Barash, John Kelly, Bence Kollanyi, Lisa-Maria Neudert, and Philip N. Howard, "Polarization, Partisanship and Junk News Consumption over Social Media in the US," Data Memo 2018.1. Oxford, UK: Project on Computational Propaganda, February 6, 2018, http://comprop.oii.ox.ac.uk/research/polarization-partisanship-and-junk-news/.

18. Fact Checker, *Washington Post*, https://www.washingtonpost.com/graphics/politics/trump-claims-database/?utm_term=.72fec2e67c1f.

19. "Fort Hood Shooting: Transcript of Barack Obama's Statement," *The Telegraph*, November 6, 2009, http://www.telegraph.co.uk/news/worldnews/barackobama/6511386/Fort-Hood-shooting-transcript-of-Barack-Obamas-statement.html.

20. Statement of Barack Obama, Hyde Park Herald, September 19, 2001, https://docs.google.com/file/d/0B-5-JeCa2Z7hVFVmQTR3ZUZjMUU/edit.

21. See Limbaugh Transcripts, October 13, 2011, September 12, 2012, October 11, 2012, August 30, 2013, May 11, 2014, January 7, 2015, February 5, 2015.

22. Jim Acosta, Kevin Liptak, "Obama Proclaims: 'We Are Not at War with Islam,'" *CNN.com*, February 19, 2015, http://www.cnn.com/2015/02/18/politics/obama-speech-extremism-terror-summit/.

CHAPTER FIVE

1. Limbaugh Transcripts, July 22, 2009.

2. Angie Drobnic Holan, "Tax Cut for 95 Percent? The Stimulus Made It So," *PolitiFact.com*, January 28, 2010, http://www.PolitiFact.

com/truth-o-meter/statements/2010/jan/28/barack-obama/
tax-cut-95-percent-stimulus-made-it-so/.

3. Limbaugh Transcripts, January 28, 2009, February 9, 2009, February
13, 2009, February 27, 2009, March 2, 2009, March 24, 2009.

4. Joe Miller, "The Stimulus Bill and ACORN," *FactCheck.org*, February 6,
2009, http://www.factcheck.org/2009/02/the-stimulus-bill-and-acorn/.

5. Robert Farley, "In Theory, ACORN Could Compete for Some Home
Rebuilding Money in Stimulus Plan," *PolitiFact*, February 2, 2009, https://
www.politifact.com/truth-o-meter/statements/2009/feb/02/john-boehner/
theory-acorn-could-compete-some-home-rebuilding-mo/.

6. The updated version read: "Illegal immigrants who lack Social
Security numbers could not get tax credits under the $800 billion-plus
economic stimulus package making its way through Congress." Both
versions are in Jeremy Holden, "AP Cited Only Single Anonymous
Republican Official in Support of Stimulus Falsehood, *MediaMatters.
org*, January 30, 2009, http://mediamatters.org/research/2009/01/30/
ap-cited-only-single-anonymous-republican-offic/147121.

7. Peter Weber, "The U.S. Auto Bailout is Officially Over. Here's What
America Lost and Gained," *The Week*, December 10, 2013, http://theweek.com/
articles/454749/auto-bailout-officially-over-heres-what-america-lost-gained.

8. Limbaugh Transcripts, April 22, 2010, October 6, 2011, November 1,
2011, July 27, 2012.

9. Chris Good, "Tea Partiers Dress Up in Union Gear," *The Atlantic*,
June 24, 2010, https://www.theatlantic.com/politics/archive/2010/06/
tea-partiers-dress-up-in-union-gear/58697/.

10. Limbaugh Transcripts, September 22, 2010, November 12, 2010.

11. Ibid., October 6, 2010, December 9, 2010, and December 17, 2010.

12. Helaine Olen, "Barack Obama and the Federal Government Are Not
Taking Your 401(k)," *Forbes*, December 19, 2012, http://www.forbes.com/
sites/helaineolen/2012/12/19/barack-obama-and-the-federal-government-
are-not-taking-your-401k/#6f07500d4e5d.

13. Jonathan Capehart, "The GOP Better Listen to Colin Powell,"
Washington Post, January 14, 2013, https://www.washingtonpost.com/blogs/
post-partisan/wp/2013/01/14/the-gop-better-listen-to-colin-powell/?utm_
term=.e640d59dc82c.

14. Limbaugh Transcripts, July 12, 2011, July 13, 2011, July 14, 2011, July
20, 2011, July 25, 2011, August 1, 2011.

15. Ibid., January 21, 2009, January 23, 2009, January 29, 2009.

16. Ibid., June 24, 2009. Here are the additional examples: July 23, 2009,

November 23, 2009, December 17, 2009, January 8, 2010, February 22, 2010, March 3, 2010, March 12, 2010, March 24, 2010, April 1, 2010, April 2, 2010, July 7, 2010, April 3, 2012, April 4, 2012, February 20, 2014, March 13, 2014, April 11, 2014, April 21, 2015.

17. Jess Henig, "The 'Real' Uninsured," *FactCheck.org*, June 24, 2009, http://www.factcheck.org/2009/06/the-real-uninsured/.

18. Katie Sanders, "Illegal Immigrants Are Covered under the Health Care Law, Email Chain Says," *PolitiFact.com*, July 9, 2013, http://www.politifact.com/florida/statements/2013/jul/09/chain-email/illegal-immigrants-are-covered-under-health-care-l/.

19. Angie Drobnic Holan, "Joe Wilson of South Carolina Said Obama Lied, But He Didn't," *PolitiFact.com*, September 9, 2009, http://www.politifact.com/truth-o-meter/statements/2009/sep/09/joe-wilson/joe-wilson-south-carolina-said-obama-lied-he-didnt/.

20. Limbaugh Transcripts, July 22, 2009, August 3, 2009, August 4, 2009, August 6, 2009, August 7, 2009, August 10, 2009, August 13, 2009, August 17, 2009, September 9, 2009, September 30, 2009, December 10, 2009, March 21, 2010, March 17, 2010, October 13, 2010, December 1, 2011, October 1, 2013. Additionally, a caller referenced ACORN on July 23, 2009.

21. Adam C. Smith, "Protesters in Ybor City Drown Out Health Care Summit on Obama's Proposal," *Tampa Bay Times*, August 6, 2009, http://www.tampabay.com/news/politics/protesters-in-ybor-city-drown-out-health-care-summit-on-obamas-proposal/1025529.

22. The memo is available at Lee Fang, "Right-Wing Harassment Strategy Against Dems Detailed In Memo: 'Yell,' 'Stand Up And Shout Out,' 'Rattle Him,'" *ThinkProgress*, July 31, 2009, https://thinkprogress.org/right-wing-harassment-strategy-against-dems-detailed-in-memo-yell-stand-up-and-shout-out-rattle-him-94e9af741078.

23. Staff Report, "Two Charged in Scuffle at St. Louis County Meeting Found Not Guilty," *St. Louis Post-Dispatch*, July 12, 2011, http://www.stltoday.com/news/local/govt-and-politics/article_972c5eb0-accb-11e0-8614-001a4bcf6878.html. See also Eric Boehlert, "The Kenneth Gladney Charade Collapses," *MediaMatters.org*, July 11, 2011, https://mediamatters.org/blog/2011/07/13/the-kenneth-gladney-charade-collapses/181483.

24. Cited in Sides, Tesler, Vavreck, *Identity Crisis*, pp. 175–76.

25. Ibid., 176.

26. Sally Kohn, "Thank Ronald Reagan and Bill Clinton for Donald

Trump's Dog-Whistle Ways," *Time*, August 16, 2016, http://time.com/4452596/donald-trump-dog-whistle/.

27. The studies are cited in Nareissa Smith, "Identifying Discrimination at Work: The Use of Field Experiments," *Atlanta Black Star*, October 10, 2017, https://atlantablackstar.com/2017/10/10/working-black-emily-gets-job-lakeisha/. See also Janell Ross, "Trump Once Had a Dream: He Would Start Over Again as 'An Educated Black.' About that . . . ," *Washington Post*, June 21, 2016, https://www.washingtonpost.com/news/the-fix/wp/2016/06/21/trump-once-had-a-dream-he-would-start-over-again-as-an-educated-black-about-that/?utm_term=.294d5dbf332f.

28. Sarah Binder, "The History of the Filibuster," Brookings Institution, April 22, 2010, https://www.brookings.edu/testimonies/the-history-of-the-filibuster/.

29. Robert Schlesinger, "Reconciliation, Hypocrisy, and a Shamelessness in Health Reform," *U.S. News & World Report*, March 10, 2010, https://www.usnews.com/opinion/articles/2010/03/10/reconciliation-hypocrisy-and-a-shamelessness-in-health-reform. See also Julie Rovner, "Health Care No Stranger To Reconciliation Process," NPR, February 24, 2010, http://www.npr.org/templates/story/story.php?storyId=124009985.

30. Louis Jacobson, "Rush Limbaugh Says HHS Secretary Kathleen Sebelius Was the "One Person" to Determine Fate of 10-Year-Old Lung Patient Sarah Murnaghan," *PolitiFact.com*, June 11, 2013, http://www.politifact.com/truth-o-meter/statements/2013/jun/11/rush-limbaugh/rush-limbaugh-says-hhs-secretary-kathleen-sebelius/.

31. See Limbaugh Transcripts, May 20, 2013, June 25, 2013. He mentioned the SEIU and the AFL-CIO getting funds as well on both dates.

32. Glenn Kessler, "No, CBO Did Not Say Obamacare Will Kill 2 Million Jobs," *Washington Post*, February 4, 2014, https://www.washingtonpost.com/news/fact-checker/wp/2014/02/04/no-cbo-did-not-say-obamacare-will-kill-2-million-jobs/?utm_term=.96ffcde510a2.

33. Congressional Budget Office, "The Budget and Economic Outlook: 2014 to 2024," February 2014, p. 117, http://cbo.gov/sites/default/files/cbo-files/attachments/45010-Outlook2014_Feb.pdf.

34. Glenn Kessler, "No, CBO Did Not Say Obamacare Will Kill 2 Million Jobs," *Washington Post*, February 4, 2014, https://www.washingtonpost.com/news/fact-checker/wp/2014/02/04/no-cbo-did-not-say-obamacare-will-kill-2-million-jobs/.

35. "Income, Poverty and Health Insurance Coverage in the United States:

2016," United States Census Bureau, September 12, 2017, https://www.census.gov/newsroom/press-releases/2017/income-povery.html.

CHAPTER SIX

1. Kevin Robillard, "Trump: 'Self-Deportation' Cost Votes," *Politico*, November 26, 2012, https://www.politico.com/story/2012/11/trump-romneys-crazy-policy-of-self-deportation-cost-votes-084238.

2. Alexander Burns, "Choice Words from Donald Trump, Presidential Candidate," *New York Times*, June 16, 2015, https://www.nytimes.com/politics/first-draft/2015/06/16/choice-words-from-donald-trump-presidential-candidate/?_r=0.

3. Justin Berrier and Eric Schroeck, "Fox Runs With Right-Wing Group's Absurd 'Estimate' that '2,158 Killed by Illegals Every Year,'" *MediaMatters. org*, May 6, 2010, https://www.mediamatters.org/research/2010/05/06/fox-runs-with-right-wing-groups-absurd-estimate/164326.

4. Limbaugh Transcripts, April 27, 2010, May 21, 2010, July 1, 2010, July 29, 2010, August 13, 2010, June 26, 2012, April 1, 2013, May 14, 2014, June 12, 2014, July 24, 2014, October 20, 2014, July 7, 2015, July 22, 2015, July 29, 2015, https://www.rushlimbaugh.com/archives/.

5. Tal Kopan, "What is VOICE? Trump Highlights Crimes by Undocumented Immigrants," *CNN.com*, March 1, 2017, http://www.cnn.com/2017/02/28/politics/donald-trump-voice-victim-reporting/index.html.

6. Michael T. Light, Ty Miller, "Does Undocumented Immigration Increase Violent Crime," *Criminology*, Vol. 56, 2 (2018), 370-401. Alex Nowrasteh, "Criminal Immigrants in Texas: Illegal Immigrant Conviction and Arrest Rates for Homicide, Sexual Assault, Larceny and Other Crimes," CATO Institute: Immigration Research and Policy Brief, February 26, 2018, No. 4, https://www.documentcloud.org/documents/4450775-CATO-Illegal-Immigration-and-Crime-in-Texas.html. See also Mike Maciag, "Analysis: Undocumented Immigrants Not Linked With Higher Crime Rates," *Governing Magazine*, March 2, 2017, http://www.governing.com/gov-data/safety-justice/undocumented-immigrants-crime-effects-study.html; and Alex Nowrasteh, "There Is No Evidence of an Illegal Immigrant Crime Wave: Why the 'Elusive Crime Wave Data Shows Frightening Toll of Illegal Immigrant Criminals' Is Flawed," CATO Institute, July 7, 2017, https://www.cato.org/blog/there-no-evidence-illegal-immigrant-crime-wave-why-elusive-crime-wave-data-shows-frightening.

7. Maria Santana, "Five Immigration Myths Debunked," *CNN.com*, November 10, 2014, http://money.cnn.com/2014/11/20/news/economy/immigration-myths/index.html.

8. The A week later, the May 6, 2010 show included more on immigration and related accusations of Obama dividing Americans as well as more clips of Sharpton.

9. Limbaugh Transcripts, April 28, 2010, May 11, 2011, May 3, 2013, May 6, 2013, July 2, 2014.

10. Steven Nelson, "Trump Confirms Demand for Border Wall Funding as Shutdown Looms," *Washington Examiner*, December 20, 2018, https://www.washingtonexaminer.com/news/white-house/trump-confirms-demand-for-border-wall-funding-as-shutdown-looms.

11. "Obama's Remarks on Immigration," *New York Times*, July 1, 2010, http://www.nytimes.com/2010/07/02/us/politics/02obama-text.html.

12. Warren Richey, "Terrorism and the Mexico Border: How Big a Terror Threat?" *Christian Science Monitor*, January 15, 2017, https://www.csmonitor.com/USA/Justice/2017/0115/Terror-and-the-Mexico-border-How-big-a-threat.

13. Through the end of 2016, 844,931 people filed initial requests and 741,546 were accepted. Data accessed July 12, 2017, at https://www.uscis.gov/sites/default/files/USCIS/Resources/Reports percent20and percent-20Studies/Immigration percent20Forms percent20Data/All percent20Form percent20Types/DACA/daca_performancedata_fy2016_qtr3.pdf.

14. Jeffrey S. Passel and D'Vera Cohen, "As Mexican Share Declined, U.S. Unauthorized Immigrant Population Fell in 2015 Below Recession Level," *Pew Research Center*, April 25, 2017, http://www.pewresearch.org/fact-tank/2017/04/25/as-mexican-share-declined-u-s-unauthorized-immigrant-population-fell-in-2015-below-recession-level/.

15. Amy Sherman, "Did Marco Rubio Flip Flop on Amnesty?" *PolitiFact Florida*, January 29, 2016, http://www.politifact.com/florida/statements/2016/jan/29/marco-rubio/did-marco-rubio-flip-flip-amnesty/.

16. Frank Newport, "Few in U.S. See Guns, Immigration as Nation's Top Problems," *Gallup*, April 15, 2013, http://www.gallup.com/poll/161813/few-guns-immigration-nation-top-problems.aspx.

17. Robert Farley, "Does ACA Give Incentive to Hire Immigrants?" *FactCheck.org*, December 5, 2014, http://www.factcheck.org/2014/12/does-aca-give-incentive-to-hire-immigrants/.

18. Calvin Woodward, "AP FACT CHECK: Trump's Mythical Terrorist

Tide from Mexico," *Associated Press*, January 8, 2019, https://www.apnews.com/4a7792c523ab4b5984893b38c988d70b.

19. Limbaugh Transcripts, August 12, 2013, January 8, 2014.

20. Donald J. Trump, Twitter Post. June 18, 2018, 6:02AM, https://twitter.com/realDonaldTrump/status/1008696508697513985,

21. Tom Newton Dunn, "Migrants 'Harm UK': Donald Trump Says Britain Is 'Losing Its Culture' Because of Immigration," *The Sun*, July 12, 2018, https://www.thesun.co.uk/news/6766947/donald-trump-britain-losing-culture-immigration/.

22. Caitlin Dickson, "Is Obama Really the Deporter-in-Chief? Yes and No," *Daily Beast*, April 30, 2014, http://www.thedailybeast.com/is-obama-really-the-deporter-in-chief-yes-and-no.

23. Allison Graves, "Fact-check: Did 3 Million Undocumented Immigrants Vote in This Year's Election?: *PolitiFact.com*, November 18, 2016, http://www.politifact.com/punditfact/statements/2016/nov/18/blog-posting/no-3-million-undocumented-immigrants-did-not-vote-/.

24. Limbaugh Transcripts, February 6, 2014, February 7, 2014, May 27, 2014.

25. Ibid., June 17, 2014, June 27, 2014.

26. Ibid., June 30, 2014, July 2, 2014, July 3, 2014.

27. Eugene Kiely, "Rick Perry Misuses 'Criminal Alien' Data," *FactCheck.org*, August 7, 2014, http://www.factcheck.org/2014/08/rick-perry-misuses-criminal-alien-data/.

28. Limbaugh Transcripts, July 30, 2014, August 4, 2014. Limbaugh also brought up the Ebola virus on August 7.

29. Ibid., October 1, 2014, October 2, 2014, October 3, 2014, October 7, 2014, October 8, 2014, October 10, 2014, October 14, 2014, October 16, 2014, October 17, 2014, October 24, 2014, October 28, 2014.

30. Ibid., October 13, 2014, October 15, 2014, October 20, 2014, October 27, 2014, October 29, 2014, October 30, 2014.

31. Elise Viebeck, "Ebola Is 2014 October Surprise," *The Hill*, October 15, 2014, http://thehill.com/policy/healthcare/220774-ebola-is-2014-october-surprise. See also Russell Berman, "The Quiet End to the U.S. Ebola Panic," *The Atlantic*, November 11, 2014, https://www.theatlantic.com/health/archive/2014/11/the-quiet-end-to-the-us-ebola-panic-craig-spencer/382623/.

32. James Poniewozik, "Fox News and Trump Reboot a Fearmongering TV Drama from 2014," *New York Times*, October 23, 2018, https://www.nytimes.

com/2018/10/23/arts/television/fox-trump-midterms-caravan.html

33. Limbaugh Transcripts, November 13, 2014, November 19, 2014, November 20, 2014.

34. Ibid., February 11, 2015, February 13, 2015.

35. Ibid., 2/18/15, 2/26/15.

36. Ibid., July 10, 2015, July 14, 2015, July 15, 2015.

37. Louie Villalobos, "Tennessee Republican Senator Bob Corker Calls Conservative Talk Radio Hosts Tyrants," *USA Today*, December 21, 2018, https://www.usatoday.com/story/news/politics/2018/12/21/bob-corker-calls-ann-coulter-rush-limbaugh-tyrants-shutdown-looms/2389666002/. Coulter does not have a radio show, but is a frequent guest on various media outlets.

CONCLUSION

1. Barack Obama, Remarks at Southern New Hampshire University Commencement, May 19, 2007, transcript available at http://www.presidency.ucsb.edu/ws/?pid=76991.

2. Barack Obama, State of the Union Address, January 12, 2016, transcript available at https://obamawhitehouse.archives.gov/the-press-office/2016/01/12/remarks-president-barack-obama-%E2%80%93-prepared-delivery-state-union-address.

3. "Rush Limbaugh's File," *PolitiFact*, http://www.politifact.com/personalities/rush-limbaugh/.

4. Scott Shane and Sheera Frenkel, "Russian 2016 Influence Operation Targeted African-Americans on Social Media," *New York Times*, December 17, 2018, https://www.nytimes.com/2018/12/17/us/politics/russia-2016-influence-campaign.html.

5. Steven Levitsky and Daniel Ziblatt, *How Democracies Die*, (New York: Crown, 2018), 144. See also Amanda Taub and Max Fisher, "Russian Meddling Was a Drop in an Ocean of American-Made Discord," New York Times, February 18, 2018, https://www.nytimes.com/2018/02/18/world/europe/russia-us-election.html.

6. Tom Kludt and Brian Stelter, "White Anxiety Finds a Home at Fox News," *CNN.com*, August 9, 2018, https://money.cnn.com/2018/08/09/media/fox-news-laura-ingraham-tucker-carlson-white-nationalism/index.html.

7. Robb Willer, Matthew Feinberg, and Rachel Wetts, "Threats to Racial

Status Promote Tea Party Support Among White Americans," *SSRN*, May 4, 2016, https://ssrn.com/abstract=2770186. See also Amy Chua, *Political Tribes: Group Instinct and the Fate of Nations* (New York, Penguin Press, 2018), 170.

8. Brenda Major, Alison Blodorn, and Gregory Major Blascovich, "The Threat of Increasing Diversity: Why Many White Americans Support Trump in the 2016 Presidential Election," *Group Processes & Intergroup Relations*, October 20, 2016, https://doi.org/10.1177/1368430216677304. See also Ezra Klein, "White Threat in a Browning America," *Vox*, July 30, 2018, https://www.vox.com/policy-and-politics/2018/7/30/17505406/trump-obama-race-politics-immigration.

9. Diana C. Mutz, "Status Threat, Not Economic Hardship, Explains the 2016 Presidential Vote," *Proceedings of the National Academy of Sciences of the United States of America*, April 23, 2018, http://www.pnas.org/content/early/2018/04/18/1718155115.

10. Bradley Jones and Jocelyn Kiiley, "More 'Warmth' for Trump among GOP Voters Concerned by Immigrants, Diversity," *Pew Research Center*, June 2, 2016, http://www.pewresearch.org/fact-tank/2016/06/02/more-warmth-for-trump-among-gop-voters-concerned-by-immigrants-diversity/. See also Jascha Mounk, *The People vs. Democracy: Why Our Freedom Is in Danger & How to Save It* (Cambridge, MA: Harvard University Press, 2018), 175.

11. Dowell Myers, Morris Levy, "Racial Population Projections and Reactions to Alternative News Accounts of Growing Diversity," *The ANNALS of the American Academy of Political and Social Science*, Vol. 677, Issue 1: 215-228, April 25, 2018, http://journals.sagepub.com/doi/full/10.1177/0002716218766294.

12. Lynn Vavreck, "Why This Election Was Not About the Issues," *New York Times*, November 23, 2016, https://www.nytimes.com/2016/11/23/upshot/this-election-was-not-about-the-issues-blame-the-candidates.html?rref=collection%2Fsectioncollection%2Fupshot&action=click&-contentCollection=upshot&region=stream&module=stream_unit&version=latest&contentPlacement=1&pgtype=sectionfront&_r=2.

13. Ian Haney López, Anat Shenker-Osorio and Tamara Draut, "Democrats Can Win by Tackling Race and Class Together. Here's Proof," *The Guardian*, April 14, 2018, https://www.theguardian.com/commentisfree/2018/apr/14/democrats-race-class-divide-2018-midterms.

14. For more, see "Race-Class: Our Progressive Narrative," May 21, 2018, *Demos*, https://www.demos.org/publication/

race-class-our-progressive-narrative. See also Ian Haney López, Anat Shenker-Osorio, "The Answer to GOP Dog Whistles? Democrats Should Talk More About Race, Not Less," August 22, 2018, *Washington Post*, https://www.washingtonpost.com/outlook/the-answer-to-gop-dog-whistles-democrats-should-talk-more-about-race-not-less/2018/08/22/7cfa4d3a-a184-11e8-8e87-c869fe70a721_story.html?noredirect=on&utm_term=.4006f42bb63a.

15. Philip D. Morgan, *Slave Counterpoint: Black Culture in the Eighteenth-Century Chesapeake and Lowcountry*, (Chapel Hill: Omohundro Institute and University of North Carolina Press, 1998). See also Ian Reifowitz, "Rush Limbaugh and the Long, Sordid History of Pitting Whites Against Blacks in America," December 2, 2013, *Huffington Post*, https://www.huffingtonpost.com/ian-reifowitz/rush-limbaugh-and-the-lon_b_4369335.html.

16. Keri Leigh Merritt, *Masterless Men: Poor Whites and Slavery in the Antebellum South* (Cambridge: Cambridge University Press, 2017). See also Robin Lindley, "Poor Whites and Slavery in the Antebellum South: An Interview with Historian Keri Leigh Merritt," November 5, 2017, History News Network, http://historynewsnetwork.org/article/167224.

17. Patricia Cohen, "Even in Better Times, Some Americans Seem Farther Behind. Here's Why," September 14, 2018, *New York Times*, https://www.nytimes.com/2018/09/14/business/economy/income-inequality.html.

18. The previous two sentences are paraphrased versions of lines delivered by the fictional President Andrew Shepherd in one of my favorite movies, *The American President*. (1995) The screenplay was written by Aaron Sorkin.